On Broadway

On

Performance Photographs by Fred Fehl

The Dan Danciger Publication Series

Broadway

Text by William Stott with Jane Stott

University of Texas Press, Austin

Images in this book were taken from originals
preserved in the Hoblitzelle Theatre Arts Library
in the Humanities Research Center, The University
of Texas at Austin.

Library of Congress Cataloging in Publication Data

Fehl, Fred.
  On Broadway.
  Includes index.
  1. Theater–New York (City). I. Stott, William,
1940– II. Stott, Jane, 1940– III. Title.
PN2277.N5F4   770'.9'7902097471   78-8389
ISBN 0-292-76010-8

Designed by Richard Hendel & Catherine Lenox

Set in Palatino by Ann Hidalgo Manley

Printed in the United States of America by
Edwards Brothers Incorporated

With Previously Unpublished Comments, Reminiscences, and Speculations by

CHARLES ADAMS BAKER, producer; President, Macmillan Performing Arts; former theatrical agent

GEORGE BALANCHINE, choreographer

MARGARET BARKER, actress

A BROADWAY OLD-TIMER

YUL BRYNNER, actor

RED BUTTONS, comedian

VIRGINIA SPENCER CARR, biographer, teacher, writer

HAROLD CLURMAN, director, critic, writer

IMOGENE COCA, comedienne

MARC CONNELLY, playwright

HUME CRONYN, actor, writer, director

MELVIN DOUGLAS, actor

MILDRED DUNNOCK, actress

WALKER EVANS, photographer

TOM EWELL, actor

NANETTE FABRAY, actress

JOSÉ FERRER, producer, director, actor

JOHN FISCHER, editor, writer

WILLIAM GIBSON, author

WILLIAM GREAVES, filmmaker, director, producer, actor, TV host, teacher of acting for film and television at the Lee Strasberg Theatre Institute

HERBERT GREENE, producer, conductor, composer, arranger

JULIE HARRIS, actress

HELEN HAYES, actress

JOHN HEMMERLY, high school drama teacher

SEYMOUR HERSCHER, Broadway business manager

ALAN HEWITT, actor, theater historian

GUSTI HUBER, actress

GENE KELLY, dancer, actor, director

WALTER KERR, drama critic, author

BETHEL LESLIE, actress

ARMINA MARSHALL, producer, actress, writer; co-director, the Theatre Guild

RUSSELL MERRITT, film historian

FREDERICK O'NEAL, actor, director, administrator; President, Actors Equity, 1964–1973; President, Associated Actors and Artistes of America (AFL-CIO)

ALFRED PALCA, writer, producer

DORIS PALCA, museum executive

GREGORY PECK, actor

HAROLD PRINCE, theatrical producer, director

PHILIP PROCTOR, actor, writer, record producer, comedian, member of the Firesign Theatre

Q, the interviewers, Bill and Jane Stott

JOHN RAITT, actor

TONY RANDALL, actor

JESSICA TANDY, actress

GORE VIDAL, writer

SAM WATERSTON, actor

FLORENCE WILLIAMS, actress

Contents

Fred Fehl (photo by Hans Geiger).

Introduction: Fred Fehl and Theater Photography

The pictures in this book are by Fred Fehl, one of the most important theater photographers of his time and the first in America to make a career of what he calls *performance* photography.

Fehl was born in Vienna and grew up there during the 1920s. These were harrowing years for the new Republic of Austria. The nation was a successor state to the Habsburg Empire, which, having fought the World War not merely on the losing side but with murderous incompetence, fell to pieces in 1918. In its first decade Austria faced postwar chaos and recrimination; staggering unemployment, inflation, and graft; the death of tens of thousands of its citizens from disease and starvation; even incipient civil war.

These problems touched Fehl lightly. His family was of the comfortable middle class, his father a prominent dentist and long-time vice-president of the Austrian dental association. His parents admired Goethe (Dr. Fehl collected his work) and enjoyed music, opera, theater, art. From early youth Fred accompanied them to performances, and at age 13 he began to go alone, sometimes four and five times a week. His parents didn't mind because they lived in the heart of the city, near the theaters, and because he still got back in time for supper. This was one happy consequence of Austria's hard time: electricity and gasoline being in short supply, theaters started at six or seven so that people could go directly from work and get home early.

A five-minute walk down the block, with a left turn into the Ringstrasse, and Fred was at Vienna's Burgtheater. Five minutes more brought him to Max Reinhardt's new Theater der Schauspieler in the Josefstadt, where every production caused a sensation and where an actor with a lead part one night–Otto Preminger, say, or Oscar Homolka –might have only a few lines the next. A five-minute walk with a right turn from the Ringstrasse, and he was at the Staatsoper where Richard Strauss conducted his own work or Mozart or Wagner, and where Fred, a standee, would come away throbbing from the exertion of listening so hard. Tall for his age and well developed from hiking and skiing, he sometimes appeared as an extra in crowd scenes; he remembers playing a soldier with an enormous sword in *Lohengrin*, standing near Leo Slezak and Maria Jeritza, and feeling the sudden sound of their voices hit his face like a spotlight.

In the summers Dr. Fehl would take Fred on trips to the art centers of Europe. They toured Italy, France, Spain, the Low Countries, and, most often, Germany, seeing Goethe's city, little Weimar, symbol of German culture, where in 1919 the national assembly started the country's danse macabre with democracy; seeing the great cities: Hamburg, Berlin, Leipzig, Dresden, Frankfurt, Nuremberg, Munich. On weekends and holidays the Fehls visited their relatives in Czechoslovakia, where Dr. and Mrs. Fehl had been born in the Moravian town of Nikolsburg, near the Austrian border. Dr. Fehl was a trustee of Nikolsburg's new Museum Jüdischer Kultur, which collected information and memorabilia about

The Erechtheum, the Acropolis, 1935. A cruise photo.

Bruno Walter at the Salzburg Festival, 1935.

important Jews born in the province. Of these, the most conspicuous was Sigmund Freud, who was interested in the project and donated books, papers, and mementos. Drs. Freud and Fehl regularly discussed the development of the museum in Freud's apartment-office beside a butcher shop in the Berggasse, Vienna's junkyard district.

Dr. Fehl was a persistent amateur photographer and on their summer trips introduced Fred to the hobby. Their first camera was a cumbersome 5 × 7, which they carried, with tripod and clanking appurtenances, in and out of cathedrals, across cities and rivers, up the Palatine, the Capitoline, and others of the sacred Seven Hills. In 1925 a German camera came on the market specifically designed to be small enough to take mountain climbing; Dr. Fehl soon bought one. The new camera was the 35mm Leica, and it would revolutionize photography. Together the Fehls experimented with it, began to know its possibilities.

In the late 1920s, after a year of law school, Fred joined the Vienna sales office of a German textile firm. He proved so good at the work that by 1935 he was branch manager, responsible for marketing throughout Austria, Czechoslovakia, Hungary, Yugoslavia, Romania, Bulgaria, and Turkey. He enjoyed his job, particularly the travel, and took his Leica everywhere, snapping souvenirs. He had a quick eye for the interesting: pictures that he made of port cities on a Mediterranean cruise were used by the Italian line in its brochures (the line "paid" him on a subsequent cruise with a first-class stateroom at tourist rate).

A person's life is incoherent only in the living of it; looked back upon, it makes perfect sense. And Fehl's life now took a casual, inevitable turn. During the summer of 1935 he was at Salzburg for the Festival. Everywhere he went in the streets, cafés, parks, hotels he saw actors and musicians he recognized from their performances in Vienna. Like most art lovers, he adulated artists for the joy they gave him. But never before had he been so close to them, camera in hand. Unobtrusively he began taking pictures: Bruno Walter coming from the concert hall, Lotte Lehmann on a street corner.

The results were handsome, but unexpected. When at leisure in the light of day, these masters, who looked so commanding on stage, seemed quite like normal people; the magic of their art did not cling to them. And Fehl realized then that he had seen this magic nowhere but in actual performance. Certainly the portrait photos in the theater lobby –smooth-faced actors with frozen smiles, conductors with half-raised batons and eyebrows–did not capture it. As early as 1924 Max Reinhardt's photographer Hans Böhm had taken unposed production pictures without supplemental lights; in the late 1920s and early 1930s Erich Salomon, Felix Man, and other photojournalists with the *Münchner Illustrierte Presse* had made "candid" pictures during performances. Fehl, who hadn't noticed this work, decided to try the same thing.

That fall a friend in the Vienna Philharmonic invited him to attend a morning rehearsal conducted by Wilhelm Furtwängler, and Fehl brought his Leica. He stood to the side of the stage, shooting the orchestra at work, particularly Furtwängler the disciplinarian, his face one moment beatific, the next enraged. When he developed the pictures, Fehl was astonished at how alive they were. As he recalls: "It became a

Wilhelm Furtwängler leads the Vienna Philharmonic, 1935. The concertmaster is Arnold Rosé.

Marian Anderson in concert in Vienna, 1937.

great hobby to me. I took the Philharmonic during rehearsals with Walter, Klemperer, Toscanini. I hadn't seen anybody do it before. They didn't mind what I was doing because I used available light, and this little camera–what did they care about it? I took pictures at the theater also. I would go to a show once, upstairs. And if it was interesting, I bought an orchestra seat and shot during the regular performance." No amateur would be allowed to do this today, but Fehl was using a camera so new that rules against its use had not been established. This pastime kept his spirits up during dark days.

In March 1938 he was in Istanbul on business. At three one morning his hotel phone rang, and when he answered, his company's local representative said, "Hitler marched into Austria," and hung up. Fehl canceled the remainder of the trip and returned to Vienna, determined to emigrate. The Nazis had ruled Germany for five years, and the Fehls knew what the Jews of Austria could expect: harassment, unctuous contempt, arrest, concentration camp (for their "protection"), torture, abrupt disappearance, even death. Not being politically prominent, the Fehls were not at first molested–though others were, including the dying Freud. They sold off their past lives for what they could get, paid taxes several times over, and wangled exit permits. But they had no place to go. Through Fred's business associates, they had applied for visas to the United States and England, but these would take months if not years to come through. Their relatives in Nikolsburg would take them in, but Czechoslovakia no longer allowed Jews to enter. When the Fehls left Vienna in September 1938, they went by bus to the Austro-Czech frontier. There, cleared for departure, they dawdled for a last meal, walked into the forest, across the border, and to a Czech post where Max Fehl, Fred's uncle, had bribed a guard.

By the time the Fehls got there, Nikolsburg was not safe. Hitler was threatening to invade German-speaking southern Moravia, and Czechoslovakia had mobilized to put up a fight. So the Fehls and their relatives –Fred's uncles, aunts, and first cousins; in all a party of twenty-five–immediately moved northward to the much larger city of Brünn (now Brno). Two weeks later at Munich, the British and French surrendered the Czechs to Hitler, and the Third Reich grew another 30 percent without a shot being fired. In December, before the Nazis had occupied Brünn, Fred received a visa to England. It was not a permanent visa; he could stay in Britain only until the United States allowed him to immigrate; more important, it was a visa for him only, not for his parents. But there was no question of his not taking it. The Fehls' relatives had been slow making arrangements to escape; they had done nothing in early 1938 when visas still could be obtained. Now in despair they were sending their children out. Several of Fred's cousins would soon go to Britain, the youngest through save-the-children agencies, the older girls as household help. Fred was needed there as a sort of big brother to hold the broken family together. He said good-bye to his parents and relatives, promising to see them in America.

His nine-month wait in London while his number crept to the top of the U.S. visa list was the worst period of Fehl's life. He couldn't work; his transient status did not permit it. He could do nothing but live thriftily off business acquaintances; try to comfort his cousins, ease their adjustment to a new country, a new language, the loss of their parents; and watch the world go wrong: Germany grabbing all Czechoslovakia in March, Hitler and Stalin pledging to be friends in August.

Fehl reported to the American consulate for his visa on the warm thundery morning of Friday, September 1, 1939. Hitler had marched into Poland at daybreak; Britain and France were about to respond; there would be a second great war. London was crowded, but people were calm and, as Fehl remembers, elaborately polite. Children stood in rows outside their schools, each child carrying a sack with underwear, food for twenty-four hours, and a gas mask. Four hundred thousand children would be evacuated to the countryside that day; 1.2 million by Sunday. All at once there seemed to be soldiers everywhere. Some helped the police and civil defense workers carry bedridden Londoners from their lodgings, for the aged and infirm were also going to safety. Nobody hurried; many people moved slower than usual as though trying to work into their bones what peace felt like.

Fehl was scheduled to sail for the United States via Canada the next day on the British ship *Athenia*, but someone more important bumped him from his berth. On September 3, the day the French and British declared war, the *Athenia*, two hundred miles west of the Hebrides, was sunk by a German U-boat in the war's first conspicuous atrocity against civilians. Of the 1,400 people aboard, 112 died.

Fehl embarked September 5 on the Dutch *Statendam* and crossed the Atlantic without incident. He came into New York harbor at sunrise on September 14, feeling, he remembers, that he might never be happier. It was Rosh Hashanah, the Jewish New Year, and a blimp turned slowly over the East River. Seeing the name Goodyear on its side, Fehl thought, "This country is good to the Jews."

America has been good to him. By the spring of 1940 he had created for himself a new profession combining his love of theater and his love of photography. That May his parents arrived from Czechoslovakia via Genoa. And that summer he married Margaret Kopekin, a pianist and teacher of piano, who has been of constant support to his work.

Twice in the 1950s and twice in the 1960s Fehl visited Europe. But he has never gone back to Austria, Czechoslovakia, or Germany and never intends to. The Museum Jüdischer Kultur was of course destroyed by the Nazis. Fehl's eighteen relatives who were caught in Brünn–his uncle Max among them–disappeared into the death camps.

Once in America, Fehl needed immediately to make a living–more than a living since to bring his parents from Europe he had to show he could support them. He set up as a free-lance photographer specializing in 35mm unposed portraits of children in their homes and at their games. "It was the easiest thing to get into," he says. "And it's always popular: parents want pictures of Baby." Enlarged to 5 × 7 or 8 × 10, these "candid camera" photos, as people called them, had started into vogue as family pictures and were looked upon as too intricate for amateurs. Fehl was a quick success.

With a reliable income he could afford to try his kind of theater photography, performance photography, the work he wanted most to do. But here he ran into a double problem: people didn't think it could be done, or they didn't think it worth doing.

At that time theatrical photography in America was still the province of studio photographers using large-format cameras, tripods, big negatives, slow shutters, special lighting, and immobilized actors. A good deal of "theater" work, then as now, actually took place in the studio. There photographers made lobby portraits–close-ups in the fashionable

Two-year-old Gabriel Pinski, 1939. Fred Fehl: "He was the most beautiful and charming child I ever photographed. When I married Margaret in 1940, he became my nephew. Now he has a doctorate in physics and works for a computer corporation."

hard-edge style of deadpan actors before matte-silk backdrops (a generation earlier the fashionable portraits were blurred, the actors impassioned, and the backgrounds leafy). There, too, photographers made rehearsal, or "preproduction," photos in the way the first production pictures had been done: they brought together the main actors of a play, staged, lit, and photographed them, in costume or not, making gestures from their roles—but without movement, without scenery, and often without much relation to the script.

Before a show opened in New York the theater photographer photographed it on stage. Even then, though, he treated the stage like a studio. He and the show had an appointment, the Photo Call, during which the show stood still for its "production" pictures. The Photo Call began after an evening performance—that is, between eleven and midnight—in the first week of a show's tryout run out of town. According to union rules, the Call could take up to four hours, and full stage, property, costume, and light crews had to be present, on time-and-a-half wages. (The actors themselves were not paid, as publicizing the show was considered part of their jobs and useful to their careers.) The producer furnished coffee, sandwiches, and sweet rolls; cast and crews wandered backstage or slumped in house seats, waiting to do what the photographer bid. He put up an 8 × 10 camera six to twelve rows back in the orchestra, framed it to cover the whole stage, photographed the final set, and then called for actors to gather at some lively moment. He re-blocked them, arranging their places, gestures, and expressions for the camera, trying to catch the "good side" of any actor worried about it (the stage photographer Joseph Abeles says, "When two actors have the *same* good side, you're in trouble"); sometimes added characters to the group if important actors had not yet entered; moved the camera or set up another—usually on stage—if he wanted a tighter shot; upped the light levels and deployed assistants holding 1,500-watt studio floods; told the actors to take their places; had one or more cheat right or left; called, "Ready. Set. Ho-o-old it. Okay!" and then retook the shot as a precaution. Having done the last scene, he worked backward to the first, so that when he finished the opening set would be up for the next performance.

Press agents used production photos for publicity on the theater's billboards, in magazines and Sunday supplements, and occasionally on posters. Such photos, as collected, say, in Stanley Appelbaum's *The New York Stage: Famous Productions in Photographs, 1883–1939* (1976), give a superlative idea of a show's visual detail: what the sets, costumes, actors looked like. But the photos themselves are rigid and dry—as though the air had been pumped out of them. The actors are diminished by their surroundings and communicate little of the production's atmosphere, its "feel," and nothing of the excitement of actual performance. "Those deadly posed shots," Garson Kanin has written, "made almost every production resemble a tableau in Madame Tussaud's Wax Museum." The morbid effect was intensified because the negatives were usually retouched. Joseph Abeles points out that retouching was much commoner then, for young actors as well as old. "You see the eyes and nose and mouth plainly," he says, "but the rest of the face hasn't a line on it, not even a laugh line. The faces look embalmed on the photograph." It is precisely the *conviction* of living theater that the posed pictures miss. José Ferrer remembers being "always appalled at the artificiality, the quality of unreality of theatrical photography in my youth. The pictures were stiff, frozen, and utterly lacking in believability."

In the thirties many people felt as Ferrer did, even theater photographers. There was a frenzy of interest in unposed, informal, "natural" pictures because suddenly, with the new 35mm cameras, such pictures were possible. These cameras were small, easy to carry and use. They took roll film of many exposures and could make pictures in a series nearly as fast as snapping fingers. Their small negative allowed a lens of short focal length, which increased depth of field and thus made it easier to capture movement. Most important, the short focal length permitted the lens to have an f2 or even f1.8 aperture; this was seven times larger—"faster"—than the f4.5 lens standard on studio cameras and hence could take pictures in dim light. As the decade began, Erich Salomon and Felix Man, the first "candid cameramen," offered *Time* and *Fortune* readers unprecedented glimpses of the great off-guard: Benito Mussolini (puffing out his cheeks in amazement at what he is reading), the Supreme Court in session (never photographed before or, apparently, since), the War Reparations Commission at The Hague (a half dozen old men dozing on their chests), President Hoover in 1932 (lithe and thoughtful, his cigar held like a painter's brush). In the mid-thirties Carmel Snow, editor of *Harper's Bazaar*, and Condé Nast, publisher of *Vogue* and *Vanity Fair*, hit upon unposed pictures as a way of humanizing fashion and the very rich. Soon, most issues of these magazines had informal candids, taken outdoors, of big-jawed models or the Vanderbilts doing fairly normal things while wearing the proper clothes. Then, in 1936, came *Life* and, hard upon it, a parade of imitators, all struggling, as Henry Luce boisterously announced, "to see the world . . . to see and be amazed." The field for new kinds of photography was thrown open.

In this golden age of experimentation, photographers tried out the new fast cameras on performances of every sort: theater, ballet, nightclub, ballroom, burlesque, folk dance, even movie (they simply took pictures of the pictures on the screen). Performance photographs—often so called—appeared in magazines and newspapers throughout the country. By 1937 the *Leica Manual* was encouraging its readers to "record important bits of action in their favorite plays" and telling them how: sit in the orchestra and on the side; get closer to dramas than to musicals; put the lens at f2 and the shutter at 1/4 second if things are dark, 1/200 if things are bright; and realize that results are not guaranteed: "Experience has taught that plenty of film should be used." Jacob Deschin's *Making Pictures with the Miniature Camera* (1937) suggested the same technique, then cautioned: "FINALLY: Try to be as unobtrusive as possible during your shooting and, if you have one, leave the camera in the ever-ready case, as this will help somewhat to soften the click of the release."

From 1934 onward the national theater magazines, *Stage* and *Theatre Arts*, regularly carried performance pictures. The men and women who published one or more such pictures include Bouchard, Alexey Brodovitch, Butcher, Robin Carson, Montgomery Clift, Alfred A. Cohn, André Da Miano, Eileen Darby for Graphic House, Dietrich, H. Foster Ensminger, Erbit, Toni Frizzell, Ruth Frank (*Theatre Arts*, 1936: "The difficulty of taking action shots without flashlight in Carnegie Hall—where the feat is said never to have been accomplished successfully before–prevented any more than these three quick-action pictures from coming through the camera adequately"), Bob Golby, Maurice Goldberg, Gray-O'Reilly, Hansen-Pavelle, Roland V. Haas, Herman-Pix, Ilse Hoffmann, Rudolf H. Hoffmann, Karger, James N. Keen (of his picture of an Ohio burlesque show in *U.S. Camera, 1939,* he wrote: "Although I am a professional news photographer, stage photography is my hobby. This photo was made from the fifth row"), Keystone-Heyer, J. Winton Lemen, Andre La Terze, Henry M. Lester, Lester-Pickett, Maley, Gjon Mili, Barbara Morgan, John T. Moss, Munkacsi, Glenn H. Pickett, Jerome Robinson, Ralph Samuels, Schall (a Frenchman who crossed the United States in 1935, said *Vanity Fair,* "armed only with his camera and one English phrase 'Okay, baby'"), Jimmy Sileo, W. Eugene Smith, Richard Tucker, Alfredo Valente, Valente-Pavelle, the Vandamm Studio.

The experiment failed. *Stage,* which had published more performance photos than all other national magazines combined, folded in 1939, and fewer and fewer live-action theater pictures appeared elsewhere. G. R. Thomas of Vandamm, the most important theater photography studio, had himself done performance shooting. In 1941 he wrote: "The candid camera just won't do the job. For consistent publicity work the action and lighting must be carefully planned"–with, that is to say, the actors posed. The reason was simple: though the 35mm *camera* was fast, the materials it worked with were not. Stage lighting of the time, though it used many more lights than today, was about 25 percent dimmer. Black-and-white film was eight times slower, and there was no dependable "push" development. Larry Madison, then a photographer and later one of America's most successful advertising and documentary film makers, remembers that "under very low light levels we had to use pretty harsh developers and develop for a long time to build up enough emulsion or silver bromide deposit to get a print." Often there was *no* print; whole rolls would be underexposed, blank. Carl Van Vechten took his Leica to an August 1, 1932, performance of the revival of *Showboat* and brought home a strong blurred picture of Paul Robeson singing "Old Man River." But most of the other negatives did not come out, and Van Vechten, who loved candids, went back to photographing in his studio under floodlamps.

Performance candids, when they did come out, were dark, heavy in contrast, with little shadow detail and a great deal of grain. And by 1940 such photos were not what editors were buying. Newspapers with high-speed presses tried to avoid them because their large areas of black drew so much ink that they smudged the press bed and made ghosts down the sheet. In the late thirties magazines cut back using them for a less technical reason: *Life* was not using them much.

Life had always been of two minds about 35mm. On the one hand, the magazine declared itself bold, experimental–the world champion of new ways of seeing. On the other hand, its editors were keenly aware that *Life*'s runaway success with the American audience (for years not enough copies could be produced to meet the demand) was due in some measure to the fact that the magazine was not like its European predecessors, mainly the *Münchner Illustrierte Presse* and the London *Weekly Illustrated.* These older journals, also very successful in their markets, were printed on inexpensive newspaper stock and ran lots of candid photos done in available light, which photos tended to be dark and of low definition. (The photos were reproduced, moreover, by a coarser half-tone process than commonly used in America.) It was conventional

Carl Van Vechten's performance candid of Paul Robeson singing "Old Man River" in the 1932 revival of *Showboat.*

wisdom—with some evidence to back it up—that a mass-market picture magazine would not go in the United States if it appeared on newsprint. *Life* became possible only when a quality "coated" paper was devised that did not smear when printed at high speed. This paper accepted any kind of picture—light or dark, posed or candid, sharp or shaggy, "hot" or "cool"—and *Life* published all kinds.

But in 1938 and 1939 the "sharp" pictures, always more common, began pushing the others out. By the early forties Phillip Andrews, a photo editor and 35mm partisan, could write: "Today the candid photograph is hard to find in *Life* or *Look*, or in any other of our numerous picture magazines. What the public wants to see, or at least what it is being shown, is not an underexposed, overdeveloped picture of an executive scurrying down a dimly-lighted hallway but a stage-managed news photo, which, though informal, is as brilliantly, beautifully lighted as a studio portrait." Experimenting was over for the duration. *Life* had found the image of America it wanted to retail. It was the optimistic America of Norman Rockwell and the Hollywood still photographer: a land where everyone was clear as a bell, posed, flaccid, glossy. It was a nation streamlined—or, better, "cleanlined," Henry Dreyfuss' word for the aesthetic that inspired him and his fellow industrial designers of the thirties. In this America men and machines were seen *smoothly*, seen on several sides at once but without edge or shadow, thanks to supplemental lighting (the characteristic portraits of the time—of Kansas farmers, say—were done outdoors in the sun with reflectors and fill-in flash) and thanks also to retouching (a chief complaint about 35mm from studio photographers was that the negative was too small to "improve"; said Thomas of Vandamm, "I hate to think what would happen to my business if I showed some of the ladies and gentlemen with whom I work as they really look"). It was a monumental America, static and unassailable.

And 35mm could not capture it. Available-light pictures made the world look drab, haphazard, sad, and temporary—in a word, un-American. Having been hailed as a panacea just a few years earlier, 35mm was now condemned. "The candid-camera is the greatest liar in the photographic family," wrote Lincoln Kirstein in 1939. "It drugs the eye into believing it has witnessed a fact when it has only caught a flicker." (And, specifically of live-action ballet photography, "Under the guise of an objective and frank reporter, the candid-camera distorts, alters, and ultimately destroys the very performances it pretends to document.") Fast-lens shooting, which took an actuality without having to ask it to slow down, was seen not as a liberation from artificiality but as a contemptible gimmick, dangerous ("Today the Leica in steady hands can be as deadly as the revolver," E. B. White observed in 1937) and laughable and, according to the cartoonists, downright lewd. It was even criticized on patriotic grounds. Edwin Rosskam took the pictures for his 1939 documentary book *Washington Nerve Center* with "small cameras," but he wouldn't say which cameras: "We are not going to name our equipment. It is all German equipment, and we refuse to do anything further in providing publicity for German goods which could be easily manufactured in the United States."

Life and the publications it influenced did not give up using 35mm. The Leica had become a standard tool of newsphotographers, *the* standard tool in Europe, and *Life* led off each issue with "The Week's Events," a section of hard news. Ninety percent of these events were

"Er—I'm afraid that's a little *too* candid, Mrs. Baker."—1937 *Esquire* cartoon by E. Simms Campbell.

political or disasters (or both). Sometimes when they were political and often when they were disasters—particularly, of course, World War II— the pictures of them were available-light 35mm. But in the rest of the magazine, the part people enjoyed, the "back of the book" where *Life* spent most of its ingenuity and money and where readers learned about debutantes and draftees and zootsuits and Australia and "The Movie of the Week" and cooking "variety meats" (sweetbreads, brains) and financiers and Betty Grable and typhus—in the rest of the magazine the pictures were posed, artificially lit, and nearly always from view cameras and large negatives.

Available-light photography was out, and so was movement. *Life* had found a way to overcome it. Rather than show a pole vaulter in motion, his body blurred, *Life* stopped action, caught him frozen in space, muscles extended, mouth torn open, and skin gleaming with the light hitting it from either of two new inventions: multiple synchronous flash or Speedlite, the first-generation strobe. Bob Feller's fastball, Billy Conn's left, a pirouette, a bullet's flight, a sneeze's spume—all were stopped in air. Reducing tremendous action to stasis became so much the vogue that when, in 1945, Alexey Brodovitch published "candid" ballet shots in which he slowed his shutter to exaggerate the motion blur, the poetic results were not merely unusual but astonishing.

Thus, when Fred Fehl began performance photography early in 1940, he entered an unpromising, even a discredited, field. He would ask press agents for permission to shoot during a dress rehearsal or performance, and they would tell him to come to the Photo Call. He would say he didn't want the actors posed. And they would say, usually in just these words, "You can't take pictures without extra light." "Let me try," Fehl would respond. But the press agents knew what the candid camera could do—or so they thought—and they didn't give him a chance. He photographed a semi-professional production at the Young Men's Hebrew Association, then took the pictures to Hans Jaray, Adrienne Gessner, and Arnold Korff, Viennese actors who were appearing on Broadway in Dorothy Thompson's short-lived propaganda play *Another Sun.* "Please let me take pictures," Fehl asked his fellow refugees. They persuaded the rest of the company to let him shoot during a performance. The results were good, and he took the best pictures to Karl Bernstein, a veteran press agent then handling Vinton Freedley's revival of *Liliom* with Ingrid Bergman, Burgess Meredith, and Elia Kazan. Bernstein let him work during a Saturday matinee, March 30, 1940. Fehl dates his career on Broadway from that afternoon.

The *Liliom* photographs turned out well. Bernstein ordered some for the lobby and said, "Why don't you take the prints by *Theatre Arts*?" Fehl said, "What's *Theatre Arts*?" Bernstein explained that it was *the* American theater magazine, which published a dozen or so pictures each month. Using Bernstein's name, Fehl got in to see Hermine Issacs, an associate editor and daughter of the magazine's editor-in-chief, Edith Issacs. She looked at the pictures a moment and then, Fehl remembers, she asked,

> "How did you take these pictures?" I said, "During a performance." "Without light?" "Yes, yes, without light. In action."
> She had never seen anything like them. She said immediately that she'd give me a full page with two pictures. And she said, "We would like more—more pictures like these." I said, "I will be glad

to, but give me a letter of recommendation saying that you're interested in any pictures I can take."

She wrote the letter, and it was my passport to the press agents. From then on I had no difficulties getting in.

Once in the theater Fehl worked like other performance photographers, literally and figuratively in the dark, having to guess at exposures and hit a moving target when it was not really moving. But he had two advantages. First, his years with the Leica had taught him what it could do and what it could not. He didn't make the common mistake of sitting back a few rows, trying to take pictures that would resemble, in content and framing, traditional production photos. He realized that, given the technology of the time, he could not get a clear shot with many people in it. His stock-in-trade had to be individuals and couples and trios. He made a virtue of necessity and moved closer than previous candid cameramen. His second advantage was his long experience with the arts. He knew how plays worked. He had an almost musical sense of pace, of when a climax would occur and an actor take a significant—and photographable—pause. He captured these moments in pictures which, though necessarily less sharp than posed ones, were far more lively, impulsive, compelling.

The special vitality of his work was recognized by many theater people. Throughout the early forties *Theatre Arts* drew attention to it. The November 1940 issue ran the picture reprinted here of Grace George in *Kind Lady* with this caption: "Much of the tension latent in the role of

Grace George in the 1940 revival of *Kind Lady*.

this lady who is held prisoner in her home by a group of criminals is captured in this candid camera shot." The January 1941 issue carried the photograph of the Helen Hayes–Maurice Evans *Twelfth Night* reproduced later in this book and said about it: "The lyric and romantic quality with which Stewart Chaney, in his scene and costume designs, and Margaret Webster, in her direction, have imbued this Shakespearean revival is well recreated in the lights and shades of this candid camera shot." José Ferrer was struck by the warmth and energy of Fehl's pictures of his performance in the 1940 revival of *Charley's Aunt*. "From then on," Ferrer says, "I insisted that he be called for all the shows that I was in, using what leverage I might have with the management. When I became a producer myself, I relied on him exclusively for my shows." Elia Kazan writes that Fehl was the first photographer to "capture the scenes I directed in the theatre on film with the precision of the living moment." When Fehl photographed the dress rehearsal of Kazan's 1948 production of *Sundown Beach*, one of the cast members amazed by the results was Julie Harris. She remembers: "It was my first experience with a photographer taking pictures during the performance, because professional companies called in photographers then, and there'd be a photographic session and the pictures would be *posed*. When I saw Fred's pictures, it was a revelation to me because they were so full of feeling, and I thought, 'That's the only way to take pictures of actors—when they're working.'"

Fehl built his career on just this premise: "Only in performance," he insists, "can you see an artist's highest emotional expression." In his remarkable candid close-ups of the forties we see actors for the first time as they appear to us on stage—glowing with energy, deeply within their passions and new selves. Against his somber backgrounds their faces blaze like incandescent lamps, and we feel, almost like heat upon us, the power of their art, their charisma.

People had done available-light performance photography before Fehl, but he was the first to be good enough to make a living doing only it. Indeed, until faster films and emulsions came on the market in the late fifties, it was a profession in which he had no peer. Other photographers tried their hand at it, found they couldn't compete, couldn't get the pictures he got, sometimes didn't get anything at all, and dropped out. Fehl, in contrast, handled not only theater but dance, a much tougher art to capture with the tools then available. In Broadway circles he came to be known, in a pun on his last name, as "Fred without Fail," the man who always got the picture.

This was how Fehl worked. When he saw an interesting show announced, he went to its press agent and offered his services. In the early years press agents would say they had already hired the production photographer. Fehl would say yes but not to do performance pictures, and offer to shoot the dress rehearsal or a performance out of town on "spec." The press agents would pay him nothing unless they liked one or more of his pictures, in which case they could buy rights and prints from him as they did from any free-lance photographer. Press agents, having nothing to lose but a possible photo in *Theatre Arts*, generally said okay.

Fehl much preferred to work dress rehearsals because he could move about in front of the first row. Sometimes, however, directors refused to have a camera shooting then, and he had to cover a performance with an audience. On these occasions he sat front row center or, if the front row was too low, in the first row of the balcony. He disliked the balcony not only because of the distance but also because shooting down foreshortened the performers, made them look big-headed and stubby.

Traditional theater photographers watched one or two performances to pick out moments to restage for the camera. Fehl, in contrast, almost never saw a show before he shot it. At first he used one Leica with a 50mm lens and another with an 85 or 90mm telephoto lens; in the early forties he added a third camera with a 135mm lens for head shots.

Old-style theater photographers worked autocratically, the center of attention, bending the show to the camera's needs. Fehl did just the opposite. He took pains to be unobtrusive so that the actors would forget about him and give themselves to their parts. Julie Harris and José Ferrer both remark how inconspicuous he was—"like part of the scenery," Ferrer says. Marcel Marceau said he liked Fehl's pictures of him because he could never relax in a studio the way he did on stage, where there seemed to be nobody present but the audience. Casts were always told when Fehl was working out front. Nevertheless, when he returned a couple of days later with pictures to sell, time and again an actor would say, "When did you take these? I didn't know you were shooting."

Shooting Fehl's way was as much a performance for him as for the actors. He remembers: "It was tremendous, hair raising. I got more exhausted than the people on stage. Because I was so *in* it, so going with it, so feeling what they were doing. And concentrating, concentrating: which is the right movement? Now? If you take the high point a second too soon it's not good yet; if you're a second after it's no good anymore. Which camera is right? Has the light changed? What is my exposure? You couldn't read it: you have to get the knack of guessing it through your fingers. And all this time you can't be thinking, because you haven't time to think. If I ever thought when I was going to shoot, I'd never shoot." The dress rehearsal over, Fehl would drive home (if that was possible), develop the film, sleep three hours, then get up and spend the day printing 5 × 7 proof copies to show the press agent the next afternoon.

In 1944 the producer Edward Choate, an early fan of Fehl's work, contracted him to take pictures of the Edward Chodorov play *Decision*. It is probable that this was the first time a performance photographer was hired as a Broadway production photographer. Thereafter, though Fehl continued to free-lance, most of his work was done on contract. As production photographer he received a flat fee for covering a show. Payment of this fee gave the press agent the right to use any of his pictures in show publicity (it did not give the press agents *prints* of the pictures: prints were sold separately at rates spelled out in the contract). The negatives themselves, their copyright, and all residual rights stayed with Fehl. More than fifteen years after the original production, he continued to sell permissions to reprint his famous *West Side Story* pictures.

By the late forties his theater pictures were appearing not only on marquees and billboards and in *Theatre Arts*, but also with articles and reviews in the New York papers, *Cue*, *People Today*, *Newsweek*, and *Time*, in *Look*'s photo essays on the latest hits, and as a monthly one- or two-page feature on the Broadway scene in the *New York Times Magazine*. His *Times* features, which began in the early forties in the rotogravure section, were done on special assignment; the pictures the *Times* chose of

*Tom Prideaux, *Life*'s theater editor, recalls that the magazine customarily had a three-hour call after a straight play, a four-hour call after a musical. In that time its photographer could take eight to fourteen different moments from the show. Prideaux and the photographer would see the show several times beforehand and make a shooting script of what they wanted. They gave a copy of the script to the stage manager, who arranged the order in which the shots were taken so as to minimize setups, give actors time to change costumes, and let those who were only in one or two pictures go home early. The producers paid the stagehands' overtime because *Life* was wonderful publicity and because, Prideaux explains, "they knew from experience that *Life* (although we never guaranteed publication) usually printed the theater pictures we shot. If ever we had to reshoot a show due to our own failing (I recall only two or three instances of this in 30 years) we paid the stagehands' bill for the second call." Prideaux adds that, to avoid "the frozen look of a posed picture, we always asked the actors to run through two or three lines, or a few motions, of any scene we wanted, and we would shoot them in mid performance, so to speak."

a show could not be used by its press agent until the paper published them.

During the 1949–50 season Fehl added a new technique to his repertoire. At the dress rehearsal of the January 1950 production of *The Man*, he used multiple synchronized strobelights. He set four strobes on tripods equal distances apart in front of the stage and fired them simultaneously as he took pictures. "Strobelight gave the advantage," he says, "that I could light up the stage uniformly, left to right, front to back. You will notice in the pictures I took with strobelight the background is perfectly clear, which you do not see with available light." Adding a fourth camera, with wide-angle lens, he now was able to photograph whole sets and chorus scenes like the traditional theater photographer, and still do it "candidly," while the show went on—indeed, while the chorus was in the air. Not only this, the light from the strobes was so intense that he could step his lens down, increase the telemagnification, use much larger negatives (2 1/4 × 2 1/4, even 2 1/4 × 3 1/4)—in fact do all these things at once—and get fine-grain close-ups of the actors.

As noted, strobelight had been used for a decade to record athletic feats. It was seldom used, however, for the performing arts. Barbara Morgan wrote in 1941 that it was aesthetically wrong for all but "acrobatic" dance pictures because its 1/10,000-of-a-second duration created an "ultra stopped effect" that exaggerated "muscle strain" and gave bodies a "mechanically hard contour." Morgan, who believes that the "spark and feeling" of dance only come across in performance, made her remarkable dance photos of the late 1930s and early 1940s by having dancers perform in her studio and lighting them with floodlamps and with multiple flashbulbs, which have a much longer duration—about 1/30 of a second—and hence a "softer," more flexible light. In the 1940s Gjon Mili, the strobelight pioneer, sometimes covered Broadway for *Life*. He had used strobes to capture ballet leaps (in color) as early as 1940 and no doubt often used them for theater work. It is likely that a small portion of this work was candid, with unposed actors, since *Life* had exclusive photo calls, after shows opened on Broadway, where Mili could take scenes any way he pleased.* But most stage photographers didn't use strobes until the early 1950s, when they replaced flashbulbs as the light source for quick, posed shots.

Among his theater photographs Fehl is fondest of those he took with strobelight for such shows as *Darkness at Noon*, *Mrs. McThing*, *The Solid Gold Cadillac*, *Inherit the Wind*, *The Diary of Anne Frank*, *No Time for Sergeants*, *Separate Tables*, *West Side Story*, *A Touch of the Poet*. Gone from these pictures are the dramatic chiaroscuro, the evocative softness of his earlier work. The strobe photos are sharper, far richer in tonal contrast, and—because the small aperture keeps everything clear—more compressed on the picture plane. Margaret Webster was so delighted at the pictures Fehl had taken of her 1950 production of *The Three Sisters* that she wrote thanking him; the pictures were done with strobelight, and her words excellently set forth its advantages: "The photographs are not only a faithful and expressive record of the actual performance, without any of the artificiality of posed pictures, but they are extremely sharp and clear, and therefore very good for reproduction purposes. This is the first time that I have met the two qualities in combination." Strobes allowed performance photos to be technically as neat as posed photos.

Strobes had, however, two important drawbacks. First, they violated the stage lighting. Like the hand-held floods of the old-style theater photographers, they could give an inexact impression of the mood of a show, particularly of a drama, and throw extraneous shadows. Second, the flash always threatened the actors' concentration, and in a dress rehearsal building toward the opening a loss of concentration can be disastrous. It is testimony to the confidence actors had in Fehl that he was able to use strobes as often as he was (apparently no other Broadway photographer used them for performance shooting). But even he worked most of the time without them.

By the late fifties, fast emulsions and developers had changed all theater photography. Most shows still used photo calls with posed pictures, but negatives were smaller (2 1/4 × 2 1/4 or 35mm), shutters faster, supplemental lighting reduced, and cameras off tripod. In the early sixties, single-lens reflex cameras with built-in meters took the guesswork out of low-light shooting, and Broadway tried to protect itself against the onslaught of photo amateurs by putting in *The Playbill* the ominous sentence, "THE TAKING OF PICTURES IN THIS THEATRE IS STRICTLY FORBIDDEN." By the mid-sixties virtually every production was photographed in dress rehearsal—often photographed to a fare-thee-well. Now when he worked a show Fehl sometimes found the front rows crawling with camera people: the latest hot-shots, pros breaking in (or out), hopeful free lances, hobbyists who were relatives of the producer or bedfellows of the star. The congestion was almost a bigger nuisance than the competition.

Margaret Webster (Masha), Cavada Humphrey (Olga), and Louisa Horton (Irina) in *The Three Sisters*, Woodstock Playhouse, 1950.

Erik Bruhn and Alicia Markova in "Les Sylphides," the American Ballet Theater, 1955. One of the most often reprinted of ballet pictures.

Fehl didn't need these impediments. He already had his hands full with other work. Through the fifties and sixties he had photographed scores of famous musicians in rehearsal and performance, usually for the *New York Times*. He had been permanent photographer to the American Ballet Theater since 1940, to the New York City Opera since 1944, to the New York City Ballet since 1948. Indeed, in the trade he had become better known as a photographer of dance than of theater. He was a contributing photographer to *Dance Magazine* and *Dance News*, and had photographed more than sixty of the leading companies, early–Martha Graham, Ballet Russe de Monte Carlo, José Limón–and late–Paul Taylor, Robert Joffrey, Alvin Ailey. He had collaborated on a book with Melissa Hayden (*Melissa Hayden Off Stage and On*, 1963) and was working on one with Erik Bruhn for Dance Perspectives (*Beyond Technique*, 1968). As interest in the dance surged during the sixties he was more in demand than ever. Furthermore, photographing dance was not the grind that theater photography was. Dance was all in Manhattan, so he didn't have the hassle of driving out, shooting, driving back, developing, and printing in a day and a half. A dance company's run was publicized with pictures taken the year before or earlier, and new dances, having no dress rehearsal as such (because the costumes are seldom ready), could not be photographed until the premiere.

Fehl preferred photographing dance because it, of all the performing arts, is most gloriously *visible*. But he had loved photographing theater –loved it so much that for years he took time from his vacation to cover summer stock as well, though he lost money doing it. Having shot shows as early as he did, he had seen remarkable things: *Gypsy* in such bad shape that its dress rehearsal could not get through act one, *Visit to a Small Planet* before Cyril Ritchard spoke to the cat, *The King and I* when it was five hours long and did not have "Shall We Dance?" and Richard Rodgers and Yul Brynner crouched upstage discussing the problems they faced. He had photographed stars who disappeared from their production the next night and dozens of shows (and two actors) that died on the road. He had seen the Broadway hits of three decades and some flops–*Truckline Café*, for instance–that still haunt him.

Yul Brynner and Richard Rodgers discuss *The King and I* after the New Haven dress rehearsal.

He withdrew from stage work gradually. In 1965 he stopped applying for new shows when he had other commitments at about the same time (formerly he would have done both jobs) or couldn't get the contract he wanted or wasn't interested in the people involved. The last shows he covered were in early 1970, productions by the visiting Comédie Française. He continues working today as a performance photographer of ballet and opera.

During the years he worked on Broadway, Fehl photographed nearly one thousand shows. This was by no means every one. Some shows he couldn't get into: the press agent did not want performance pictures, occasionally because the aging stars demanded that their pictures be retouched. Some shows he had to choose between: they were having dress rehearsals at the same time hundreds of miles apart ("I made mistakes," Fehl says with a smile. "I didn't always choose *then* what I would choose now"). And some shows he passed over because they were not worth photographing free lance: the smell of disaster hung too heavy on them; nobody would want their pictures, not even the actors. For whatever reason, there are shows missing from Fehl's Broadway record—and this book—that one would pay in blood to have his pictures of: *The Skin of Our Teeth, Oklahoma!*, the Paul Robeson *Othello*, the Laurette Taylor *Glass Menagerie*, the Laurence Olivier *Oedipus, A Streetcar Named Desire, Guys and Dolls, Long Day's Journey into Night, Who's Afraid of Virginia Woolf*.

Nevertheless, Fehl is likely *the* Broadway photographer of his time. No other photographer covered so much. No other photographer got so many of the important shows. His pictures appeared in tens of thousands of newspaper and magazine articles and hundreds of books—appeared everywhere the Broadway stage was paid attention to. Fehl's name is not known outside the world of performing arts, but his theater pictures *are*. More than any other person, he created the image that persists of a generation of Broadway shows. And as José Ferrer observes, "More than any single photographer, he changed the style of theatrical pictures."

Before Fehl, the usual Broadway picture was posed. After him, the usual picture was done his way. There were technological and economic reasons for this change, but the main reasons were commercial and aesthetic: Fehl's kind of photography did the job better.

The job of theater photography is to help the press agent sell tickets. "The press agent is in charge," Fehl says. "Every picture I took was negotiated through a press agent." Press agents who hired Fehl or allowed him to shoot wanted straightforward pictures of a production—pictures that would show possible ticket buyers what it was like and, at the same time, excite them about it, stimulate their curiosity. These press agents did not want "artistic" photographs where tricky darkroom work put the principals in silhouette or vignette or washed everything with an impressionist mist. They did not want a photographer who made the performance more "visual" by shooting it against grey velour drapes or actual brick walls. Other photographers did stunt work of this sort, sometimes to great acclaim, but not Fehl.

He was a literalist. What you saw in his pictures was what you saw if you went to the show. He scrupulously respected the American tradition that the theater photographer shoot a performance only as the audience can see it. In England, where production costs are relatively

Paul Muni relaxes by playing drunk during an intermission in the dress rehearsal of *Inherit the Wind*.

A *Folies Bergère* girl gets ready for the technical rehearsal.

less and theater photography more prestigious, this tradition does not hold; photographers like Angus McBean and Tony Snowden cross the proscenium and shoot from on stage, *within* the performance, getting close-ups from angles unavailable to the audience. "In this country you're always limited to photographing from the house," says Harold Prince, who prefers British theater photography. He adds: "I think probably that's the producer's fault, or the director's. We restrict our photographers; we tie their hands. We don't give them the time they need. We generally make them work during a dress rehearsal, when I, as director, am much concerned about the production, which hasn't opened yet. And photographers are in my way; they're wandering around in my way, and I wish they'd get out of my way. In England they get much more time and attention. *And* respect." To many Americans, though, British stage photographs are forced, unsettling. The viewer feels himself inserted where he is not supposed to be. The actors look hammy doing their tricks in such an intimate space and for a camera right at their ear. And the pictures, though unobjectionable perhaps in a magazine where a drama's plot is given step by step and the camera becomes a sort of engaged onlooker (*Life* sometimes used the British technique this way), seem false and wrong in ads or outside the theater –*existentially* wrong, as the Hollywood stills on the marquee in the forties and fifties looked wrong when one came out of a movie because they showed scenes from angles and at moments that never appeared on the screen.

Fehl didn't cover shows from on stage because that is not the American tradition. He didn't cover shows *backstage* because that was not his job. He was a theater photographer, not a photojournalist; he shot the performance itself, not "stories" about it. Magazine and newspaper photographers, in contrast, were usually after a show's sidelights, the odd goings-on behind the scenes, the personal lives of the players. Fehl never looked for "off-stage" candids, though occasionally, when a dress rehearsal was held up, he might notice something worth a picture: a scowling *Folies Bergère* chorus girl glueing herself in her costume, Paul Muni playing drunk to amuse the *Inherit the Wind* cast, Rouben Mamoulian thinking about the arrangement of curtain calls for *St. Louis Woman*, Orson Welles showing how a thug leans against a wall in *Native Son*. Sometimes, too, the press agent might decide that people backstage– the director, say, or the author–were conspicuous enough to draw customers and ask Fehl to do posed shots including them. Typical results are Fehl's pictures of Maxwell Anderson, Harold Clurman, and Elia Kazan preparing *Truckline Café*, Rodgers and Hammerstein with the *Me and Juliet* company, John Gielgud and Peter Shaffer with the leads in *Five Finger Exercise*.

The point always was to provoke interest. Photos of big-time actors are of course interesting in themselves, but our interest multiplies when the actors are caught in the throes of a plot unknown to us. A Broadwaygoer of the 1950s would have recognized most of the actors in the accompanying pictures from *Happy Hunting*, *Fallen Angels*, and *Mrs. McThing*. Looking at each picture before having seen its show, he would have wondered, for example, why that small boy (Brandon de Wilde, already prominent because of his work in *The Member of the Wedding*) exasperates Helen Hayes and startles the meek roughneck (Ernest Borgnine, still an unknown). How is Nancy Walker driven to such a funny rage? What wisecrack has Ethel Merman for Daisy the horse? How do they handle a horse on stage? Are there housebroken horses?

But the actors do not need to be famous or the show any good for the photo to work—if *it* is good. *Journey to the Day* was a 1961 summer theater production which, with a different cast, ran twenty-nine performances on Broadway in 1963. *Diamond Orchid* lasted five performances on Broadway in 1965. We may not recognize the actors in either photo-

Brandon de Wilde, Ernest Borgnine, and Helen Hayes in *Mrs. McThing*.

Nancy Walker in *Fallen Angels*.

Ethel Merman and Daisy in *Happy Hunting*.

Nancy Marchand in *Journey to the Day*, 1961, Westport Country Playhouse.

Jennifer West and Bruce Gordon in *Diamond Orchid*.

Mary Martin and Ezio Pinza in *South Pacific*. Mary Martin (1959): "It is easier to produce a great tone when the body is in vigorous tension. Like Wagnerian opera. You know how Tristan will clutch Isolde to his breast and sing, and then Isolde will clutch Tristan and sing. That's not passion—they just want to grab hold of something to sing against."

graph yet still be intrigued to know what caused the one woman's puzzled grief, the other couple's gay—is it entirely gay?—contortion.

Such photos not only stir our interest; they also give us information about each show so that we can decide *how* interested we are. Are we in the mood to watch a couple climb over each other? Do we want to see someone cry? Can even Ethel Merman save a show in which they have her playing to a horse? Is Nancy Walker as a bored haute bourgeoise too absurd—or just absurd enough? At most basic, the photos offer a rough rating guide of the audience each show is for. Helen Hayes is G–family entertainment. Despite her evening gown, Ethel Merman is, too; the kids will love the horse. The other shows require discretion (PG). *Journey to the Day* will bore the young, and *Diamond Orchid* is an outright No for preteens.

The usual procedure for theater photographers, especially those doing performance work, was to show the press agent contact prints of all negatives made of a show. Fehl did not do this. Instead, he took an extra day and made high-quality 5×7 prints from the negatives he deemed of possible interest. He made these proof prints for two reasons. First, he thought it hard for the press agent to judge a picture's effect when it was one tiny image in lock step with many others on a page. Second, he wanted to edit what the press agent saw. Fehl considered it his responsibility to make a show and its performers look their best. When a photo was obviously no use to the press agent—like the powerful but grotesque one of Mary Martin and Ezio Pinza printed here—Fehl did not show it to him.

The press agent thumbed through the proof prints, selecting those he wanted copies of. Occasionally he or Fehl would take them to the stars for their approval: the photo of Merman and the horse has Merman's initialed "OK" on the back. Some press agents themselves marked the prints to record their verdict. A press agent for *Illya Darling* tore half across Fehl's close-up of Melina Mercouri hugging two young men to her. The picture was exciting and good of Mercouri, but it was rejected (one assumes) because Mercouri's gesture and face and the men's lowered heads made her look maternal and thus gave away what the press agent wanted kept secret: she was old for the part of a romantic heroine. Nat Dorfman, press agent for *The Heavenly Twins*, put a blue X on the pictures he refused, and we see why he Xed the picture of Faye Emerson and Gaby Rodgers. The women seem to have lost their concentration. Rodgers' face is empty, rather chillingly so (which is perhaps interesting). Emerson's face is slack and heavy on its bones; she is bored–bored not as an actor acting boredom: really bored. The contrast with the picture of Emerson and Jean Pierre Aumont in the same play could not be sharper; here are performers at full energy of attention. Dorfman made not a mark on this print.

Good show photos are photos that make a show look worth seeing. This book has a wide and representative selection of Fehl's best photos, the ones press agents chose to billboard their shows. And these pictures suggest that there are patterns in theater photography: certain kinds of images recurrently sell certain kinds of shows because they feel appropriate.

Consider drama first. The force of a drama comes from its plot, and of course a plot, which is built over time, cannot be shown in a photograph, which is of an instant. The accompanying picture from *Decision* has two men arguing. The high social and human consequences of their dispute are unknown to us until we see the play or read, for instance, the caption that accompanied the picture in the April 1944 *Theatre Arts*.

Ethel Merman's OK on the back of Fehl's picture of her and Daisy. Fehl stamped his name, address, and phone number on the back of all show photos.

Melina Mercouri in *Illya Darling*.

The Heavenly Twins, 1955. *Left*, Faye Emerson and Gaby Rodgers. *Right*, Jean Pierre Aumont and Emerson.

"Fascist and liberal—both American—confront each other in Edward Chodorov's *Decision* in the persons of a crooked lawyer and a fighting school superintendent. The lawyer Allen (played by Howard Smith) has just made it clear that superintendent Riggs (Raymond Greenleaf) shall either resign as chairman of a citizen's committee which is preparing to expose political leaders behind a local race riot or suffer the consequences of a trumped-up charge of rape. Riggs' refusal to surrender leads to his murder. *Decision* is a forceful statement in melodramatic terms of the playwright's conviction expressed by the superintendent to his soldier son: 'I believe we are living, now, in the midst of a very real civil war—a war that must be decided before you come home for good—or you will come home to the ashes of the cause for which you fought'"—Caption from *Theatre Arts*, April 1944

Julie Harris in *Marathon '33*.

Similarly, the extraordinary portrait of Claude Rains in *Darkness at Noon* reproduced later in this book does not inform us of the play's circumstance: that an old Bolshevik, Rubashov, is being hounded to death by the brutal system he created in hopes of bringing justice and brotherhood to the world. The picture does not show us what the play is about —and yet deeper and more fundamentally it does. For it shows us someone with fearful courage facing up to the darkness of his fate—Man Suffering, Man Alone.

As Rubashov in the play gains tragic stature by his isolation, so Rains in this picture gains power because the scenery and costuming are darkly undefined. The reduction of extraneous detail forces our attention on his face, which is his character's soul, intricate with meanings we immediately grasp but have to struggle to put in words. Molière said that theater needs only a platform and a passion or two. W. B. Yeats remarked that actors performing in picture-box sets look smaller than life. Thornton Wilder argued that décor, particularly "realistic" décor, vitiates whatever happens on stage. Fehl's pictures of plays like *Death of a Salesman* and *Sweet Bird of Youth* suggest that, as regards drama, these men were right. Actors in drama gain by loss of detail. Their faces, like Julie Harris' in *Marathon '33*, are freed to be more eloquent when some of the world is stripped from them. Thus, in handling "serious" plays the canny photographer works rather as the sculptor does, carving away excrescences, cutting down to the pure shape of emotion.

In handling comedy the photographer seeks the same kind of telling expressions—"high moments," Fehl calls them—and because of the way comedy works, such expressions and the emotions they represent are usually more *legible*, less ambiguous than in drama (as an example, contrast Nancy Walker, p. xxvii, with Julie Harris, this page). But there is an obvious difference between most good comedy pictures and most good drama pictures. In comedy pictures detail counts. A character is not seen isolated from his environment, like Rubashov. On the contrary, environment—scenery, costume, make-up—is an important part of his meaning. Look at the picture of Menasha Skulnik in *The Fifth Season*.

Menasha Skulnik in *The Fifth Season*.

Much of the humor of this radiant, leering figure comes from what is about him: the cold (but "normal") room with magazines curling from disuse and a pointless mask on the wall, the martini shaker with nickle-plate top and complex mixing guide on the side, the bulky suit of good cloth and burlesque pants. Skulnik makes the sort of life the theater public knows—cocktail time in the rising middle class—look full of un-expected diversion.

Many literary critics, Alvin Kernan and Northrop Frye prominent among them, have argued that comedy and drama happen in quite dif-ferent worlds. The comic world is crowded with things and full of light. The world of drama is darker, emptier, more constricted. Comic heroes belong to their world; the heroes of drama stand—or try to stand—apart

John Garfield in *Golden Boy*.

Theodore Bikel and Kurt Kasznar in *The Sound of Music*.

from theirs. In consequence, it feels correct that most successful comic photos are more widely framed: look at Helen Hayes on the telephone in *Mrs. McThing*, Cyril Ritchard with Rosemary in *Visit to a Small Planet*, the leads in *No Time for Sergeants*, Shirley Booth in *By the Beautiful Sea*, Ruth Gordon in *The Amazing Adele*, Bobby Clark everywhere. The characters these actors impersonate are seen in their locales and seen from an apparent distance–which is right, since we are to laugh *at* them, whereas we are to empathize *with* the heroes of drama, whom we see most memorably from closer.

Of course it also feels correct that comic pictures are brighter, since light not only makes details visible but also creates a cheerful mood. Indeed, a picture's light or dark tone seems almost by itself to define a show's genre. John Garfield's expression in the accompanying picture from the 1952 revival of *Golden Boy* was not meant as comic; he is Joe Bonaparte, and this is tragedy. But the picture's abundant lighting (from strobes) encourages us to misread the play's intent and think that he is kidding. Conversely the dark tone of the picture of Theodore Bikel and Kurt Kasznar in *The Sound of Music* makes us think Kasznar's anger and the show more serious than both were. Because the picture might mislead potential customers, one press agent Xed the back of the proof print. Another press agent wrote "OK" over the X. The picture was so good that it needed to be used, even though it was off-tone with the show.

Musical comedy pictures follow the comedy pattern. But there is a special picture unique to the musical. The most famous example of such a picture is Fehl's most famous photograph and the most widely reprinted show photo of all time. The picture is from *Damn Yankees*; it is of Gwen Verdon in a black undergarment, hands on hips, head high and slightly to the side, fiercely singing "Whatever Lola Wants." The photo shows what vaudevillians called the "give" moment, the moment when the performer turns directly to the audience and plays to them, often acknowledging their presence. Such moments are highlights of musical theater, and they are always represented in a musical's publicity photos. In many "give" pictures the performers look directly at the audience, as Judy Holliday and Peter Gennaro do in the *Bells Are Ringing* picture. Such eye contact makes only more evident the appeal that is in all these pictures: hey (they say) look us over; see how hard we're working; we really shake our heels for you.

What the "give" picture seeks to communicate–energy, life, commitment–is what performance pictures of drama and comedy and musicals are always giving. In these pictures there is an unmistakable candor. The actors are actually acting; they are not pretending to act so that their picture can be taken. Their concentration is on their roles or other actors or the audience, not on whether the camera has their good side. However sharply they are seen, they still are veiled by their performance.

Performance photography has become the standard Broadway technique because its pictures are–as Harold Prince says, snapping his fingers–"*active*." In these pictures, bodies are out of repose. Foreheads and mouths and necks are working. Eyes glow with darting about or inner agitation. Faces do not *have* expressions: they are crossed by them. And the excitement of live theater, which is due to the immediacy of living actors, comes across, strains against, seems almost to defeat the stillness of the photographic medium.

THE GIVE MOMENT

Above left, Judy Holliday and Peter Gennaro dancing the "Mu-Cha-Cha" in *Bells Are Ringing*.

Above right, Paula Lawrence and Ethel Merman sing the show-stopping "By the Mis-sis-sis-sis-sis-sis-sis-sis-sin-e-wah" in *Something for the Boys*.

Left, The Jets blow "Cool" in the 1964 City Center revival of *West Side Story*.

Earlier we said that when Fehl shot a theater production it was a performance for him too. That is the way he saw it. He explains:

> A photographer cannot be compared to a creative artist, like a composer or choreographer. But I think he can be compared to a *re-creative* artist, like a musician or a dancer or an actor. He is also a performer. A good picture, like a good performance, is a combination of re-creating and creating. The re-creating is that you photograph what is there, what they do on stage; the creating is *how* you photograph it. So I consider myself a kind of an artist.
>
> There is another reason I say this. Maybe it sounds funny, but when I work I have to be inspired. The lights have to be good, the location has to be good, but just as important if not more important the production has to touch something in me. If an actor or a dancer inspires me I can shoot and shoot and shoot. Otherwise . . . Sometimes I am at a performance and my wife, Margaret, whispers to me, "You haven't taken a picture yet." And I say, "They haven't done anything yet. Not to me."

In the pages that follow, Fehl is performing at the top of his art. The shows his pictures re-create for us are sometimes world famous, sometimes forgotten. Fifteen of them ran more than one thousand performances, which seemed like forever on the old Broadway. These shows entered our conversations, gave us songs to sing, changed the clothes we wore. Other shows passed in a fortnight or less, leaving Fehl's memorable glimpse of them and little else.

Hit or miss, the shows are all long dark. The Broadway they were done on, the Great White Way, has updated its act and lost much of its glamor and influence. Certain of the theaters the shows were done in have been razed for more profitable ventures, like pornography and parking cars. The actors who did them have moved on to other engagements, out of show business, into retirement or the grave. "Movies we can see again, TV is taped, but Broadway's strength," says novelist and screenwriter William Goldman, "is that the people are alive." Broadway's strength and frailty.

Here in Fred Fehl's photographs the people are alive, downstage, lustrous, ready to please. They appear to us immediately present, out of time (and yet, because we know so many of their faces and their fates, poignantly *in* time, too). For as long as anyone cares to look, their performance will go on.

William Stott

A Note on the Photographs and the Comments That Accompany Them

The photographs in this book are from negatives or prints in the Fred Fehl Collection of the Hoblitzelle Theatre Arts Library in the Humanities Research Center of the University of Texas at Austin. Fred Fehl and Bill Stott chose the pictures for their photographic and historical interest. The shows appear in chronological order of their opening, the date of which is given in American style (month/day/year), with the exception of *Du Barry Was a Lady*, *The Male Animal*, and *Separate Rooms*, which Fehl photographed during their Broadway runs, after his photographs of *Liliom* had launched his career.

The comments with dates are from published sources, mainly fugitive periodicals. The comments by Yul Brynner, Red Buttons, Imogene Coca, Tom Ewell, Nanette Fabray, Herbert Greene, Gene Kelly, Bethel Leslie, Gregory Peck, John Raitt, and Bessie Mae Sue Ella Yaeger are from unpublished interviews conducted over the last four years for the Oral History Project on the Performing Arts at Southern Methodist University. The comments by Charles Adams Baker, George Balanchine, a Broadway Old-Timer, Harold Clurman, Marc Connelly, Hume Cronyn, Melvyn Douglas, Mildred Dunnock, John Fischer, William Gibson, William Greaves, Julie Harris, Helen Hayes, Seymour Herscher, Alan Hewitt, Gusti Huber, Walter Kerr, Armina Marshall, Russell Merritt, Frederick O'Neal, Alfred Palca, Doris Palca, Harold Prince, Philip Proctor, Tony Randall, Jessica Tandy, Gore Vidal, Sam Waterston, and Florence Williams are from conversations and correspondence undertaken for this book.

The Shows

Ingrid Bergman (Julie) and Burgess Meredith (Liliom) in the Theatre Guild's revival of Ferenc Molnar's play. Shy Julie is falling for braggart Liliom. The mismatch ends sadly. Benno Schneider directed. 56 performances. This was Bergman's Broadway debut.

ALAN HEWITT: The production wasn't as good as you'd think. The casting was wrong. In the play Julie is frail and refined, and Liliom big and virile. But Bergman was such a tall, strong Julie, that at the first pass Meredith, a short fellow, made at her, she would have led one from the floor and let him have it, and that would have been the end of that.

Liliom 3/25/40

ALFRED PALCA: I don't remember what play it was–probably *Golden Boy*–but I was once standing outside a theater, looking at the names of the people in the cast, and I became aware there was somebody standing right beside me. I looked and there was a fellow about my height and a little bit older, and he said, "That's me!" and he pointed to his name in the cast. It was Kazan. He was so proud. Later, when I saw his work as a director–wow! He really grabbed audiences. He got intensity from everybody. He did in acting what Jerome Robbins was able to do in dance: fill the theater with excitement.

Elia Kazan (the Sparrow) and Meredith. Kazan played the villain, who leads Liliom into committing a murder. *Carousel*, Rodgers and Hammerstein's 1945 musical, was based on *Liliom*.

Du Barry Was a Lady 12/6/39

Ethel Merman (May Daly) and Bert Lahr (Louis Blore). Blore, a nightclub washroom attendant, dreams that he is Louis XV and that Daly, the star of the club's floor show, is his paramour Du Barry. Cole Porter wrote the songs. B. G. De Sylva produced and wrote the book with Herbert Fields. Edgar MacGregor directed. Sets and costumes by Raoul Pène du Bois. The big number: "Friendship." 408 performances.

BROADWAY OLD-TIMER: This was just before—or was it after?—the bit where Lahr is chasing Merman round and around the bed, and he falls behind and she *passes* him, a lap ahead!

The Male Animal 1/9/40

Regina Wallace (Myrtle Keller), Matt Briggs (Ed Keller), Elliott Nugent (Tommy Turner), Ruth Matteson (Ellen Turner), and Leon Ames (Joe Ferguson) in James Thurber and Nugent's comedy about academic life and standing up for one's rights. The authors had been classmates (class of 1920) at Ohio State University. Co-editors of the college paper, they had agreed to write a play together someday. In the summer of 1939 both happened to be in Hollywood and decided the time had come. *The Male Animal* premiered in Los Angeles and tried out across the country. Only a modest hit in its Broadway run, it shows signs today of becoming immortal. Herman Shumlin produced and directed. 243 performances.

Separate Rooms 3/23/40

Alan Dinehart as Jim Stackhouse, a gossip columnist, is delighted to see Glenda Farrell as his sister-in-law, Pam, fall adoringly upon Lyle Talbot as Don, his brother. Playwright Don married Pam, the icy star of his first success; until Jim hatches a scheme, Pam shares her bedroom with a Chihuahua, not with Don. Dinehart, Farrell, and Talbot were taking a holiday from successful movie careers. Dinehart wrote this farce with three screenwriters: Joseph Carole, Alex Gottlieb, and Edmund Joseph. Bobby Crawford produced. William Friedlander directed. 613 performances, an enormous moneymaker.

There Shall Be No Night 4/29/40

KANSAS CITY STAR (12/14/41): The capacity audience that attended *There Shall Be No Night* at the Music Hall last night did not know of the sudden news and attendant drama that had struck backstage shortly before the start of the performance.

Alfred Lunt, co-star with Lynn Fontanne in the production, received a long distance telephone call from Robert E. Sherwood, author and one of the producers, to close the company's tour Thursday in Rochester, Minn., due to the fact that the content of the plot is opposed to America's war interests at the present time.

There Shall Be No Night is woven around Russia's invasion of Finland in 1939. Russians, and behind them, the Nazis, are the villains of the piece. The Finns are the heroes.

These were Mr. Sherwood's sentiments in 1939 and during the subsequent year. Now, however, everything is different. The Finns, formerly deep in the affections of the people of the United States, are allied with Germany. Russia is putting up a gallant fight against the Nazis, and has the support and cheers of Americans.

There has been speculation among insiders in the theatrical world, accordingly, as to how long *There Shall Be No Night* could run, or how long Mr. Sherwood would allow it to run. A candid comment heard the other day was "One hiss and off it goes." Mr. Lunt and Miss Fontanne are not actors at whom one hisses without considerable thought and bravery, but Mr. Sherwood, who long has been in the front rank of the "All Out for America" crew, came to a decision in the matter.

Alfred Lunt (*center*) as a Finnish Nobel Prize–winning neurologist, Kaarlo Valkonen; Lynn Fontanne as his American-born wife, Miranda; and Richard Whorf as an American correspondent patterned on Edward R. Murrow. Kaarlo is about to broadcast to America a speech condemning Hitler. By the end of the play the Russo-Finnish war has claimed the life of the Valkonens' only child, a soldier son. Hearing this, Kaarlo renounces his scientific training, straps on a pistol, and goes to his death at the front. Miranda prepares to burn her house and die defending her garden with a rifle. The Lunts toured Robert Sherwood's topical melodrama around the United States, giving nearly 1,400 performances. Fontanne later called the play "the most rewarding and exciting" of their career. Lunt directed. The Theatre Guild produced. Whorf did the sets.

Love's Old Sweet Song 5/2/40

On the porch Doro Merande (Leona Yearling), *at center* Walter Huston (Barnaby Gaul, a lovable carnival flim-flam man), *at right* Arthur Hunnicutt (Cabot Yearling). The Yearlings, Okies in California, have 16 children, one of whom is at left. This, William Saroyan's third Broadway play, ran 44 performances.

ALAN HEWITT: The play would have been a success if Saroyan had left it alone. He insisted on being co-director with Eddie Dowling, and couldn't stop changing things around. He rewrote freely, redirected—he even brought in people off the street, people who had never seen a theater before, and insisted they be cast in the play. By the second week in Philadelphia, though, the play was in fairly good shape. The Theatre Guild decided, "By God, we've overcome the problems. Now let's just play it and let everybody get used to it." And the New York opening was postponed for a week while we went to Baltimore to smooth everything out. But Saroyan just couldn't stop making changes and we came into New York a mess instead of being a fairly neat play.

Walter Huston could have stopped Saroyan—he had the power to—but he was tractable, terribly tractable and amenable—many of the great actors are. They aren't troublemakers. If they like the director and the actors they're working with, they'll say, "Well, all right, I've got enough to worry about with my own part. I'll just go ahead and do this, and we'll see."

I had a terribly funny monologue in the play. Terribly difficult, too, because I had to memorize the then 74 names on the masthead of *Time* magazine. "Editor of the magazine is Henry R. Luce; managing editors of the magazine are Manfred Gottfried, Frank Norris, T. S. Matthews; associate editors are Carlton J. Balliett, Jr., Robert Cantwell, Laird S. Goldsborough, David W. Hulburd, Jr., John Stuart Martin, Fanny Saul, Walter Stockly, Dana Tasker, Charles Wertenbaker; contributing editors of *Time* magazine are Roy Alexander, John F. Allen, Robert W. Boyd, Jr., Roger Butterfield, Whittaker Chambers, James G. Crowley, Robert Fitzgerald, Pearl Kroll, Louis Kronenberger," and so on and so on. Try to make a narrative of that! A mere 37 years ago, but once you have beaten that stuff into your mind, it can stick.

Keep off the Grass 5/23/40

Jimmy Durante, Ilka Chase, and Ray Bolger in a revue by many hands. Harry Kaufman produced for the Shuberts. George Balanchine choreographed. 44 performances.

At center Jackie Gleason, *at right* Emmet Kelly.

GEORGE BALANCHINE: I remember a very interesting story about this number. It's called "Horse with the Handsome Behind" and was written by Vernon Duke and Ira Gershwin first for *Ziegfeld Follies*. It was just a little song I staged—and it was nothing. Nothing happened in it or anything. And they throw that out. Later when we did *Keep off the Grass*, Harry Kaufman was an aide to Shuberts and he said to me, "George, I've got wonderful property I bought." So I said, "What did you buy?" He said, "Oh, it belongs to me now." I said, "What?" "'Horse with the Handsome Behind.'" All right, second time! Does he think maybe it's dirty? Who knows? So I staged it *again*. Awful! So awful!

Journey to Jerusalem 10/5/40

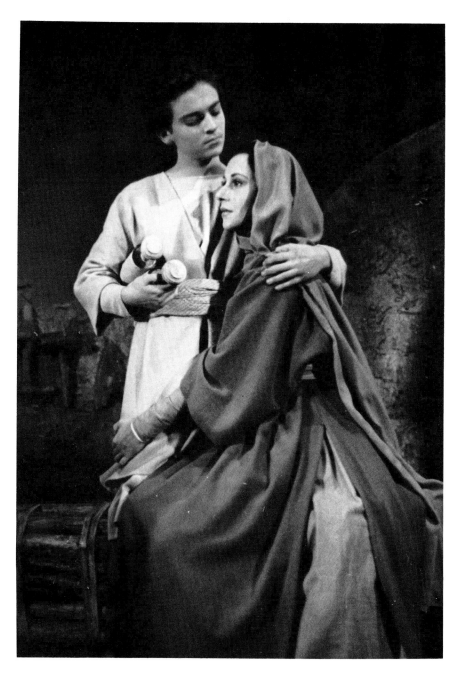

Sidney Lumet as Jesus, called "Jeshua" in the play, assures Arlene Francis as Mary, called "Miriam," that he is happy to be the Messiah. Maxwell Anderson's play, directed by Elmer Rice, ran 17 performances.

Charley's Aunt 10/17/40

José Ferrer ("Babbs"–Lord Fancourt Babberley) impersonates Donna Lucia d'Alvadorez, a rich widow from Brazil, "where the nuts come from." This revival of the 1892 Brandon Thomas farce brought stardom to Ferrer. Joshua Logan directed. Day Tuttle and Richard Skinner produced. 233 performances.

JOSÉ FERRER: It was a very athletic production. I lost five pounds every night. Of course it was all water; I put it right back on.

Cabin in the Sky 10/25/40

GEORGE BALANCHINE: The book was not *Cabin in the Sky*; it was *Little Joe*. And Lynn Root wrote it and Lynn Root knew Vernon Duke. Duke's name was Dukelsky, a Russian, a friend of mine from years and years, from Monte Carlo we worked together. He was a composer, but he played very well jazz and he composed, like, songs. So Vernon told me, "Why don't we do that?" And also Doc Bender–Bender used to be a dentist, he was a friend of Larry Hart's. All those people were on Broadway. Bender said I should direct this. And Aronson.

Q: Another Russian?

BALANCHINE: Another Russian. So three Russians decided to do this thing. We wanted to have Cab Calloway in this play. He used to be singing, you know, jive. We wanted him as the devil, but we couldn't get him–he was too rich at that time. We wanted Rochester, and Rochester wanted to do it but Ethel Waters didn't want him. So then we found this Dooley Wilson who was in the movies; he did some *Morocco*, something like that . . .

Q: Yes, he did *Casablanca*, "Play It Again Sam."

BALANCHINE: But not very well known then this Dooley Wilson. But somehow, I don't know, we started a play. Katherine Dunham, her people and company–I thought it was very nice. Somehow we started. We put some money–I just put nothing, $500 I think. And we couldn't get enough money. And Vinton Freedley finally came at the last moment. We need $5,000, so he put $5,000. We finally got the show. It cost $30,000 only. You see, we put it on Broadway without going out. We opened cold.

Q: Ethel Waters has talked about putting God into the show.

BALANCHINE: Well, God, to me, doesn't go into the show. He lets *us* go into the show. He doesn't go around like that–Super Star; Jesus Christ. Everybody wants to put them in. But they don't exist the way we think they exist.

ETHEL WATERS, *while touring with the show* (1941): Someday, somehow I hope that I can find a play in which I don't have to sing all the time. It's a long time now that I've been singing, and I'm getting tired. I don't know, either, how long my pipes will last, and this show calls for a lot of improvising and has songs that are really out of my range. Yes, I do like *Cabin in the Sky*, and I enjoy being in it, but I do want to do a straight play.

Ethel Waters as Petunia, Little Joe's right-living wife, sings ''Taking a Chance on Love,'' the show's hit number. God looks with such favor on Petunia that Little Joe just does squeeze into heaven.

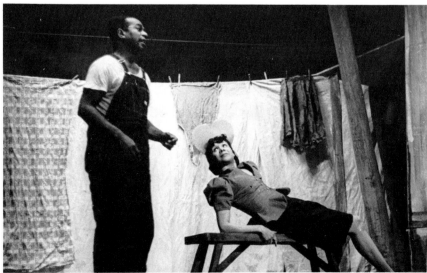

Dooley Wilson as Little Joe, a happily married man, is led into temptation by Katherine Dunham as Georgia Brown. Lynn Root's ersatz folk story had songs by Vernon Duke with lyrics by John LaTouche. George Balanchine directed. Boris Aronson did sets and costumes. Albert Lewis produced in association with Vinton Freedley. 156 performances—enough to turn a profit.

Twelfth Night 11/19/40

Q: I was interested to read in your autobiography that you say you got Viola right in the last two performances.

HELEN HAYES: It was the third performance before the last. That's the mysterious thing in the theater. It's the thing that keeps you there; it's what keeps you struggling. It makes up for all the disappointments when you get that one moment when you know it's right. I had it happen to me once in *Mary of Scotland*. And that night it was such a dramatic happening that the actors avoided me between scenes when I came off to wait for another entrance. We used to sit in the chairs in the dark and whisper and chatter. But no one spoke to me and I was not inclined to speak to anyone. Isn't that strange?

Q: Like a pitcher with a no-hitter.

Helen Hayes (Viola) and Alex Courtnay (Sebastian), the twins in Shakespeare's comedy. The Malvolio was Maurice Evans. Margaret Webster directed. Paul Bowles did incidental music. The Theatre Guild and Gilbert Miller produced. 129 performances.

HAYES: Exactly! Where everybody gets hushed; where nobody dares breathe and break the spell. It's only happened to me a few times in my whole life. And it's really extraordinary when it does happen. You just transcend craft and go right into art. You are transported into the character. And in the case of Viola, I had gotten inside Shakespeare's tale—I *knew* it. The rest of the time, you moil and toil through, and pray that it will come out *fairly* good.

The Corn Is Green 11/26/40

MILDRED DUNNOCK: She was a star if ever there was one. I never think of her as Ethel Barrymore. I always think of her as *Miss* Barrymore. She knew Richard Waring, who played opposite her. She knew me. She knew one or two other people. But the majority of the cast she didn't know. She didn't know the school kids. One day I remember she had a big scene and off-stage somebody sneezed, one of the kids. She had a roll of school plans in her hands, and when she came off she said, "Who was that?" And she rapped the child on the head with the plans. It's difficult for me to know what to say about her. She was a star. I think she was of another kind of theater than we know these days, another sort of being.

Mildred Dunnock (Miss Ronberry), Ethel Barrymore (Miss Moffat), and Rhys Williams (John Goronwy Jones) in Emlyn Williams' autobiographical play. The role of "L. C. Moffat, M.A.," a middle-aged English schoolteacher in a backward part of Wales, was the last great triumph of Barrymore's career. Herman Shumlin produced and directed. 477 performances.

DUNNOCK: I played the part of the schoolteacher and it was typecasting in a way, because I had been teaching school. Once you get typed on Broadway, every time a schoolteacher comes up, they look to you. Or once you get in a success like *Death of a Salesman*, they say, "It's a Linda Loman part." Then you get typecast for another sequence until you fall in with another part which somehow or other captures the fancy of either the critics or the people.

Q: Is this peculiarly American?

DUNNOCK: I don't really know. You see, what is America? America is so much that we don't have a great deal of personality on our own—we're almost everything. I played, for instance, a Jewish mother in the remake of the movie *The Jazz Singer*. There was not one single Jew in that picture, which was all about Jews. The Rabbi was German; Danny Thomas played Al Jolson, and he's Lebanese. The set was filled with priests almost the entire time. And I am a Protestant. Then all of a sudden I got a great many Jewish parts. In *The Corn Is Green* I was a little schoolteacher, shy and timid, and ever after that, every time a little schoolteacher came up, I was sent for.

Pal Joey 12/25/40

GENE KELLY: I didn't know it was going to be a turning point in musical history, and I wonder why I was so dumb. Right from when it opened in Philadelphia the show created a lot of argument—and musicals don't create argument. Usually, people see one and say, "That was nice," "pleasant," or "terrific." But the character of Joey made a lot of women dislike the show—mature women. They thought Joey was mean and immoral. Joey's living with an older woman, and kept by her. That's nothing now, but that was really something then. He's also making love with a young girl at the same time and having affairs with every member of the chorus. He was completely self-centered, brought up in an era in America when whatever you could do to get ahead, you did—quite a true reflection on American society. All this was thinly disguised under a veneer of intimations, but there it was, you know, all hanging out. A lot of people weren't ready for it.

Brooks Atkinson didn't like the show at all; he felt it lacked moral taste. I'll always remember the closing line of his review for the *Times*:

Janet Lavis, Diane Sinclair, Gene Kelly, Frances Krell, Van Johnson (*in background*), and Tilda Getze. Kelly in his first star role as Joey Evans, a hard-boiled on-the-make hoofer, rehearses a number, "You Mustn't Kick It Around," with the chorus girls in a sleazy Chicago cabaret. This landmark musical, the first of the genre to approach moral realism, had Richard Rodgers and Lorenz Hart's greatest score; John O'Hara adapted the musical's sardonic book from his short stories. George Abbott produced and directed. Robert Alton choreographed.

"You can't draw sweet water from a foul well." After the opening we waited for the reviews, up at Larry Hart's house, and Larry called a friend on the *Times* who read the review as it rolled off the press. As he read it to Larry, Larry didn't say anything. Being a very sentimental and emotional man, he started to cry and then went out of the room. And we thought, "Well, maybe we've got a bust on our hands."

Kelly with Vivienne Segal as Vera Simpson, a Gold Coast matron who can't get along without a man and is willing to pay for his favors. They sing "Den of Iniquity." Other memorable songs: "I Could Write a Book," "Bewitched, Bothered and Bewildered," "Take Him," "Zip," and "What Is a Man," one of Rodgers' slow remorseless foxtrots.

KELLY: The ladies from Westchester would come for the Wednesday matinees, always. I'll never forget those Wednesday matinees. They were frigidly cold; they were sub-zero. On some songs they'd just sit there grimly and stare at us and there was hardly a patter of applause. There was one song, "A Little Den of Iniquity," which I did with Vivienne Segal, sitting on pillows out "in one" by the footlights. We dreaded doing that on Wednesday matinees. But it was a pleasure to do the Friday and Saturday night shows, because then we got the swinging group. Then we got the people who came back 20–25 times to see it.

DORIS PALCA: My mother took me out of it because it was *dirty*. She didn't understand the dirty jokes so she thought it was bad for me. I never saw the end of *Pal Joey*.

KELLY: One day at rehearsal George Abbott said to Larry Hart, "Well, we've got to have more choruses." And Larry said, "Yes. Right. Fine." And he took a piece of wrapping paper and said, "Now, let's see, how does that song go?" And he wrote down four-letter nonsense words for the dummy, like, "Zip-a-da-dah-da-dee-blank. Some of a zip-da-da-bleep-da-da-dah." Then he went out. In half an hour he came back with three choruses with interlocking rhymes, interwoven rhymes, inter-rhymes, and interrhyming rhythms. And like Lincoln's Gettysburg Address, it was done on this paper bag, as far as I could see. I've never seen that fast since–I've seen fast, but nothing like that. The things just flowed out of his arm.

First act finale: Joey dreams of the posh nightclub, Chez Joey, he will build with Mrs. Simpson's money. He later tires of her and, blackmailed and disgraced, drifts back to the penny-ante life that suits him. The musical's cynicism was years ahead of its time. *Pal Joey* ran 270 performances. A 1952 revival, starring Segal and Harold Lang, ran twice as long and became, nearly a decade after Lorenz Hart's death, Rodgers and Hart's longest run.

My Sister Eileen 12/26/40

Shirley Booth plays the older, "sensible" sister, Ruth, in Joseph Fields and Jerome Chodorov's hit comedy based on Ruth McKenney's stories about two Ohio girls in Greenwich Village. George S. Kaufman directed. Max Gordon produced. The set was by Donald Oenslager. 866 performances.

All in Fun 12/27/40

Bill "Bojangles" Robinson struts his
stuff in a revue that lasted three performances. Leonard Sillman produced
and directed. Irene Sharaff did the
costumes.

Flight to the West 12/30/40

Paul Henried, Hugh Marlowe, and Arnold Moss. Elmer Rice's play was sort of a philosophical flying *Grand Hotel*. Passengers of many nationalities and political views take a Pan American Clipper from Lisbon and a Europe under threat of Nazi Fascism to the New World. Rice directed. Jo Mielziner did the sets, which included this Bauhausy lounge. The play ran 72 performances at regular prices, then cut price to a dollar top and ran eight weeks more.

PAUL HENREID, *who, himself a refugee from Hitler, played the villain, a cold-blooded German consul on the way to his post in New York* (1940): If I can show how really rotten the Nazis are, then I'll consider that I'm doing my bit.

BROADWAY STORY

When one of his plays was panned, Elmer Rice blasted the New York reviewers, calling them "senile, drunken, and degenerate." One of the reviewers, Percy Hammond, said, "Mr. Rice hasn't told all he knows about us."

Arsenic and Old Lace 1/10/41

BROADWAY OLD-TIMER: Josephine Hull went to Radcliffe—my *mother's* vintage. She was married to one of the leading men of the day who was so gorgeous, my mother said, that everyone got tears in their eyes looking at him. He was the brother of Henry Hull, the actor—you may have heard of him.

Q: Jeeter Lester.

OLD-TIMER: Right, *Tobacco Road*. Well, the brother died young, and Josephine went on to become a delicious character actress.

Jean Adair and Josephine Hull as the lovable Brewster sisters of Brooklyn, who do in friendless old men with poisoned elderberry wine. At the end of the play, Mr. Witherspoon (played by William Parke) comes to take them to a mental home. They suggest he have a drink before they leave and, as the final curtain falls, serve him elderberry wine. The *Baltimore Sun* called Joseph Kesselring's farce "the funniest play about murder ever written." Bretaigne Windust directed. Howard Lindsay and Russel Crouse produced. 1,444 performances.

Boris Karloff as brother Jonathan Brewster, another homocidal maniac. Jonathan has had a plastic surgeon reconstruct his face to make him look like the ghoulish film star Boris Karloff.

The Doctor's Dilemma 3/11/41

Raymond Massey as Sir Colenso Ridgeon in Bernard Shaw's satire on the medical profession. Katherine Cornell revived it. Guthrie McClintic directed. 112 performances.

FRED FEHL: I shot it during a matinee. After the first scene, a note came down from Raymond Massey, "Please no more pictures." Mrs. Roosevelt was in the audience, and the cast was nervous. They didn't want any distractions. I stopped of course.

Five Alarm Waltz 3/13/41

BROOKS ATKINSON (1941): Mr. Kazan is getting to be a self-conscious actor with purple patches and many little curlicues on the side. Cast as the mad genius of the play, he has to act several scenes costumed in a pair of drawers, and it is pleasant to observe that he has a nice little thicket of black curlicues smack in the middle of his chest. Since nature gave him those, he is entitled to them and is herewith handsomely congratulated. But what worries the art lover are the little fancies in his acting style that look as if they had come out of a book. Mr. Kazan's acting in this drama is studiously spontaneous.

Elia Kazan as Adam Boguris, a wacky Bulgarian-American novelist modeled on William Saroyan, and Ann Thomas, who wheels a baby carriage advertising baby carriages. Lucille S. Prumbs' comedy ran four performances. Robert Lewis directed. This was Kazan's last appearance as an actor.

WALTER KERR: I saw Kazan play Eddie Fuseli, the gangster in *Golden Boy*, when I was still in college in Chicago, and I was stunned. I mean, I was so startled by this performance: highly stylized—way beyond anything else in the show. Mesmerizing—you couldn't take your eyes off of him. Damn good. And he got a contract and went out to Warner's.

Then he quit that because he realized that he was going to be cast as taxi drivers for the rest of his life—because he wasn't a handsome leading man. He finally decided that because of the way he looked he was going to be limited and typed, so he decided to go into directing instead.

Louise Platt (Brooke March) and Kazan. Brooke is Adam's wife, a successful playwright.

ELIA KAZAN (1974): I was a very limited actor. I was intense, an intensity that came from all the pent-up anger in me. I didn't have much range. I was like an instrument with only three or four very strong notes. I was referred to in one review as "the proletarian thunderbolt."

Native Son 3/24/41

Director Orson Welles shows an actor how to lean against a wall like a leering hoodlum. Richard Wright and Paul Green dramatized Wright's sensational novel. Welles and John Houseman produced. James Morcom did the sets. 114 performances.

Bigger in prison, awaiting the electric chair. "When I killed that girl," he tells his lawyer, "I didn't mean to kill her. I killed her 'cause I was scared and mad. I had been scared and mad all my life. But after I killed her, I wasn't scared no more – for a little while! I was a man! That made me feel high and powerful and free!"

Anne Burr as Mary Dalton, a rich girl, and Canada Lee as Bigger Thomas, her family's chauffeur who accidentally kills her.

Q: I thought I might say something like, "Welles always says he learned film making by 'studying the old masters: John Ford, John Ford, John Ford.' This picture shows he brought Ford to his plays, too. The backlit jail comes from *Young Man Lincoln*."

RUSSELL MERRITT: The trouble with the Welles-Ford connection is that the photograph doesn't look like much of anything in *Young Man Lincoln*, not even the jail scene.

Q: That's backlit.

MERRITT: A little bit; that was common practice by the 1930s. But what's special in this picture is the positioning of the actor and the stark anti-naturalistic set. The source for both is German Expressionism, which exerted tremendous influence on the American stage in the early thirties, thanks to Max Reinhardt and the German silent films. I've never been persuaded that Ford was an important influence on Welles.

Q: Why does he claim it?

MERRITT: Camouflage. Few artists enjoy talking about their most profound sources of inspiration, least of all a showman like Welles. And of course he does admire Ford.

Watch on the Rhine 4/1/41

Paul Lukas (Kurt Müller, a German anti-Nazi underground agent) and Mady Christians (Sara, his American wife) in Lillian Hellman's strong propaganda play. The Müllers arrive from Europe, Sara's first time home in 20 years. They stop near Washington, D.C., with Sara's mother. When a Roumanian ne'er-do-well threatens to expose Kurt to the Nazis, Kurt kills the man in cold blood. He then says good-bye to Sara and their children and returns to Germany to carry on the fight against Hitler. Herman Shumlin produced and directed. 378 performances.

MARC CONNELLY: It was Paul's best job. I think it was his *apologia pro vita sua*, really. He was chemically right for it, you know–because he was in retreat from life. The play is ten times as good as it was ever credited with being.

ALFRED PALCA: The Blacklist killed Mady Christians. But that's not an anecdote–that's history.

ALAN HEWITT: The Blacklist hurt Mady Christians severely and most unfairly. She had left behind in Germany a husband who was a Nazi, divorced him for his politics. She was liberal, progressive, a maverick, but certainly not a Red. People like her, willing to be a minority of one in a vote–oh, God, you've got to suspect them!

But it wasn't only the Blacklist, one must be fair about this. Theater history is full of important ladies who couldn't find good parts once they got around age fifty–there just aren't that many parts. Laurette Taylor for years couldn't find anything to do. Then there was that miracle of her return to life in *The Glass Menagerie*, which is one of the most incredible performances that anyone of my age ever saw. Mady didn't get a miracle.

Anne of England 10/7/41

JESSICA TANDY: We had *wonderful* costumes. What I remember most vividly was one day when Flora Robson had slapped my face—

HUME CRONYN: In the play, I hope.

TANDY: In the scene, oh, yes. There was an argument about giving brandy to the Queen. I was giving it to her, and Flora Robson, as the Duchess of Marlborough, said I shouldn't and slapped my face. And there I was still holding this cup. Gilbert Miller, who was directing, said, "I don't understand. Why do you just so quietly go and put that cup down? You would do something violent." And I said, "Well, I could throw it right in her face. Would you like that eight times a week over these very expensive costumes?" "Oh," he said, "no! I think maybe you'd better not. What you're doing is just fine."

CRONYN: That was just after I met you. Was it '42?

TANDY: No, that was '41.

CRONYN: '41—just after, one year after. I met you in 1940.

TANDY: I was still trying to make it on my own.

CRONYN: I was still trying to get you to agree to marry me. [*They laugh.*]

Barbara Everest as Anne, Queen of England, and Jessica Tandy as Abigail Hill, a calculating lady of the bed-chamber. Abigail turns the Queen against her long-time friend and confidant the Duchess of Marlborough. The Duke of Marlborough—the *first* Duke, Winston Churchill's heroic ancestor—resigns from the army in disgust, and England seeks peace at any price from the France of Louis XIV. For England, dark days lie ahead. Contemporary analogy didn't rescue Mary Cass Canfield and Ethel Bordon's play: seven performances. Gilbert Miller produced and directed. Mstislav Dobujinsky did sets and costumes.

Let's Face It 10/29/41

Eve Arden as Maggie Watson and Vivian Vance as Nancy Collister, middle-aged married women who pine for the company of young servicemen on a near-by base. Herbert and Dorothy Fields drew the book from *The Cradle Snatchers*, a 1925 farce. Cole Porter did most of the songs, the best-remembered of which is "Farming." Edgar MacGregor directed. Vinton Freedley produced. 850 performances.

Danny Kaye does his hilarious "Melody in 4-F," a patter song about the woes of an Army draftee. The song, which had perhaps a dozen words of straight English, was by Kaye's wife, Sylvia Fine.

Blithe Spirit 11/4/41

Clifton Webb as Charles Condomine fails to convince Peggy Wood as his wife, Ruth, that the spirit of his dead first wife, Elvira, has come to annoy them. Noël Coward wrote this "improbable farce," as he called it, to give Londoners something to laugh at during the Blitz. John C. Wilson produced and directed on Broadway. Stewart Chaney did the sets. 650 performances. *Blithe Spirit* is Coward's most frequently produced play.

ALAN HEWITT: *Blithe Spirit* needs absolutely first-class actors to play it–otherwise, forget it. Amateurs should never attempt it. The kind of high style it needs is almost a vanished art.

People know Webb from the movies–the Belvedere series where he pushes the oatmeal in the baby's face–but it's almost forgotten that he began as a dancer of an elegance equivalent to Fred Astaire's. He'd started as an opera singer in Boston and then began dancing in Paris in the early 1920s at Les Ambassadeurs, a famous nightclub. He came back to the States as a dance leading man.

A notable fact: both Webb and Cole Porter, two of the most sophisticated Americans of this century, were born in Indiana–Webb in Indianapolis and Porter in Peru, which is probably pronounced "Pee-rue."

Leonora Corbett as Elvira teases Mildred Natwick as the wacky bike-riding medium Mme Arcati, whose incompetence summoned Elvira from the dead. Natwick found the dress for Mme Arcati in a heap of discarded clothes at the Salvation Army.

Theatre 11/12/41

Cornelia Otis Skinner as an aging actress who has an affair with a young man to convince herself that she still has appeal. She then goes back to her husband. Guy Bolton and Somerset Maugham made a mediocre comedy of Maugham's mediocre novel. John Golden produced and directed. 69 performances. Skinner, famous for her one-woman shows, first appeared on Broadway in the 1921 dramatization of Blasco Ibáñez's *Blood and Sand*. She had three lines. The play's star was her father, Otis Skinner, at age 66 portraying his last romantic lead, the love-crazed toreador played by Rudolph Valentino in the 1922 film. Cornelia Otis Skinner later wrote of opening night: "During one of Father's curtain calls he caught sight of me standing off at the side, came over to me, snatched up my hand, and to my panic and delight led me onto the set and down to the footlights, where he made a gesture which indicated that he was therewith introducing his daughter to the public and we both bowed, first to the house, then to each other. The curtain came down. Father squeezed my hand, dropped it, smiled, and said, 'Well, Miss, you've made your New York début. From now on–' he waved me off the stage –'you're on your own,' and he strode back for another solo call."

Junior Miss 11/18/41

NEW YORK HERALD TRIBUNE (3/22/42): "The first acting I ever did?" Miss Peardon looked back into the dim past when she was ten. That was when it began, she said. "My father had a business appointment at a broadcasting studio, and I went there to meet him. I had long curls. Somebody pulled them and asked me, 'Little girl, how would you like to be in radio?' I said, 'If other children can do it, I guess I can.'

"So they put me on a program and pretty soon they moved me over to the *March of Time*. I did all kinds of voices. The first of them all was Snow White, and I learned many foreign accents and dialects, too. I did a Russian one for Stalin's daughter. Daddy helped me with some of them, especially French, because he had lived in France. When I was twelve, some one at the studio told me the Theatre Guild was looking for a child to play the little French girl in *Jane Eyre* with Katharine Hepburn. I went to the Guild, and they took me."

Patricia, accompanied by her mother, toured for months in *Jane Eyre*. It was Pat's first stage engagement, *Junior Miss* being her second, and she became devoted to Miss Hepburn. The feeling was mutual. When the play closed without coming to Broadway, the star sent her a note which said: "Dear Patricia, When I am old and you are famous, as you will be if you persevere, you can give me a job. Affectionately, Aunt Katie."

Philip Ober as Harry Graves, Patricia Peardon as Judy, his 13-year-old daughter, and Barbara Robbins as Grace, his wife, in Jerome Chodorov and Joseph Fields' comedy about a Little Miss Fixit who gets her parents into hot water and out again. Peardon, 17, wore two sweaters and padded clothes to give her the "chunky" look of a girl just coming to womanhood. Moss Hart directed. Max Gordon produced. 710 performances and forever after in little theaters.

Angel Street 12/5/41

Vincent Price and Judith Evelyn as Mr. and Mrs. Manningham. Kindly sinister Mr. Manningham is trying to drive his wife insane. Patrick Hamilton's smash hit thriller was produced and directed by Shepard Traube. It was made into the 1944 movie *Gaslight* with Charles Boyer and Ingrid Bergman. 1,293 performances.

SEYMOUR HERSCHER: The famous derby that was left on the table one day by mistake turned out to be the greatest suspense item in the show. The detective has to hide when the husband comes in. But in rehearsal the detective left his hat on the table by mistake, and everybody said, "Oh, my God, the hat!" Then they said, "Leave the hat there! Leave the hat there!" and had the detective run back for it later. From then on, audiences would shout, "The hat! the hat!" It was the big directorial triumph of the show.

FLORENCE WILLIAMS: I used to visit *Angel Street* backstage because I had several good friends in the company. I had done summer stock with Leo G. Carroll, who played the detective, and one Saturday night quite late he called me, very excited.

"How are you, Florence?"

"How are *you*, Leo?" I said, wondering what was going on.

"Are you doing anything just now?"

"No, not much." I was between jobs at the time.

"Well, would you consider making me a couple of shirts?"

I'd often helped with costumes and done some dressmaking for friends. "Shirts?"

"Yes, two shirts for the play." That Friday Leo had seen a dress rehearsal of the road company. The actor playing his part got a huge laugh after a line about being very conservative by taking off his jacket and showing a loud plaid shirt. Leo wanted that laugh! "I bought the material," he said. It was seersucker so he could wash and drip-dry it in his dressing room after each performance.

I said, "Leo, how about the wardrobe mistress?"

"Oh, she said it would take her weeks to get them."

"And when do you want the shirts?"

"Monday." He couldn't wait!

I made the shirts, by Monday.

Leo G. Carroll as Inspector Rough convinces Mrs. Manningham that her life is in danger. He is holding her broach, which belonged to a woman her husband murdered.

VARIETY (12/17/41)

After an air raid warning in New York City, someone said that the Nora Bayes Theater should be the safest place to go, because, "It's never had a hit."

Banjo Eyes 12/25/41

Eddie Cantor in a musical adaptation of *Three Men on a Horse*, the George Abbott–John Cecil Holm comedy about a greeting card poet who's a genius at the race track. 126 performances, but the show could have run much longer had Cantor not left for an operation. Hassard Short directed. Albert Lewis produced. Vernon Duke and Harold Adamson's show-stopping song: "We're Having a Baby."

The Rivals 1/14/42

WALTER KERR: In *The Rivals* he got laughs mainly by visual business. I don't know whether I've ever laughed quite so hard—well, maybe at Buster Keaton films—as I did at Bobby in the letter-writing scene. He's being made to issue a challenge, and he's trying to dash it off, to be heroic about the whole thing. He had this tiny pen, and the tricks he played with the quill pen and the ink pot and the parchment! I can't tell you what they are now; I don't remember them in detail. But they were absolutely fascinating and simply hilarious. So without saying a word for about five minutes he had the audience screaming.

Q: That wouldn't happen nowadays.

KERR: Who can do it? Who can do it? People aren't being trained in it anymore. Thrown into a situation, they can't stand there and do it all by themselves. Beatrice Lillie is out of commission now; she could do it and was doing it within my period of reviewing.

Bobby Clark as Bob Acres pauses to think about the duel he has gotten himself into. Eva Le Gallienne directed this Theatre Guild production, with songs, of Richard Brinsley Sheridan's comedy. Mary Boland was Mrs. Malaprop; Walter Hampden, Sir Anthony Absolute. At the end of his career Clark said Bob Acres had been his favorite part. 54 performances.

FRED FEHL: Clark was always running about, always moving. It was very difficult to catch him.

Cafe Crown 1/23/42

Sam Jaffe (Hymie the busboy at Cafe Crown) and Morris Carnovsky (David Cole, long-time star of the Yiddish theater). Cole wants Hymie's backing for his new venture, a modern-dress version of *King Lear*. Cafe Crown and its habitués were based on the famous Cafe Royal at 12th Street and Second Avenue, gathering place for New York's Yiddish-speaking artists and intellectuals. H. S. Kraft's comedy was directed by Elia Kazan. 141 performances.

BROADWAY STORY

During an actors' strike a producer saw on the picket line a character actor who had often worked for him. Furious, the producer turned to an assistant and said, "Don't ever hire that son-of-a-bitch again until we need him."

THE THEATRICAL AGENT

Charles Adams Baker: I was head of the legitimate stage department at William Morris for 23 years, an agent for performers and playwrights and directors and choreographers. Your obligation as an agent is to get employment for your clients: *you're* the employee. You have to use your experience and discretion to decide what is proper to create and maintain a career. You don't want just *any* job, because the wrong one will kill someone quicker than none at all. In the best sense an agent really has a sublimated parental role, like a psychiatrist or clergyman. You're the one father figure in a world of cutthroat commerce—unless there are stage parents around, in which case the career is impossible. They never understand how the industry works.

A Kiss for Cinderella 3/10/42

Luise Rainer in a short-lived revival of the James M. Barrie romance about a London charwoman who does her part in the First World War by adopting an assortment of orphans. Rainer, Vienna born and a product of Max Reinhardt's theater, was the first performer to win two Oscars: in 1936 as Best Actress for *The Great Ziegfeld* and in 1937 as Best Actress for *The Good Earth*. Lee Strasberg directed. 48 performances. The original Broadway production, in 1916, starred Maude Adams.

Keep 'Em Laughing 4/24/42

Q: How can we explain Moore and Gaxton to—

ALAN HEWITT: Gaxton and Moore. First the straight man, then the comic. Burns and Allen, Abbott and Costello, Martin and Lewis.

Q: Gaxton and Moore—right. But how can we explain them to today's young people?

HEWITT: You can't. God, I'm glad I was born when I was so I saw *great* comedians instead of the junk they put on television now.

Victor Moore and William Gaxton in a sketch in a revue produced by the Shuberts. 77 performances.

Uncle Harry 5/20/42

LIFE (7/13/42): Theatergoers today, looking for escapist entertainment, seem to prefer a quiet, homey murder among the antimacassars as a relief from the news of mass slaughter on every front.

Eva Le Gallienne as a woman who allows herself to be executed for a perfect murder committed by her brother. Joseph Schildkraut played the brother, Uncle Harry. Lem Ward directed Thomas Job's thriller, which ran 430 performances. Le Gallienne and Schildkraut had been Broadway stars since the original production of *Liliom*, in 1920.

Vickie 9/22/42

MILDRED DUNNOCK: The first time I played with Uta and Joe was in *Seventh Heaven* in Mt. Kisco. I played the sister. I don't remember her name, but she was an absinthe drinker and she was a *really wild woman*. I always took the theater rather seriously, and Joe and Uta lived near by and they were wonderfully gay people—not that they didn't take the theater seriously, they did—but they were much gayer than I. I was playing this drunk tough strong woman, and I remember Uta had a crucifix hanging on her neck. In one of the scenes I went over to her and ripped this crucifix off and threw it on the floor. And she burst into laughter. I was so upset; I just couldn't bear it. I thought she thought I was a lousy actress. So they went off to lunch. They had a car with the top down and a flock of spaniel dogs. When they came back in again, Joe came over to me and said, "You were upset, weren't you?" He's a very sensitive person. "You were upset that Uta did that." And I said, "It's stupid of me, but I just feel as though she thinks I'm a dopey actress." And he said, "Oh, no, we think you're one of the best actresses we know. She just did that because you had so much fierceness in you." It cemented us; we became very close friends.

Uta Hagen as Vickie Roberts, a meddlesome war worker, and José Ferrer as her beleaguered husband in a farce that poked fun at women in uniform. Ferrer co-directed with Frank Mandel, the producer. 48 performances.

Hagen and Mildred Dunnock as Mrs. Dunne, a severe leader of worthy causes.

Count Me In 10/8/42

WALTER KERR: *Count Me In* was the first time we were exposed to the mechanics of a Broadway production. I was teaching at Catholic University in Washington at that time, and I collaborated with a graduate student, a friend of mine, Leo Brady, on this show for the university theater. It got such good notices from the Washington critics that all of a sudden people began flooding down from New York. We had a flock of offers on the show, but it was badly muffed. Neither one of us knew how to handle this situation—you know, getting the right Broadway producer out of the ones offered to you, casting, rewrites—we had no notion of rewriting out of town. None! Because in the university, you stage the show and when it opens, it opens. So we got into Boston with this dreadful mishmash and we didn't know how to cope with it.

The play had a slight narrative line: a family trying to engage in war activity—needless to say, this was the beginning of the war. *Count Me In*: that's the point. And so Mama is starting to be an air-raid warden; Daddy is doing this; and Sonny is going off to be a pilot, whatever. And then some Japanese spy material came into it. All that sounds idiotic now, except that's the kind of joke-plot that you used in a musical those days.

But what had been a sly, small, intimate show in Washington was blown up into a monster, and when you made it that big it wouldn't work anymore. We were mis-directed, mis-cast—in spite of the fact that we had a lot of wonderful people: Charlie Butterworth, Luella Gear, Hal LeRoy, Junie Price, Mary Healy, Gower and Jeanne. I mean, my God! you could have gotten a show out of that layout. But we were just a couple of green kids and control was taken right out of our hands instantly.

An acrobatic interlude in a musical with book by Walter Kerr, Leo Brady, and Nancy Hamilton, and music by Ann Ronell and Will Irwin. The Shuberts and Ole Olsen and Chic Johnson produced. Robert Ross directed, under Harry Kaufman's supervision. The critics liked best Irene Sharaff's costumes and Robert Alton's choreography. 61 performances.

Rosalinda 10/28/42

Shelly Winter (Fifi), Oscar Karlweis (Prince Orlofsky), Virginia MacWatters (Adele), Ralph Herbert (von Eisenstein), and Gene Barry (Falke). Von Eisenstein has just recognized Adele, his wife's maid, in one of his wife's gowns, at Orlofsky's ball. Von Eisenstein shouldn't be there either; Falke tricked him. This *Rosalinda* was an Americanization of Max Reinhardt's celebrated 1929 Berlin production of Johann Strauss' 1874 *Die Fledermaus*. Reinhardt's production caused a world-wide resurgence of interest in the operettas of Vienna's ''waltz king.'' In Berlin, Karlweis had played Orlofsky, a role traditionally given to a contralto in male attire. In Berlin and New York the music director was Erich Wolfgang Korngold, a Strauss authority who, in the United States, became a Hollywood composer. The book and lyrics for the New York production were by Gottfried Reinhardt, John Meehan, Jr., and Paul Kerby. Felix Brentano directed. George Balanchine choreographed. Lodewick Vroom and the New Opera Company produced. 520 performances. MacWatters was later a prominent opera singer. Herbert sang and directed at the Met. Barry went from operetta to drama to films to television. And Shelly Winter became Shelley Winters. The music critic Olin Downes called her, ''vocally speaking, the most distinguished stylist of the evening. Her air in the second act was one of the occasions when applause momentarily held up the show.''

Counsellor-at-Law 11/24/42

Paul Muni in one of his great roles: the mercurial George Simon, a Jewish immigrant who has risen from poverty on the Lower East Side to be New York's foremost criminal lawyer. Joan Wetmore played Simon's high-born prig of a wife. Muni had originated his part eleven years earlier, when the play ran 412 performances. For this revival, which ran 258 performances, Elmer Rice, the playwright and director, updated the text and called it a "comedy" rather than a "drama." Comparing the two productions, the *New York Journal American*'s John Anderson wrote: "It is worth noting, I suppose, that the one serious social criticism in the play, which comes with the young radical's bitter arraignment of George Simon as a traitor to his class, produced last night only uproarious laughter. It didn't seem funny in the apple-vending year of 1931."

ELEANOR ROOSEVELT, *backstage after a performance* (1942): In Great Britain, they give their finest actors knighthoods. In Japan, deserving artists are designated as national treasures. Here we have nothing to give you but our applause and our affection and our gratitude. But if I had the power, Mr. Muni, you would be declared an American knight and one of our national treasures.

Something for the Boys 1/7/43

Ethel Merman as Blossom Hart, a defense worker who can receive military radio messages through the fillings in her teeth. This Herbert and Dorothy Fields–Cole Porter musical had amusing things happen to three people who inherit a ranch by Kelly Field in Texas. Hassard Short and Herbert Fields directed. Jack Cole choreographed. Michael Todd produced. 422 performances. The hit song: "Hey, Good Lookin'."

WALTER KERR: That's a marvelous picture. The *lift* in the eyebrows—an exploding quality.

THE "NEW ART FORM"

Q: What accounted for the end of the musical revue?

Walter Kerr: Oklahoma! That's what happened. Strong story—or what was thought to be a strong story. Today you look at *Oklahoma!* and say, *"That's* a strong story? It's all about who's going to buy a girl a basket for the picnic lunch!" Nevertheless, at the time it was a cohesive, coherent, virile narrative, with dances that matched. Agnes de Mille is a very strong choreographer. In fact, I think no one has ever done quite as sexual work in ballet for musical comedies as Agnes—*good* sexual work, honest sexual work. Stronger narrative lines demanded songs that flow out of the story motivation, character motivation. Very often the songs got to doing the exposition as well—which is where I go up the wall. It drives me crazy when somebody sings, "I need a job, I gotta have a job by five o'clock." When I hear that I want to give it all up and go back to "I Love Louisa."

The amazing thing that happened is that the story show, like *Oklahoma!*, killed off the clown show—what I call the clown show. The clown show is the older fashion musical revue which stars an Ed Wynn or a Bea Lillie or a Fred Allen or a Bert Lahr—or three of them together. A revue, too, had a continuity; the fact that it's all songs and sketches doesn't mean that it doesn't need a thread. But the thread was the personalities. A revue would normally have three big stars: you take these three people and you watch them all night. Clifton Webb turns up in one sketch as John D. Rockefeller; Fanny Brice turns up in another as a revolutionary. You're watching them do different things—the same people do different things—and come together in different ways. They have solo spots, but they also play together. And that's fun, when you suddenly see these two personalities merge. And then eventually all three will turn up in something. So you're watching something progress.

Q: And the plot is where will they turn up or what will they be like when they turn up again?

Kerr: That's the fun of it. It is the people who give it its continuity. The book show killed off the clowns, and when your clowns are gone, who can hold a revue together? Eventually it got harder and harder for Bert Lahr to find a clown show for himself. The book show drove them out. And so you find Bert Lahr playing *Godot,* as Bobby Clark played Molière.

BROADWAY STORY

A wardrobe mistress was given an opening-night ticket to *Oklahoma!,* and after the show someone asked her what she thought of it. "You call *those* seams?" she sniffed.

VARIETY (1/27/43)

Reports that there are infrequent disturbances among enlisted men admitted gratis are surprising to some theater managers. The men are most apt to fall asleep being in the habit of retiring early.

Tomorrow the World 4/14/43

Skippy Homeier as Emil Bruckner, a Nazi-educated 12-year-old in a Midwestern college town, and Shirley Booth as Leona Richards, his uncle's fiancée, whom he once calls a "Jewish whore." James Gow and Arnaud d'Usseau's play stirred up great controversy. Elliott Nugent directed. Theron Bamberger produced. The set was by Raymond Sovey. 499 performances.

GRACE HALL, *wife of a clergyman* (1944): The play certainly gives you something to think about. It makes you wonder if we Americans are actually going to be able to bring the indoctrinated Nazi children into a democratic way of life.

ALAN HEWITT: Up to this play, Shirley had been principally a comedienne. Now she was playing drama and showing how well she could do it. It's a lot easier to go that way, from comedy to so-called "serious" theater, than in the other direction. Comedy is much more difficult; ask any actor who has done both.

Sons and Soldiers 5/4/43

GREGORY PECK: My impression of Max Reinhardt was of a very great man past the peak of his powers. But there were still embers glowing there of a big, big creative talent, of a warm and loving disposition, of a man who is used to a lot of power but who had adjusted to no longer having it. He had been the genius of German theater, and then of course a refugee from the Nazis. He was living in a modest New York hotel.

He would sit out in the orchestra during rehearsals and usually relay his directions up to the actors through a very lovely woman named Lili Darvas, who had been with his company in Germany. He never shouted out directions; he always conveyed them. Either he would make the long walk up through the orchestra onto the stage and take you quietly off to one side, or, more often, he would send Lili Darvas up. He never directed actors so that anybody who happened to be standing around could hear it, especially if he had something critical to say. He loved actors and was far too sensitive to do things that way.

I remember best an incident where he *did* walk all the way up from the back row of the orchestra and take me aside. I was playing a young fellow and I had a scene which called for quite a bit of dialogue. I had to laugh at one point and then cry, and then do both at the same time. That can be done, and human beings do behave that way sometimes. But as a young actor of twenty-three or twenty-four, it was hard to shed all my self-consciousness and just go ahead and do it.

And I was having trouble. I was faking the laughing or the crying or possibly both. It just wasn't right. I wasn't professional. As a professional you deliver; you do what the author wants you to do. But I was holding back on my emotions. I was afraid to let go. It was rather embarrassing because everyone could see that the scene wasn't coming off the way it should.

So he paddled all the way up and he took me off to one side and he said, "I know what you're going through, young man, but you must throw your self-consciousness to one side and just play, just pretend. We don't mind if you don't do it well the first few times, but you won't do it well at all unless you stop taking yourself too seriously. It's play-acting." And he said, "After all, we in the theater are privileged. We can go on play-acting and pretending all of our lives. Most people have to stop doing it when they're grown up, but we don't have to stop. It's just play, it's play, that's all it is."

And that was the key that unlocked the door for me.

HAROLD CLURMAN: The play was almost totally ruined by Norman Bel Geddes' set, and he knew it because he took his name off the program. The set was unwieldly and made everything awkward; it had no intimacy and the play needed intimacy. Very few sets ruin a play but that one did. Well, that happens.

58

Stella Adler (Catherine Carnrick) and Gregory Peck (Andrew Tadlock) in the Irwin Shaw play, directed by Max Reinhardt. 22 performances.

Andrew (to Catherine, his mistress). When you chuckle it's as though the whole female sex, all the women who ever lived and loved men, were in this room. God bless the female sex. When I die, no matter how I die, I'll remember this afternoon, and I'll say, "I'm glad, I'm glad!"

The Two Mrs. Carrolls 8/3/43

Victor Jory as Geoffrey Carroll and Elisabeth Bergner as Sally, his second wife. Geoffrey is trying to kill Sally with slow poison. Martin Vale's melodrama ran for two years, thanks to Bergner's surprising, low-keyed performance. A product of the Reinhardt theater, she was one of the greatest European actresses of the century. Reginald Denham directed.

MILTON BERLE ("The Berle-ing Point," *Variety*, 9/1/43)

Hitler will be remembered in history as The Hotfoot in The March of Time.

What's Up 11/11/43

Jimmy Savo as the Rawa of Tanglinia. The plot of this musical comedy has him caught in a measle quarantine at a girls' finishing school in Virginia. One of the schoolgirls with a love problem calls President Roosevelt for advice. George Balanchine directed. 63 performances.

ALAN HEWITT: Savo was unique. He was a dear little man. His vaudeville number, his hallmark, was "River, Stay Away from My Door." He did pantomime to this. He would kneel down and, bending over, push the river away from the door. It was the sweetest thing you ever saw in your life. He had this beatific little Italian face, a chubby body, and these enormous eyes. He was an adorable comedian. Most unusual.

GEORGE BALANCHINE: It would be now a smash, because it's a very funny show. You laughed. That was Fritz Loewe and Alan Lerner, their first show. Every song was beautiful. But at that time there were no Names, only young nice talented people. Except Jimmy Savo. Jimmy Savo had a name, but not a name that people grabbed, you know.

Q: Did that experience persuade you not to direct any more?

BALANCHINE: No. I am not director, really. It is not my business to direct words. I can stage, I can see if something is well dressed–I can do this. But I cannot direct dialogue, certainly American dialogue. It is not my business. George Abbott is a great man; he finds how to make funny lines. You need someone like that.

Q: But you did direct *Cabin in the Sky*.

BALANCHINE: *Cabin in the Sky* I did direct, but you see we had a dialogue supervisor. I did all this, the idea, how it looks and, you know, the whole thing. Only I did not do the conversation. Also, the sound, you know, blacks talk a certain way. How can anybody . . . ? They do themselves very well without me. No, I was just placing people and dressing them.

Winged Victory 11/20/43

ALFRED PALCA: I knew a lot of these fellows because I was in *This Is the Army*, the other soldier show from World War II, the one Irving Berlin wrote. You know something funny? Last night was the 35th anniversary of the opening of the show. The company had a reunion at Sardi's. Doris and I were supposed to be in Europe until today, so when I was invited to this dinner I said, "I can't go." And I forgot about it until last night when I was out on Broadway and a woman whose husband was in our company said, "Why aren't you down at Sardi's?"

Q: Did you run down?

PALCA: No, I didn't.

DORIS PALCA: You should have.

The graduation ceremony, the awarding of pilots' wings, at the end of act one. Moss Hart wrote this pageant play for the Army Air Force in three weeks and staged it in 17 days. The cast was made up of 300 soldiers, 41 of their wives, and nine professional actresses. Sgts. David Rose did the music, Harry Horner the sets, Howard Shoup the costumes, Abe Feder the lighting. Lt. Leonard de Paur was choral director. The U.S. Army produced. *Winged Victory* and *This Is the Army* raised millions of dollars for Army Emergency Relief. 212 performances, then long tour.

ALAN HEWITT: The strictly military people involved in it—the colonels and majors—thought all these guys were goof-offs. They didn't have any respect for them as actors and felt they had to chew their asses off all day long to make them feel like soldiers. Finally people like Moss Hart and Irving Berlin told the colonels, via Washington and the Pentagon, "The most important thing these fellows have to do is the show at 8:30—not do close-order drill and calisthenics. They're in the army to give a show and you clowns are not to tire them out so they have no energy."

THE PLAYBILL: *Red Buttons* is a graduate of the burlesque circuit who acquired his stage name by virtue of his initial night club appearance in bellboy costume.

"The Yuletide Follies," a GI Christmas celebration on a South Pacific island. At center is Pvt. Red Buttons; with him are the Slate Brothers, Pvts. Henry and Jack. They are doing a parody of the Andrews Sisters.

Carmen Jones 12/2/43

Luther Saxon (Joe) and Muriel Smith (Carmen Jones) in Oscar Hammerstein II's hit adaptation of Bizet's *Carmen*. The all-Negro cast included many people who had never appeared on stage before. Saxon had been working in the Philadelphia Navy Yard, and Smith in a camera store. Hassard Short and Charles Friedman directed. Eugene Loring choreographed. Robert Shaw directed the singing, Joseph Littau the music. Howard Bay did the sets, and Raoul Pène du Bois the costumes. Billy Rose produced. 502 performances.

Glenn Bryant, as the heavyweight
contender Husky Miller, sings Hammerstein's adaptation of the famous
Toreador Song. *"Toréador en garde!
Toréador, toréador"* becomes "Stan' up
an' fight until you hear de bell, stan'
toe to toe, trade blow fer blow!"

The show-stopping quintet "Whizzin'
Away along de Track." Smith is at
center; the others are Edward Lee Ty-
ler, Dick Montgomery, June Hawkins, and Jessica Russell. In Bizet's opera
the quintet sings of how advantage-
ous it is to have women help on a
smuggling venture.

The Voice of the Turtle 12/8/43

Elliott Nugent as Bill Page, a good-humored Army sergeant, meets and spends the weekend with Margaret Sullavan as Sally Middleton, a young actress, in this hugely popular three-character comedy written and directed by John van Druten. Alfred de Liagre, Jr., produced. 1,557 performances.

MARY MCCARTHY (1946): *The Voice of the Turtle,* while not a serious or particularly well-written play, makes an original contribution to the stage. John van Druten has discovered for the theatre a new American type, a type with whom we are all familiar in life but have not seen behind the footlights. This is the character played by Margaret Sullavan; she is the well-brought-up American girl who, at twenty-one, has had two affairs, yet remains at heart a virgin, an innocent, a perennial spinster who will always be more in love with her apartment, her flowers, her possessions, her treasury of quotations from poetry, than with any man she sleeps with, whose bed the morning after a sexual adventure will always be made up, with the spread indented under the pillows, while coffee for two drips in the Silex and toast pops out of the electric toaster. This is the eternal college girl, who will be windswept and hatless at forty, and whose old age no one so far can predict.

Jackpot 1/13/44

Nanette Fabray (Sally Madison) leads a chorus of war workers in "The Last Long Mile," the first song of this Guy Bolton–Howard Dietz–Vernon Duke musical. Sally offers herself as first prize in a war-bond rally. Three Marines win her, then can't decide how to divide the spoil. Naturally she goes to the one who's handsomest and the singer. Vinton Freedley produced. Roy Hargrave directed. The best-remembered song: "Sugar Foot." 69 performances.

Jerry Lester, Betty Garrett, and Benny Baker, the show's comedians. The musical's first act finale was a Charles Weidman ballet parodying the dances in *Oklahoma!* It was called "Grist for de Mille."

THE PLAYBILL: *Betty Garrett* is a St. Joseph, Mo., girl who spent her early days on the West Coast. She came east to dance with Martha Graham's group, appeared in *Meet the People*, *Let Freedom Ring* and *Of V We Sing*. During the World's Fair she did a chaste strip tease in a Pullman car four times a day in the famous pageant "Railroads on Parade."

Jacobowsky and the Colonel 3/14/44

Oscar Karlweis (S. L. Jacobowsky, a Jewish refugee originally from Poland) and Louis Calhern (Colonel Tadeusz Boleslav Stjerbinsky, a Polish aristocrat). As France is falling, Jacobowsky and the Colonel, opposites in class and character, team up to outwit the Nazis and get vital information to London. Karlweis, himself born in Poland, had been a refugee in Berlin, Vienna, Prague, Paris, and Lisbon. He arrived in New York in October 1940 knowing two word of English, "beefsteak" and "money." After the war he returned to Germany where he was an actor, director, and translator of American plays. Elia Kazan directed and the Theatre Guild produced the S. N. Behrman adaptation of this Franz Werfel comedy. Behrman cut this line from Werfel's text:

Jacobowsky. No, Colonel! I am no better than anyone else. But I *do* have one advantage over you. I can never be Hitler, never as long as the world lasts. But you could easily have been Hitler, and you still could be. At any time!

415 performances.

Anna Lucasta 6/8/44

(at the 135th Street Library Theater)

8/30/44 (on Broadway)

FREDERICK O'NEAL: It's a funny thing: that play was written for a Polish-American cast. We had it in our files for two or three years, and then the author's agent called us and said, "Look, what do you think about making this a play about blacks?" Abe Hill, the co-organizer of the American Negro Theater, and I finally got Harry Gribble interested in it. And then Abe worked on it, and John Proctor, and I did too; during rehearsals I think I wrote most of my own lines. But it was mainly Harry. Phil Yordan, the author, had said, "Go ahead; do anything you like."

It was quite a success. This play in our theater was one of the first off-Broadway productions reviewed by the daily press. And we got wonderful reviews. People began to come up to Harlem to see it, and eight people were bidding for the rights to present it on Broadway. Phil Yordan came to see it and he didn't like it–because it wasn't his play anymore. It was as different as day and night. When we went to Broadway, I said to Harry Gribble, "Why don't you see if you can't get co-authorship?" Harry said, "He won't give it to me. He doesn't like it, but he insists that his name be on it." At that time Philip Yordan was a rewrite man for Columbia Pictures; now he has several production companies. Harry Gribble is 84 years old and in retirement.

Earle Hyman (Rudolf) and Hilda Simms (Anna). An innocent agricultural student from a prosperous Southern black family, Rudolf comes North to look for a wife and falls in love with Anna, a prostitute and the Lucastas' only unmarried daughter. Harry Gribble directed. John Wildberg produced.

O'NEAL: Earle came to the American Negro Theater when he was only seventeen, in 1940 or '41. And he got sort of hooked on Ibsen. He became interested in everything Norwegian. He studied the language–became fluent in it. Years later he went to play with the Norwegian State Theater. He played with them for some time and then won the award for the best artist of the year—I forget what year it was now. And that award is not restricted to performing artists, but includes architects, historians, and so on. As a matter of fact, the only other performing artist to win it was Charlie Chaplin. There's a bust of Earle in the State Theater in Oslo. He goes back and forth now, working in the language.

Rosetta LeNoire as Stella, Anna's sister; George Randol as their father; Georgia Burke as their mother; and Frederick O'Neal as Frank, Stella's husband. Greed in his heart, Frank defends Anna's right to reform her life and make a new start with Rudolf. When the play was done in Harlem, Anna didn't get a new start: she committed suicide. When the play came to Broadway, the ending was changed: Anna and Rudolf began a happy life together. The play ran more than two years in New York and more than a year in London.

O'NEAL: When we did the play in London, Jack Hylton, the producer, took us all to the races. You know, racing is different in England—you get served lunch and dinner and champagne. Well, Georgia Burke, who played the mother, loved the races. Wherever we played, if there was horseracing, she was there. We went directly from the races that day to our evening performance. In one scene, Earle and Hilda are on the sofa in the living room by themselves, and just as they are about to kiss, Georgia is supposed to come in the door and slap her hands together—because she's all for it—and say, "Halleleulia!" Well, when she came in this time, Georgia still hadn't gotten over the racetrack and that champagne, so she said, "Helllllllo!" Earle and Hilda were supposed to draw quickly away, very embarrassed. That night they put their heads in their hands and broke out laughing.

Song of Norway 8/21/44

Q: Is there a difference between working with ballet dancers and musical comedy performers?

GEORGE BALANCHINE: First of all, ballet people, you know what training they have, you know they dance a certain way–one way. It's a different type of entertainment, the ballet. Musical comedy is a story, it's a comedy, requires acting, singing. Opera is different. Opera is not musical comedy, really. But *opéra-comique*–like in France, they call it "operetta"–it's the same as musical comedy. I did lots of them in France.

A moment from one of the dances. This Milton Lazarus–Robert Wright–George Forrest musical was based on the life and works of Edvard Grieg. Over 250 of Grieg's compositions were used in the score. The dancers were from the Ballet Russe de Monte Carlo; George Balanchine choreographed. Charles Freeman directed. Edwin Lester produced. 860 performances.

VARIETY (9/27/44)

Bramwell Fletcher introduced something new in curtain speeches at the opening performance of *Rebecca* at the Schubert, New Haven. Following several curtain calls for the players, Fletcher stepped to the footlights and held up his hands in the dramatic gesture which means silence. A hush fell over the audience expecting to hear some gracious words of appreciation. What came out was, "I have been asked to announce there will be no bus or trolley transportation available."

I Remember Mama 10/19/44

SCRIPT FROM "THE GOLDBERGS" ON WMCA (1944):

Ethel. It is jam-packed with humor, sentiment, and that something I just can't explain. . . . Call it enchantment or pleasing feeling.

Julius. You can say, IT LEAVES A PLEASANT TASTE IN YOUR MOUTH . . . IS GOOD?

Ethel. Is very good. You'll never forget MAMA. You'll have never enough praise for her. I REMEMBER MAMA, and so will you, for many seasons to come, right at the MUSIC BOX THEATRE. TERRA MARTA. IT'S SOLID. IT'S EARTHY. IT'S WHAT YOU NEED THIS OR ANY OTHER NIGHT. I REMEMBER MAMA.

Julius. Forget anything, Ethel?

Mady Christians (Marta, "Mama"), Frances Heflin (Christine), Ellen Mahar (Aunt Sigrid), Carolyn Hummel (Dagmar), Ruth Gates (Aunt Jenny), and Marlon Brando (Nels). Nels tells Dagmar that the cat on her lap is a male.

Mama. Nels, how you know?
Nels. I looked!
Dagmar. How can you tell?
Nels. You can.
Dagmar. But how?
Mama (quickly warning). Nels, you do not say how!

This nostalgic comedy was written and directed by John van Druten, and produced by Rodgers and Hammerstein. 714 performances.

THE PLAYBILL: *Marlon Brando* was born in Calcutta, India, where his father was engaged in geological research.

VARIETY (10/25/44)

Eleanor Roosevelt attended a performance of *Soldier's Wife* in the Golden, New York, and afterwards went backstage to visit the cast of the Rose Franklin play. The company manager secured a taxi for her and gave the driver $2 to wait for the first lady. Instead he scrammed. When the President's wife was ready to leave another taxi was found and as she entered the cab Mrs. Roosevelt graciously asked whether anyone was going uptown. There were many people standing under the theater canopy because of a heavy rain. A young couple accepted the invitation.

Sadie Thompson 11/16/44

Daniel Cobb, Norman Lawrence, June Havoc (Sadie), James Newill (Sgt. Tim O'Hara) in a musical version of Somerset Maugham's ''Miss Thompson.'' Ethel Merman had been slated for the role of Sadie but bowed out because she didn't like Vernon Duke's songs.

Havoc was much praised for her performance, though several reviewers couldn't forget Jeanne Eagles' corrosive Sadie in the 1922 play, Rain. Howard Dietz and Rouben Mamoulian did the book; Mamoulian directed. 60 performances.

Laffing Room Only 12/23/44

MARC CONNELLY: They weren't funny; they were just absurd. Of course, absurdity can be exploited and almost turned into something which is comedically attractive. They had tricks that were beguiling: the man coming in trying to deliver the potted plant which grows each time he appears in the theater–that's all right as what used to be called a running gag; that was funny. But the two men themselves, I thought, were outrageous. They were about as funny as the Royal Nonesuch. Do you remember the Royal Nonesuch?

Q: You mean in Mark Twain?

CONNELLY: You remember they left town quite suddenly. The Duke of Bilgewater and the Dauphin. In Twain they were funny, but in real life they must have been appalling. Well, I thought Olsen and Johnson were that, too. Olsen had hyperthyroid; or was it the other one? One of them had it.

Ole Olsen and Chic Johnson heckle the audience in their third rock-em sock-em vaudeville show. Their first, the 1938 *Hellzapoppin*, ran 1,404 performances. The second, the 1941 *Sons o' Fun*, ran 742. *Laffing Room Only* ran 232. Burton Lane wrote songs for it, one of which was ''Feudin' and Fightin','' later made famous by Dorothy Shay, the Park Avenue Hillbilly. John Murray Anderson directed. The Shuberts and Olsen and Johnson produced.

Q: I can never separate Olsen and Johnson . . .

CONNELLY: I wouldn't want to.

Q: . . . in a photograph.

CONNELLY: I don't think it matters which is which. They had enough momentum to put their show over. They were comedic emetics.

Mata and Hari, comic dancers.

A Lady Says Yes 1/10/45

Hollywood's Carole Landis makes her stage debut. Book by Clayton Ashley and Stanley Adams, music by Fred Spielman and Arthur Gershwin, staging by Boots McKenna. 87 performances.

VARIETY (12/21/44): The title of *A Lady of ?* has been changed to *A Lady Says Yes*.

CUE (1/20/45): The trouble with *A Lady Says Yes*, the latest Shubert musical to hit Broadway with a thud, is that though you pay more to see it than you would for a burlesque, you get less.

Hope for the Best 2/7/45

Franchot Tone as Michael, a folksy newspaper columnist with 11 million readers, and Joan Wetmore as Margaret, his fiancée, a sophisticated political writer. Michael wants to take up "serious" writing from a liberal slant; when Margaret pooh-poohs the idea, a factory girl doesn't and wins his love. Tone believed in William McCleery's play, had money in it, and his popularity kept it going for 117 performances. Jean Dalrymple produced.

PEGGY DOYLE, *columnist for the Hearst press* (1945): Franchot Tone is by way of being a healthy if reluctant threat to the Sinatra supremacy in the bobby sox poll.

MARC CONNELLY: Now, wait a minute. Franchot Tone, and who else was in that? I've forgotten. I can hardly remember the play—it's a Freudian thing. I've just dismissed it from my mind. It wasn't a very good play, but it was better than the critics let it be. Franchot had a kind of desperation feeling about it because he realized that it was a flop. And I'm guilty of having had a hand in putting it on because I directed it. But isn't it awful? Isn't it indicative of how you don't remember unpleasant things? I can't remember a damn thing about it except the hero was noble. The whole thing is fuzz and veiled.

Hollywood Pinafore 5/31/45

George S. Kaufman rewrote the book of Gilbert and Sullivan's *H.M.S. Pinafore* as a parody on the movie industry. Here Shirley Booth, as gossip-columnist Louhedda Hopsons, explains why she's called "Little Butter-Up." Kaufman directed. Max Gordon produced. 52 performances.

Concert Varieties 6/1/45

Katherine Dunham. This "vaudeville entertainment" was "assembled and presented by Billy Rose." 36 performances.

Zero Mostel.

LIFE (1/18/43): Mostel's proudest boast sounds like a gag but is not intended to be. "I was the first radio comic to demand a second front," he says.

IMOGENE COCA: I almost die opening nights. Opening nights to me are like death time. If someone were to come to me and say, "Do you want this to be a hit, with the understanding that you'll drop dead the second the curtain comes down?" I'd say, "It's a deal. You're on."

Imogene Coca and William Archibald in their spoof ballet "The Morning After of a Faun."

COCA: We did the regular Nijinski choreography. We always did the regular choreography of whatever ballet I was doing; we only changed little bits and pieces.

Strange Fruit 11/29/45

Mel Ferrer as the weak brooding protagonist in Lillian Smith's adaptation of her novel about race relations down South. José Ferrer (no relation) produced and directed. 60 performances.

Hamlet 12/13/45

Maurice Evans (Hamlet) and Lili Darvas (Gertrude). Major Evans had played this version of *Hamlet* with a soldier cast throughout the South Pacific. He and the director, Sgt. George Schaefer, had trimmed the play to two and a half hours. They cut the Fortinbras subplot because they felt the politics of war would bore the soldier audience. They cut the graveyard scene with Yorick's skull and the talk about how long it takes a buried corpse to rot ("some eight year or nine year–a tanner will last you nine year") because they felt the soldiers would think it "corny." They cut all references to cowardice, like Ophelia's description of Hamlet's "knees knocking together." This production ran 147 performances on Broadway, *Hamlet*'s longest run to date. Evans produced.

SEYMOUR HERSCHER: I was backstage one night when Maurice Evans played *Richard II* on Broadway. He was the producer and business manager, as well as the star. He was standing offstage waiting to go on for the marvelous scene when he kisses the ground–very emotional homecoming–and he suddenly turns to the box office man and says, "How much did we do tonight?" "$8,000." "$8,000? That's *terrible*! 'I weep for joy to stand upon my kingdom once again.'" In the same breath he was on stage and had transformed himself. That's an actor.

The Would-Be Gentleman 1/9/46

Bobby Clark (Monsieur Jourdain) in his adaptation of Molière's satire. Michael Todd produced. John Kennedy directed. The costumes were by Irene Sharaff. 77 performances.

WALTER KERR: Of course, Bobby Clark invented that famous line from *The Would-Be Gentleman*; I suppose you know it.

Q: No, no.

KERR: They're trying to teach him proper pronunciation, and it's explained to him that the alphabet is divided up into two classifications: there are consonants and there are vowels. And he said, "Hmm. That's only fair." Well, that's not in Molière, but it's very funny. Got an awful big laugh.

Truckline Café 2/27/46

HAROLD CLURMAN: I don't understand to this day why it wasn't a success. I thought it was a good play because it gave a sense of the kind of cut-off quality that the GIs felt when they got back to civilian life.

FROM THE PLAY:
[*Sage enters slowly, very tired. His clothes are dark and heavy on him. He has just come out of the sea.*]

Sage. Don't be afraid. I swam back from the pier. To give myself up. [*He looks out.*] They're still watching out there. I guess it didn't occur to them if I could swim out I could swim back again. One of you ought to go and tell them I'm here. If you don't–well, it's compounding a felony, I suppose. I might escape, you know. I might escape justice. That would be terrible. You wouldn't want that to happen. . . . Let's see–where are we? I keep having to remind myself where I am. I shot Troy–with the automatic pistol–and then gave her body to the sea. That makes me a murderer. Escaping from the law. Do you know what it feels like to be a murderer escaping from the law? No, you don't. It feels like being anybody else. It's no different. Only you know they are going to come and get you. Oh, God, oh, God, I wish I had her back. If I hadn't killed her she'd be here now. It could be almost as it was. Not quite, but pretty much. She was guilty. When we went into that cabin, I said, "Is it true?" and she said, "Yes, it's true, but don't kill me, because I love you and we can be terribly happy." Then I took out the pistol and shot her. Ten times. Five–and then five. But I wish I hadn't. I wish she were here. We could have been happy together. I'll never have anything now. [*He shakes his head as if to clear it.*] No matter. A fellow has to keep going up to the time they come and get him. I wonder if I could have some coffee.

CLURMAN: Maxwell Anderson was a gentle, sweet man, who could only be aroused once in a while. Early in my career, I said a stupid thing to him. I wanted to cut some lines of a play called *Night over Taos*–which I wasn't even directing. I said, "This speech is longer than anything in Shakespeare." He got really angry and he said, "This is my play." I agree it was a silly thing for me to have said. I think he was angry because he was often accused of writing a kind of semi-Elizabethan verse and criticized for it–so the reference to Shakespeare was not welcome.

He was a very serious and rather sad man. A big, tall, hulking fellow and a very genuine person who looked deeply hurt by something or other–the whole world. He was very romantic in his nature. He liked tiny women over whom he towered like the Eiffel Tower over a cottage. I think one of the best things he ever wrote was "September Song" because it came right out of his heart; he was getting older. It was rather sad toward the end of his life because he had a long series of failures.

Harold Clurman, director and co-producer; Elia Kazan, co-producer; and Maxwell Anderson, author. When the play was panned, Anderson took out a newspaper ad to protest the reviews: "The public is far better qualified to judge plays than the men who write reviews for our dailies. It is an insult to our theatre that there should be so many incompetents and irresponsibles among them." 13 performances.

THE PLAYBILL: *Marlon Brando* was born in Bangkok, while his father was engaged in zoological research.

CLURMAN: Marlon Brando was never better at any time later. The audience applauded him for almost a whole minute, and that's a long time in the theater.

Q: Someone said that when he came back from the murder and drowning, it was as if he had an epileptic seizure.

CLURMAN: That's that nonsense of people saying he was overacting. I always said, "I wish everybody else could overact the way he does." It was better than anything some of the English actors who are so highly praised could do. I haven't seen such acting since John Barrymore. It was terrific. It was inside of him—a psychic explosion.

Marlon Brando in the important secondary role of Sage McRae, his first Brandoesque part. Sage has come back from the war in the Pacific believing his wife, Troy, to be unfaithful. During an offstage confrontation he shoots her and then carries her body into the ocean.

St. Louis Woman 3/30/46

Pearl Bailey in her Broadway debut, a musical with book by Arna Bontemps and Countee Cullen based on Bontemps' novel *God Sends Sunday*. Cullen died while the show was trying out. Lena Horne withdrew, as did Antony Tudor, the choreographer. Rouben Mamoulian was brought in to direct, but the show didn't jell. It had haunting Harold Arlen–Johnny Mercer songs: "Come Rain or Come Shine," "Any Place I Hang My Hat Is Home." 113 performances.

A moment from a dance.

Mamoulian just before he staged the curtain call. Among his shows: *Porgy, Marco Millions, R U R, Porgy and Bess, Oklahoma!, Carousel*, and *Lost in the Stars*.

Woman Bites Dog 4/17/46

Kirk Douglas and Mercedes McCambridge as the idealistic young lovers in a Bella and Samuel Spewack comedy about conservative publishers and the Communist menace. Five performances.

Call Me Mister 4/18/46

MELVYN DOUGLAS, *who produced the show with Herman Levin*: During the war I was assigned to Army Special Services in the China-Burma-India theater. At that time Special Services covered the PXes, Information and Education, Army radio stations and newspaper, off-duty athletics and entertainment. The only stateside entertainment available to us was movies. We were receiving none of the USO entertainment; we were too far away and transportation was much too scarce.

One day the captain in charge of my division said to me, "Douglas, why don't you see what you can round up in the way of live entertainment over here?" I began scouting around. I found a small band attached to an Air Force unit in Karachi and with the aid of some old burlesque routines, gags from Joe Miller's joke book and donated clothing, put together a sort of junior high school review. I spent about three months with this spectacle, traveling through our entire theater of operations, and at each installation I searched for GIs with usable talent. The

Lawrence Winters, *center*, leads "The Red Ball Express," a ballad in tribute to the trucking line that "supplied the hungry Army with the goods" as America's soldiers advanced across Europe. The skit leading into the song complained that blacks couldn't get peacetime trucking jobs. Robert Gordon directed. 734 performances.

result was a sort of Asian Tin Pan Alley, which produced shows consisting of everything from fire-eaters to string quartets. The production center was in Calcutta from which the shows were sent throughout the CBI.

In 1945 I was sent back to the States on temporary duty to assemble new personnel and material. At Special Services headquarters in New York I came into contact with Harold Rome and Arnold Auerbach. They had been putting together sketches and ditties for distribution in the Army for the use of soldier shows. We played around with the idea of creating a show based on our combined experiences. The war ended, our conversations continued, and the result was *Call Me Mister*. The title was a natural. Everyone was damn glad to get back to civilian life. The show was a huge success, and in both original company and the national touring company all the performers, male and female, had had actual service experience.

Floorwalker Jules Munshin watches as Betty Garrett samples one of his establishment's provocative perfumes.

Garrett as a USO hostess who has rumbaed and sambaed and congaed till her spine's out of whack. "South America," she cries, "Take It Away!" The song made Garrett a star, and the Bing Crosby–Andrews Sisters record of it sold over a million copies.

Annie Get Your Gun 5/16/46

Ray Middleton as Frank Butler and Ethel Merman as Annie Oakley in Irving Berlin's greatest musical. At the end of it, Annie and Frank, rival sure-shots in 1880s Wild West shows, have a grudge shooting match, prefaced by the taunt song "Anything You Can Do I Can Do Better." Annie, the better shot, lets Frank win to keep his love. Dorothy and Herbert Fields wrote the book. Joshua Logan directed. Rodgers and Hammerstein produced. Helen Tamiris choreographed. Jo Mielziner did the sets, Lucinda Ballard the costumes. 1,147 performances.

DOROTHY FIELDS (1966): We did a lot of research on Annie Oakley and Frank Butler, and both of them apparently were about the dullest people in the world. Annie Oakley in real life used to sit in her tent and *knit*, for God's sake.

Annie's prowess with a rifle has scared off suitors. In her comic lament, "You Can't Get a Man with a Gun," she complains that she "can't shoot a male in the tail like a quail."

Annie has just shot out a dozen candles from her moving steed, Mielziner's anachronistic motorcycle. When Mary Martin played Annie in a revival, she used a real horse for this scene.

BROADWAY OLD-TIMER: There's a scene where Annie fires a gun in the air and a stuffed bird falls from the flies. Well, one night Ethel pulls the trigger and the cap misfires—no bang. But the bird falls anyhow. Ethel picked it up with a big grin. "I'll be goddamned," she said. "Apoplexy!"

"There's No Business Like Show Business"–two versions. *Above*, 1946: William O'Neal (Buffalo Bill), Merman, Marty May (Charlie Davenport), and Middleton. *Below*, the 1966 revival: Bruce Yarnell (Frank Butler), Merman, Rufus Smith (Buffalo Bill), and Jerry Orbach (Charlie Davenport).

A Flag Is Born 9/5/46

Celia Adler as Zelda and Paul Muni as Tevya, an East European refugee couple trying to get to Palestine. Prevented by the British, they die on the way. This Ben Hecht pageant drama propagandized for the establishment of a Jewish homeland in the Middle East. The play's profits ($275,000) and all money contributed at the theater went to the American League for a Free Palestine, which produced the show. Luther Adler directed. Kurt Weill composed the music. Planned for a three-week engagement, *A Flag Is Born* ran three months. When the state of Israel began, the flagship of her navy, a reconverted ocean liner, was named the S.S. *Ben Hecht*.

MARLON BRANDO (1946): You know that scene where Muni dies on stage? Well, at the beginning I'd cover him with a flag—body, face and all—and I'd stand over him, deliver my final speech, pick up a banner and march offstage to a crescendo of music. But Muni came up to me backstage the other day and suggested that I cover only his body, not his face. It would be more dramatic, he said, if the features of the old, dead Jew were seen while I made my speech.

I agreed with him, but in the next performance I forgot all about his suggestion and covered him completely, face and all. I began my big speech, and when I looked down I saw the flag crawl down his forehead, slip away from his eyes along the bridge of his nose, slowly exposing his face inch by inch. It was like magic.

I saw Muni's upstage hand, the one hidden from the audience, pulling down the flag by gathering folds in his fist. The old hambone couldn't stand not having his face in the final scene. I was afraid I'd break up, so I stopped in the middle of the speech, kneeled, pulled the flag away from his face and tucked it tenderly under his chin. His expression was beatific. Imagine! He was supposed to be dead, but he was still acting. If the curtain hadn't come down, he'd have acted out all the stages of *rigor mortis* setting in.

THE PLAYBILL: Born in Bangkok, Siam, the son of an entomologist now affiliated with the Field Museum in Chicago, Mr. Brando passed his early years in Calcutta, Indo-China, the Mongolian desert and Ceylon.

Marlon Brando played the cynical young Jew who swears to fight to achieve Zelda and Tevya's dream.

Cyrano de Bergerac 10/8/46

José Ferrer as Cyrano threatens Leo-
nardo Cimino, one of a crowd who
mock his grotesque nose, in a sur-
prise-hit revival of the Rostand classic.
Ferrer produced. Mel Ferrer directed.
Lemuel Ayers did sets and costumes,
Paul Bowles the incidental music.
193 performances.

AN ACTOR PREPARES

Bethel Leslie: I remember the first thing Garson Kanin said to me when I got on stage during rehearsals for *Years Ago*. I said, "Well, where would you like me to go?" And he said, "Where would you like to go?" And I thought, "Uh-oh, it's going to be like that." And it was. That was the first taste I had of having to create my own thing, which was good—it was also unheard of. But then Garson didn't have any nonsense around either, because if he didn't like what you were doing, then you stopped doing it very quickly. He would ask me to try to do something; if it didn't work, then it didn't work and we'd do it his way. He always had alternatives. But I think—in fact, I *know*, because I talked to him about it—that he had a theory that if actors could do something naturally, out of themselves, it would be better than something he superimposed on them.

BLACKS ON BROADWAY

Frederick O'Neal: Things are much better for black actors today than in the forties and fifties. And we in Equity made a difference. We have a committee called the Ethnic Minorities Committee; then it was called the Committee on Hotel Accommodations. It was called that because in some areas of the South and Midwest blacks were not accepted in hotels. This was one reason producers didn't want to cast blacks—they couldn't take them on the road.

There was a big problem in Washington which was one of the main road towns. Blacks played on the stage of the National Theater, but they were segregated in the audience. They were admitted to the DAR Hall, but couldn't perform on the stage. And hotels would not accept blacks. In 1946, Ingrid Bergman was playing the National Theater when she learned that blacks were admitted only on a segregated basis and she said she would never play again under those conditions. We had a big mass meeting about it at the 46th Street Theater here in New York and she spoke, Elmer Rice spoke, I spoke, and so did Robert Sherwood, Sam Wanamaker and others. Then there was a meeting of Equity. There were about 700 people there; it was the largest meeting we've ever had. A resolution was put forward that Equity would not play the National Theater as long as this policy existed. It was put to a vote and the vote was unanimous; there was not one vote against it.

For five years they played motion pictures at that theater and Equity played the Shubert, which was formerly a vaudeville house. Finally, the National was taken over by City Investment Company, the Roger Stevens people. They remodeled the theater, air-conditioned the whole place, and re-opened under the new policy. This was in 1952, and I remember the date well because President Truman was there for the opening. I always remember him being there because when a man behind him reached in his pocket for his handkerchief, about 15 security people stood up. From that time on, all the Washington theaters and hotels would accept blacks; so would the restaurants and nightclubs. It was followed by St. Louis and Baltimore. We like to think that this Equity strike was the incident that broke the dike.

Finian's Rainbow 1/10/47

David Wayne (Og, a leprechaun) and Ella Logan (Sharon) sing "Something Sort of Grandish." The E. Y. Harburg–Burton Lane–Fred Saidy musical successfully combined whimsy, social satire, and romance. When Harburg asked Lane to write the music, he said, "All it needs is something like *Porgy and Bess*." Lane rose to the challenge and produced the melodies for such songs as "How Are Things in Glocca Morra?," "If This Isn't Love," "Necessity," "Old Devil Moon," and "When I'm Not Near the Girl I Love." Lee Sabinson and William Katzell produced. Bretaigne Windust directed. Michael Kidd choreographed. Eleanor Goldsmith did the costumes. 725 performances.

WILLIAM GREAVES: David Wayne was a sensitive artist—introspective and thoughtful. His Og was both thoroughly worked out and constantly inspired. It was the best performance on Broadway at the time, and I say that having seen them all. I had an ideal part in *Finian's Rainbow*—ideal for a curious 20-year-old at least. I was on stage for seven minutes, got the biggest laugh of the evening (I was the college student who ever so slowly brought a Bromoseltzer to the ailing Southern senator, you recall?), and then was free to see the second and third acts of everything in town. People forget it but Wayne was one of the members of the 1947 study group that later became the Actors' Studio. He belonged to that astounding first class: Marlon Brando, Arthur Kennedy, Julie Harris, Jo Van Fleet, Maureen Stapleton, Dick Boone, Dorothy McGuire, Tom Ewell, Karl Malden, Kim Stanley, and what other stars have I forgotten? When the Studio accepted me in the second class the next year, I felt I had a toehold on Parnassus.

All My Sons 1/29/47

HAROLD CLURMAN: I was in Hollywood one day and I picked up a collection of recent American writings, and I read a play called *The Man Who Had All the Luck*. It had run in New York for about five days—a total failure. I wrote the author a letter and said, "I'll do your next play when I get to New York." This is very unusual because when a playwright has a failure everybody says, "*Stay away!*" But I knew he had talent and he was writing about interesting things. So he sent me *All My Sons*, and I said, "I'll do it." He also submitted it to Shumlin who asked him for this kind of change and that kind of change. And I said, "No, I'll do it." And he said, "Who'll you get to direct it?" And I said, "I'll give it to Kazan" –because Kazan and I had made a partnership. It got the Critics' prize.

ALAN HEWITT: Ed came to the theater very late. For years he'd been a radio actor and announcer in Hartford, Connecticut. When he first started playing on the stage, he would literally bump into furniture–he didn't know how to move around. But he had a wonderful natural quality and he had this voice that could cut through a 16-foot-thick concrete wall.

Arthur Kennedy (Chris, Joe Keller's son), Karl Malden (George Deever, the son of Keller's former business partner), Beth Merrill (Kate, Keller's wife), and Ed Begley (Joe Keller, an airplane engine manufacturer). George has come to tell Chris that Keller knew of the defective engine blocks his company sold the Air Force. The blocks were responsible for the death of 21 pilots. This was playwright Arthur Miller's first success. He has said that if it, his tenth play, failed, he was going to stick to other lines of work. Elia Kazan directed. 328 performances.

Dream Girl 6/23/47
(McCarter Theater, Princeton)

Lucille Ball as an overly imaginative book-shop employee and Scott McKay as a struggling writer in a touring production of Elmer Rice's hit comedy of the 1945–46 season.

ALAN HEWITT: I feel I personally discovered Lucille Ball. I had been best man at Scott's first wedding and went to see *Dream Girl* while it was up in the Bronx on a subway-circuit tour. When I saw Lucille Ball I said, "This girl is no good in the dramatic moments of the play, but she's one of the best low-crotch, pratfall comediennes I've ever seen. That's what she should concentrate on; she could make a bloody fortune at it." How right I was! If only I had been her agent.

Allegro 10/10/47

AGNES DE MILLE, *observations* (1977):
You must not bore.
A tacet in music is not a silence, it's a suspense.
There never was a bad folk dance.
Man is the only animal that dances.
You don't have to bare the whole fang to show disdain.

In a rehearsal huddle: Lawrence Langner, Richard Rodgers, Agnes de Mille, and Oscar Hammerstein II. De Mille directed as well as choreographed Rodgers and Hammerstein's musical allegory. Langner and the Theatre Guild produced. The hit songs: "A Fellow Needs a Girl," "The Gentleman Is a Dope." 315 performances.

Medea 10/20/47

John Gielgud as Jason and Judith Anderson as Medea, the role, Brooks Atkinson said, "everyone now realizes she has been destined for from the start." Robinson Jeffers adapted Euripides' tragedy. Gielgud directed. Robert Whitehead and Oliver Rea produced. 214 performances.

JOHN HEMMERLY (*said in 1957*): The night I saw her Medea, Judith Anderson played utter hysteria from her first word on. She made me feel that maybe Jason had been right to set up housekeeping elsewhere. Everybody says that she is a great actress and this her great role. I don't deny it. That's something special about the theater: it's not one night's performance, it's *every* night's performance. I didn't happen to be in a lucky audience.

TOM EWELL: I was lucky to have once been in a play where Toscanini almost fell out of a box because he was so moved by the performance of the lady I was working with, who was Judith Anderson, and where Thomas Mann, who was sitting in the front row, crawled over the footlights to kiss her gown at the end of the show. That sort of thing doesn't happen today.

THE STREETCAR STORY

Robert Downing, stage manager of the original production ("Ad Lib," Denver Post, 4/2/72): At the end of one scene in *A Streetcar Named Desire* Brando was to lift Miss Tandy in his arms, carry her to a bed and utter the line, "You and me have had this date from the beginning." Blackout.

Came the night when, as usual, Marlon picked Jessie up, spoke his line and started for the bed. No blackout.

With utter confusion, Brando carried Tandy into the set's bedroom closet. When I had managed to get the stage lights out and the curtain down, I raced behind the set to see what had happened to my stars. I found Jessica, the mild, the ever-understanding, beating wildly on Marlon's chest and screaming with all the vigor of a woman scorned: "You (unprintable) so and so! After all I've taken from you. After all your stupid improvisations! Finally, you have a chance to rape me on stage, and what do you do? You carry me into a closet."

Jessica Tandy: Oh, this story! [*Laughs.*] I say, "Why don't you go ahead and rape me?" It's not true. No, not at all. The lights did fail to go out –that's right; there *was* no blackout.

Q: And you are supposed to have said, "Here I've put up with all your stupid improvisations for weeks on end and now a *real* moment arises and you do nothing."

Hume Cronyn: "You don't live up to it!" [*Laughs.*]

Tandy: It's a lovely story, but it isn't true. First of all, I wouldn't have had time to have said anything, because I was so busy changing my clothes–chung! Quick! Ah. I wonder who started that. I mean, we might have said it in the dressing room–I would never have said "stupid improvisations" because I never would have criticized him like that –but I might have said it as a joke, you know, "Well . . ."

Cronyn: "Here's your chance, boy."

Tandy: "Here's your chance, boy," right. [*Laughs.*] But I certainly didn't say it to be serious. I've heard a lot of people tell me that–I'm always coming across that story, but you know . . .

Cronyn: These stories, they grow or are made up, and, I mean, you hear anecdotes about things you were in and you say–

Tandy: "I don't remember that at all." [*Laughs.*]

Cronyn: "I don't remember that."

Q: How do you feel about these anecdotes, though, that aren't true?

Tandy: I don't care. You're not going to stop it. [*Laughs.*] And it's probably much more interesting to people. That's what they want to hear.

Galileo 12/7/47

Charles Laughton as Galileo in his own translation of the Bertolt Brecht play. Joseph Losey directed. The American National Theatre and Academy produced. The play was expected to run beyond its "limited engagement." It didn't. Six performances.

WILLIAM GIBSON: Brecht never made a dollar for anybody on Broadway.

Crime and Punishment 12/2/47

John Gielgud (Raskolnikov) and Dolly Haas (Sonia) in Rodney Ackland's dramatization of the Dostoevski novel. Theodore Komisarievsky and Bea Lawrence directed. 40 performances.

JOHN GIELGUD (1963): When I am studying a part, I am subconsciously affected by everything I see and hear going on about me. The imagination is already geared to some of the implications of the character that is slowly being brought to life. I remember noticing a tramp lying face downwards, his face and hands buried in the dirty grass, on a sweltering day in St. James's Park, when I was walking home from a rehearsal of *Crime and Punishment*. His spread-eagled, despairing abandonment was exactly that of Raskolnikov lying on his bed in his attic after the murder.

Angel Street 1/22/48

José Ferrer and Uta Hagen as Mr. and Mrs. Manningham in this revival at the New York City Center. Richard Barr directed. *Angel Street* was the first of six shows Ferrer produced for the City Center during the latter half of the 1947–48 season. Plays at the City Center customarily ran, as this did, for two weeks.

Joy to the World 3/18/48

Alfred Drake (Alexander Soren) and Morris Carnovsky (Sam Blumenfeld) in Allan Scott's pointed comedy about a young liberal Hollywood producer, Soren, who is blacklisted for wanting to make meaningful films. Blumenfeld, a veteran independent producer, gives the play a happy ending; he shares Soren's idealism and agrees to bankroll a movie about Samuel Gompers, the father of organized labor. It was observed that Drake was like Orson Welles, Carnovsky like Sam Goldwyn. John Houseman and William Katzell produced. Jules Dassin directed. 124 performances.

HOLLYWOOD STORY

Alfred Palca: I'm reminded of the story that's told about Oscar Levant. He once went to a sneak preview of a new movie in a small town in California. And when the film was over he was in the lobby in a clump of men. He didn't realize he was with Jack Warner, the president of the company, and the director of the film, and he said he thought the picture was lousy. One of them said, "Who are you to think it was lousy?" Levant said, "Who do you have to be?"

Inside U.S.A. 4/30/48

HERB SHRINER, *one of his quips in the show*: A lot of people in Washington are afraid the Russians will start something—and a lot are afraid they won't.

Bea Lillie and Jack Haley as Indians disgusted with life in present-day America; they sing, "We Won't Take It Back." This musical revue was suggested by John Gunther's book of the same title. It had sketches by Arnold Auerbach, Moss Hart, and Arnold Horwitt, and it introduced the low-keyed Hoosier comedian Herb Shriner. Arthur Schwartz produced and wrote the music; Howard Dietz wrote the lyrics. Their hit: "Rhode Island Is Famous for You." Robert Gordon directed. 339 performances.

Eric Victor and Valerie Bettis in the satirical ballet "Tiger Lily," choreographed by Helen Tamiris. Lily (Bettis) pushes her lover off a cliff. She tells all to the court psychiatrist, Dr. Zilmore (Victor), who gets her acquitted. She then pushes him off a cliff.

The Alchemist 5/6/48

Ezra Stone (Sir Epicure Mammon) and José Ferrer (Face) in Ben Jonson's bitter comedy, a production at the City Center. Morton Da Costa directed. Deems Taylor composed incidental music.

ALFRED PALCA: Ezra was in *This Is the Army* with me. He made a fortune in radio playing Henry Aldrich, a typical American boy, when he was about 50.

Lysistrata '48   6/28/48
(Westport Country Playhouse)

Guy Spaull as Lykon is comforted—
but not enough—by June Havoc as
Lysistrata in Gilbert Seldes' updating
of Aristophanes' comedy.

The Skin of Our Teeth 8/17/48
(Westport Country Playhouse)

Thornton Wilder and Armina Marshall, as Mr. and Mrs. Antrobus, the first man and woman (and the last), wait to make their Atlantic City speeches to the Ancient and Honorable Order of the Mammals in a revival of Wilder's comedy about human survival. Marshall ran the Westport Country Playhouse, one of America's most famous summer theaters, with her husband, Lawrence Langner, who had founded it in 1931.

ARMINA MARSHALL: Thornton was totally relaxed and concentrated in his acting, and delightful to perform with. Since he was playing his own philosophy, his performance gave an added weight to the play and the audience adored it.

Thornton's enthusiasm for people, especially the young and talented workers in the theater, was inspiring and enormously helpful to all with whom he came in contact.

MARC CONNELLY: Thornton was a genius; he had wonderful ideas. But his plays needed to be organized and articulated by other people. The idea for *Our Town*, which came from his one-act play, *The Happy Journey to Trenton and Camden* – a beautiful play – was really organized by Jed Harris. I know a lot about it because I played in it myself, here and in England, and I went up to Boston when it was being tried out. Jed called me up one afternoon and told me they were desperate; they were going to close. I thought that was horrendous, so I got on a plane and they held the curtain for me at the Wilbur Theater. It was easy to hold, because there was only $125 in the house. It was a Thursday night, and the whole company was suicidal. Jed was shot to pieces by adrenaline. Thornton wouldn't even sit and talk about it. We went over to the Ritz-Carlton after the theater and Thornton said, "I'm tired." Jed said, "All right. Good night, you goddamn professor."

Boston had been a disaster. For the opening night Jed had sent Mrs. Alva Fuller, the wife of the Governor – he helped expedite the execution of Sacco and Vanzetti – several seats in the second row. She got up and left after the first act, which showed how stupid and empty the play was. And the critics the next morning had been just about as friendly.

The only suggestion I made was that Jed use a dark blue curtain instead of a black curtain for the traveler curtain at the end for the stage manager to guide across, because the black was a kind of depressant – not that that had anything to do with the play itself. The play was perfect. It has moments that are transcendental, moments that really ache with beauty. Anyway, I told him he'd be insane if he closed it. He had the Henry Miller Theater for only four nights when he brought it in. And of course the rest, as your grandmother said, is history.

Wilder as Antrobus, home from all the wars, looks forward hopefully to building new worlds.

Sundown Beach 9/7/48

Julie Harris as Ida Mae Long and Steven Hill as Thaddeus, her husband. Bessie Breuer's episodic play about war-weary men and women trying to adjust to civilian life had many juicy parts. Its actors were, as one reviewer explained, "a new group of young hopefuls called the Actors Studio." Elia Kazan directed. Seven performances.

JOHN LARDNER (1948): A high point in the play, for me, was when a young Southern wife won back her husband—halfway, at least—by reciting the bill of fare of the first meal she would give him when they got home. The part is played by Julie Harris, who intoned the words "Collard greens . . . side meat . . . black-eyed peas" with a sweet, wistful, angelic expression and an upturned profile. The "black-eyed peas," especially, were like a chord on a heavenly harmonium.

JULIE HARRIS: It was probably a case where the opening night performance fell down—we were awkward, we didn't have the spark of truth, you know. Sometimes it's not there and opening night it wasn't. And because it wasn't, we pushed too hard trying to make up for it.

Q: Is that spark less likely to be there opening nights or more likely?

HARRIS: Less likely—well, it was for me, for a long time. Because I was so frightened. So much rides on it, and everyone tells you, "You've got to be the best you've ever been." I have to be relaxed. I can be excited, but I have to be unafraid.

I played a woman from Georgia, an uneducated little girl from a farm who married a boy. He'd gone away in the Air Force, and she'd gotten involved with another man and had a child by him. The husband came home, emotionally sick, and was confronted by the situation. She really loved the boy—this other thing just *happened*, and she went to the hospital to try to win him back. Every time he looked at the child he would just freeze. It was a very moving story, and it really was the beginning in people's minds that I was a waif, a Southern waif. So when *Member of the Wedding* came along, Harold Clurman remembered *Sundown Beach* and thought of me for Frankie.

STANISLAVSKI

Broadway Old-Timer: It's one of the choice stories. Lawrence Langner invited Stanislavski to direct a production for the Theatre Guild. Stanislavski said fine. "How long do you want to rehearse?" Langner asked. "A year," Stanislavski replied.

"A year? My God, we couldn't give you a year."

"All right. Two weeks."

William Greaves: Stanislavski was interested in truth, psychological and artistic truth. His "method," particularly as Lee Strasberg has developed and teaches it, enables an actor to gain access to his own experience and thus approach, with empathy, the inner life of an imagined character, participate in the character's feelings and so make them real and convincing to the audience. Because the actor works from the depths of his subconscious, he is able to unleash larger increments of individual genius.

What hasn't been appreciated, I think, is Stanislavski and Strasberg's necessary and logical place in theater history and the architecture of the theater. In Greece actors performed on stilts and with huge masks; they had to to be seen in the amphitheaters by huge numbers of people. The Roman theaters were so large, again accommodating thousands of people, that the actors resorted to broad pantomime. In Shakespeare's time actors still had to be much larger than life to come across in the open air and sunlight. The nineteenth-century proscenium stage was more intimate, but it still kept actors removed from the audience so that they had to exaggerate what they did. But always there was an inexorable movement toward greater intimacy with the audience and, consequently, more naturalism.

Today, with film and even more with television, we get so close to actors that there is an overwhelming demand on them for absolute psychological credibility. Technological change, the change in the physical environment in which acting takes place, has changed the acting profession. And it's changed what we expect of actors, not only on TV and in movies but in theater. We look at them now *microscopically*, and Stanislavski and Strasberg were the first persons to systematically teach actors how to get by under such scrutiny.

Helen Hayes: I believe the Method, as practiced here by Strasberg and the Studio, went wrong and did a lot of damage to actors. They didn't–at least I never heard them–offer anything to lean upon for the time when God doesn't touch you on the shoulder, when inspiration fails. They didn't seem to offer any kind of technical base on which you could rest until the next magic moment came along. You have to have that in the theater; there's no getting around it. You have to have it because you cannot be in a state of high, wild, pure emotion all the time.

Q: Helen Hayes had a grudge against the Stanislavski Method because it gave actors nothing to fall back upon when they didn't feel like performing.

Harold Clurman: There's some truth to that. It's not entirely true, though. Stanislavski actors didn't, after all, play eight times a week. They played only occasionally or they changed parts. They were doing repertory.

Alan Hewitt: American actors really didn't know what Stanislavski's "method" was until a great deal of damage had been done in his name. He wrote *An Actor Prepares* and *Building a Character* at the same time. But the English translation of *An Actor Prepares* came out in 1936 and there was a 13-year gap before *Building a Character* appeared in 1949. Actors who trained during the thirties and forties got the theoretical Stanislavski but not the practical one. They had the Old Testament but not the New.

Frederick O'Neal: I studied the Stanislavski *approach* to the theater; I wouldn't say "method." That's where a lot of people get screwed up. They say they're doing the "method" but they're not. They're doing his *approach* to theater, because if you followed his "method" it would mean among other things that you had weeks and weeks of rehearsal and study which you don't have. His *approach* to it is something else again. He believes that if you really know your character and if you're concentrating on that character, you can't do anything wrong on stage. And I think he's right.

Let me give you an example. One night we were playing *Anna Lucasta* and John Proctor and I had to pick up Frank Silvera, who played his drunken father. Just as I threw one leg across the other and was picking him up, there was a noise. I don't know where that noise came from, but they heard it in the first row and we got tickled. I got tickled and John got tickled and I dropped Frank three times. I just couldn't seem to get going. And finally I said, "How much liquor did this bastard drink?" as if it was the weight that was the problem. That line was not in the script, but it came right out of the character. It's something he *would* have said.

Small Wonder 9/15/48

"Play it, Nick baby, play it for me!"
Mary McCarty encourages Tom Ewell
not to give up the bull fiddle. Among
the contributors to this revue were
Phyllis McGinley (lyrics), George
Axelrod (sketches), Gower Champion
(dances), and Burt Shevelove (director). 134 performances.

As the Girls Go 11/13/48

Bobby Clark (Waldo Wellington) and Irene Rich (Lucille Thompson Wellington, first woman President of the United States).

Lucille. Do you think you'll be happy in the White House?
Waldo. Why not? Dolly Madison was.

Waldo uses his position as First Gentleman to chase girls in this William Roos–Harold Adamson–Jimmy McHugh musical comedy cum burlesque show. Howard Bay directed. Hermes Pan choreographed. Michael Todd produced. 414 performances.

BROADWAY STORY

To accommodate all the special lights in a musical, an electrician had to rewire during the show. He could only get at the plugs by going through the women's dressing room. As he entered, he would sing out, "Close your eyes, girls, I'm coming through."

The Silver Whistle 11/24/48

Doro Merande, Phyllis Hill, José Ferrer, and William Lynn. Ferrer as Oliver Erwenter, a jaunty hobo, charms the boredom out of life in an old people's home. Hill played Miss Tripp, the home's prim superintendent; she disliked the role and left the show after Boston. Eleanor Wilson replaced her. An unexpected hit on Broadway, the play had opened at the Westport Country Playhouse in the summer and been rebuilt during a long road tryout. The author was Robert McEnroe, a 33-year-old researcher for United Aircraft. McEnroe, a southpaw, named his hero "Erwenter" because the name types easily with the left hand. The Theatre Guild produced. Paul Crabtree directed. 219 performances.

Brooks Atkinson (1948): "Mr. Ferrer is the most able, the most stimulating and the most versatile actor of his generation in America."

Red Gloves 12/4/48

Charles Boyer in his Broadway debut as a cynical European Communist boss. The play was Daniel Taradash's adaptation of Jean-Paul Sartre's *Les Mains sales*. Producer Jean Dalrymple wouldn't let Sartre see the script before the Broadway opening, but he apparently read a copy stolen while the show was in Boston. He repudiated Taradash's version, protesting that it was anti-Communist propaganda. This brouhaha and Boyer's chilling performance helped the production run 113 performances. Jed Harris directed.

CHARLES BOYER (1948): It is not anti-Communist. I would never be associated with Red-baiting. I enjoy the privilege of being a liberal and I want the world to live in peace. I don't believe peace can be obtained by Red-baiting.

Anne of the Thousand Days 12/8/48

Joyce Redman (Anne Boleyn) and Rex Harrison (Henry VIII) in Maxwell Anderson's history play. The Playwrights' Company and Leland Hayward produced. H. C. Potter directed. Costumes by Motley. 288 performances.

The Madwoman of Chaillot 12/27/48

Martita Hunt as the Madwoman and John Carradine as the Ragpicker in Jean Giraudoux's comedy about the extermination of all the bad people in the world. Giraudoux began the play in 1942 while living in Switzerland, a refugee from Vichy France. When he died in 1944, he left a note on his copy announcing that it would be presented when France was liberated. On December 19, 1945, the play opened in Paris. Maurice Valency did the English adaptation. Alfred de Liagre, Jr., produced and directed. The critics were cool to the play; the public loved it. 368 performances.

Kiss Me, Kate 12/30/48

Patricia Morison (Lilli Vanessi, "Kate") and Alfred Drake (Fred Graham, "Petruchio") in Cole Porter's greatest musical, with book by Bella and Samuel Spewack out of William Shakespeare. On the evening they celebrate the first anniversary of their divorce, Lilli and Fred are trying to open *The Taming of the Shrew*. The Spewacks said their show had a message: "It's Shakespeare's: slap your wife around; she'll thank you for it." Saint Subber and Lemuel Ayers produced. John C. Wilson directed. Hanya Holm choreographed. Ayers did sets and costumes. 1,077 performances.

DAVID GOCKLEY, *General Director, Houston Grand Opera* (1976): Why can't grand opera produce something like *Kiss Me, Kate*?

ALFRED DRAKE (1973): We got rave reviews when we opened in Philadelphia, but then Bella and Sam Spewack decided that since it obviously was a hit, it had better be polished up. So then came a process of changes one night which were removed the following night. Changes are part of the business, but if two lines are altered in a scene, occasionally it is more troublesome than a whole new scene. When we arrived on Broadway, the show was in just about the same shape it was in when we first played Philadelphia.

WALTER KERR: *Kiss Me, Kate* was kind of an in-betweener. It was almost like an old clown show, but at the same time it had a central story. In fact, it was considered a throwback at the time. I remember Mike Todd being very snooty about it, saying "old-fashioned show." So I went to see it, and heard that score, and I thought, "Ye gods, what did he mean 'old-fashioned show'? Any show that's got this score is a great show. I don't care when it was written." They said the same thing to Irving Berlin after he did *Annie Get Your Gun*. They said it wasn't in the new *Oklahoma!* vein. It was broad comedy with Ethel Merman. They told him it was old-fashioned, and he said, "Yeah, it's an old-fashioned smash."

BELLA AND SAMUEL SPEWACK (1953): You may remember that the old musical comedy consisted of a story (book), songs, dances, scenery, girls, and boys. On the other hand, the New Art Form consists of a story (book), songs, dances, scenery, girls, and boys.

"Brush up Your Shakespeare." Jack Diamond and Harry Clark, gunmen out to collect a $10,000 gambling debt from Fred Graham, sing the praises of the Bard of Stratford-on-Avon in the show-stopping comic number.

"We Open in Venice." The troup of strolling players: Morison, Drake, Lisa Kirk (Lois Lane, "Bianca"), and Harold Lang (Bill Calhoun, "Lucentio"). Among the great songs: "Another Op'nin', Another Show," "Why Can't You Behave," "Wunderbar," "So in Love," "Too Damn Hot," "Where Is the Life That Late I Led," "Always True to You (In My Fashion)."

Death of a Salesman 2/10/49

MILDRED DUNNOCK: What can I say about *Death of a Salesman* that hasn't been said 100 times? Everybody asks me, "Was it your favorite play?" No, it really wasn't. I had such enormous respect for it because the audience did. We felt when we played in it that we could do no less than our best because somehow the audience got so involved in what was happening.

ALAN HEWITT, *who was Howard Wagner in the play*: It cost us actors a reasonable amount of money to keep scotch and bourbon in the dressing room for our backstage visitors who would come in completely broken up. People were terribly shaken.

DUNNOCK: I remember we had a great deal of trouble with the so-called "Attention must be paid" scene because it's a speech that goes on for 12 or 13 minutes and it's a narrative, it's not really drama. Drama is conflict, and it's a narrative–it *tells* . . . And how to find the drama in it?

Mildred Dunnock (Linda Loman, Willy's wife), Lee J. Cobb (Willy Loman), and Arthur Kennedy and Cameron Mitchell (Biff and Happy, their sons). Arthur Miller's tragedy of the common man, directed by Elia Kazan. Kermit Bloomgarden and Walter Fried produced. Jo Mielziner did sets and lighting, Alex North the incidental music. 742 performances.

Cobb.

Kennedy and Mitchell.

We were in Philadelphia just prior to the New York opening and Kazan asked me to see him about the scene. When I came in I was told Mr. Kazan was at a concert across the street and had left a ticket for me at the backstage entrance. I arrived in the midst of a symphony, one of those symphonies that has five movements and that rises to an enormous crescendo. And as we left the hall, I said, "Gee, that symphony's like you, Gadge. That's the way you conduct, the big crescendo." And he said, "Well, I'm going to conduct tomorrow." The next day we rehearsed the "Attention must be paid" scene, and he took an old stick, I think it was the piece of an old broomstick, and he began to use it like a baton. And as I did the scene, he kept beating it and saying, "More! More! More! More! More!" Finally I was screaming at the top of my lungs, and I stopped and I burst into tears and I said, "I can't! I won't *do* it that way!" And he said, "That's *exactly* the way you will do it." And I said, "But where are all the nuances?" And he said, "Nuances? We'll come to those in a couple of months."

HEWITT: Willy Loman takes a lot out of any actor who plays him anywhere, anytime. At the end of the first public performance in Philadelphia, Lee and I met while crossing under the stage, coming from opposite directions to get in place for curtain calls. Lee had just exited to kill himself. You heard the sound of Willy's car starting up and zooming away, and then a moment later, with Jo Mielziner's marvelous transformations of light, you had his funeral on a forestage built out over

the orchestra pit. Lee was walking heavily, with his shoulders slumped and mouth hanging open from emotional and physical exhaustion. As I came past him, I said, "Been on yet?" And he looked around in a strangled way and this awful sound came from him. Then he put his hand over his mouth so they wouldn't hear him on stage and fell apart with laughter. He never forgot this and would often remind me, years later, how I had pulled him out of Willy Loman's misery and back to life as Lee Cobb.

DUNNOCK: I always say that the greatest director I worked with is Kazan, and it is because of this play. He has the capacity to make you use yourself to your fullest extent—and to fall flat on your face, but he always takes the blame for anything that's not right; you never lose face with Kazan. He also lets you be free of yourself. Linda Loman was a part I had to struggle to get, because I'm not a natural Linda Loman. His descriptions of the character helped me to be able to play her. He said Linda Loman is an old-fashioned woman; she would let her husband use her like a doormat, but never feel that he was using her. And it gave me something—I don't know whether it will mean anything to you—but it certainly seems to me to carry through as I see this picture of her. She looks—she *exists* in somebody else always; she never exists in herself. In the other pictures, too. I never really thought of it that way before. [*Laughs.*] I never looked like *that*, I don't think, really. It has a kind of childlike quality, an ingenuousness that Kazan made possible.

Kennedy, Cobb, and Dunnock.

DUNNOCK: I played with seven Willy Lomans, and Lee was, by far, the one I enjoyed playing with most. I suppose that's necessarily true because he was the person I found my character with; it was with him that I discovered the rhythm that worked for me. And he was absolutely right for the part as it was directed by Kazan. Actually, when you first read the script of *Death of a Salesman*, Gene Lockhart, who followed Lee, was much more right for the part, because he was a little Milktoast of a man. But Kazan chose to direct the play on an epic level, and so all the characters he cast were bigger than life. Lee was like a bull in a china closet, you see, and that made for a different person than Gene Lockhart. When I came to play with Gene, it nearly drove me crazy. I felt as if *I* were playing Willy Loman and he was playing Linda. I was the stronger of the two. When I'd say to Willy, "Go upstairs," he'd say to me, "Darling, you'll be all right." He was consoling *me*! It was just the nature of the beast. Lockhart was a charming, soft man; Lee was never that.

Cobb and Dunnock.

ANTA Album 1949   3/6/49

Congressionally chartered in 1935 to encourage the decentralization of American theater, the American National Theatre and Academy (ANTA) gave all-star benefit nights in 1948, 1949, 1950, and 1951. Fred Fehl was hired to cover the last three years. *ANTA Album 1949* showed a $13,000 profit.

Ray Bolger does "The Old Soft Shoe," a vaudeville routine he had done in the 1946 revue *Three to Make Ready*.

GEORGE BALANCHINE: You know, Bolger was really a thing that happened. Bolger himself was a laugh the way he was—really fantastic. He even danced!

Tallulah Bankhead as Regina Giddens, her greatest role, in Lillian Hellman's *The Little Foxes*, produced on Broadway in 1939.

MARC CONNELLY: I knew Tallulah from babyhood, damn near, and I spoke at her funeral. I knew her when she was a kid of seventeen when she used to pick up food from the Round Table at the Algonquin. She would come in and nibble, the darling! Everybody loved her and wanted her to be a success.

Leonard Bernstein, Betty Comden, and Adolph Green. The three had first come to popular notice in the early forties as members of The Revuers, nightclub entertainers who wrote and performed their own material. Another Revuer: Judy Holliday.

Grace and Paul Hartman, revue entertainers, radio personalities.

BROADWAY OLD-TIMER: When Lillian Hellman came to New York she married Arthur Kober. They got divorced and Arthur married another girl. One day a friend called Mrs. Kober, senior, and said, "How's Arthur?" Mrs. Kober, who was a very simple, gentle old Jewish woman, said, "Oh, Arthur's getting along fine. He's now married to Maggie, you know, and he comes home from the office and he kisses Maggie and they play with the baby, and then in the evening their friends come in and they play games and they have all kinds of fun." "How's Lillian?" "Oh, Lillian comes home, she comes home from the bank, and turns the key and she says, 'Hello, min*e* apartment.'" [*Laughs.*]

Oh, Jesus. It's got that Jewish cosmic knowledge in it. What a hell of a thing to say, "Hello, min*e* apartment."

James Barton in a vaudeville monologue. Barton grew up in theater,
for years playing Topsy with a traveling company of *Uncle Tom's Cabin*. He
replaced Henry Hull as Jeeter Lester in
Tobacco Road. He is probably best remembered as Hickey in the original,
1946 production of Eugene O'Neill's
The Iceman Cometh.

On leave from their usual starring
roles of Mr. Roberts and Ensign Pul-
ver, Henry Fonda (*top bunk*) and David
Wayne portray two of the seamen in
Thomas Heggen and Joshua Logan's
comedy hit *Mr. Roberts*.

HENRY FONDA (1976): I was in the Navy for four years and I hated
every minute of it. But I wouldn't change it.

Walter Hampden and José Ferrer: the Cyrano of the 1920s greets the Cyrano of the 1940s.

WILLIAM GREAVES: My scene from *Finian's Rainbow* was in an *ANTA Album*, and I sat in on everybody else's rehearsal. It was incredible seeing all the titans of the theater doing the best scenes of their most famous roles. You realize how much Broadway has changed from that time–has deteriorated, I regret to add. There was a communality in the effort, a shared interest; you felt it was born out of the love and tremendous élan of performers in their art. Today such a thing probably couldn't happen. The pall of commerce would kill it; it kills virtually everything artistic today–even the songs on the radio. What I hear the singers saying is not what the song says but rather, "Listen! Listen to the money I'm making."

South Pacific 4/7/49

MARY MARTIN, *asked her favorite role* (1977): Certainly *South Pacific*. I will never have another *South Pacific*. Everyone in the world came to see it. People came to *South Pacific* to get married, to get divorced, to get back together again. Presidents, kings, emperors came to see it.

BESSIE MAE SUE ELLA YAEGER, *a girlhood friend of Mary Martin*: Of course the rumor was that Mary and Ezio loved each other–which, of course, they did. Mary said, "Oh, well, I'm so glad people don't say we *hate* each other. That would hurt the show."

MARC CONNELLY: I was teaching up at Yale and the night it opened I met with Dick and Oscar after the show. We all gathered at Kaysey's, and I will never forget Pinza came in and apologized for having balled up a lyric–it was "Some Enchanted Evening." I don't know what he missed but he twisted some line or other. Dick Rodgers was furious but Oscar was calm and balmy. Oscar put it down as one of those minor errors. Oscar was, of course, a philosopher; he was a gentle, adaptable person. But Dick, oh, Dick was relentless. What the hell was Dick so worried about? His notes weren't confused–it was the lyrics.

CHARLES ADAMS BAKER: Ezio's contract was a very interesting one: he could not be called upon to sing an aggregate of more than twelve minutes in one evening. When you think back on that show, you think he never stopped singing, but he did. He sang exactly twelve minutes, which was wise, because if he'd had a real big singing lead, he couldn't have made eight performances a week, which he did. He was about the only opera star ever to appear on Broadway who managed that. You know, the most a star sings in opera is twice a week, if that.

Ezio Pinza (Emile DeBecque, a French planter in the South Pacific) and Mary Martin (Ensign Nellie Forbush, a Navy nurse from Little Rock) at the moment Emile and Nellie declare their love. Pinza, a former Metropolitan Opera star, has just sung "Some Enchanted Evening." This greatest of Rodgers and Hammerstein musicals was adapted by Hammerstein and Joshua Logan from stories in James A. Michener's *Tales of the South Pacific*. Logan directed and choreographed.

A dripping Mary Martin sings, "I'm Gonna Wash That Man Right outa My Hair."

JOSHUA LOGAN (1949): I owe a good deal of what I've done in *South Pacific* to Stanislavski. I saw him make singers sing as actors and I saw him use the orchestra to suggest the emotion of the scene. Until then, all I'd ever seen in opera were dull flabby people whose dramatic expression signified only that they thought their own voices were beautiful. I watched a man in *Boris Godunov* sing while jumping backward over a bed. I was 21 then. My God! It set me on fire!

BETHEL LESLIE: Josh Logan is one who gets up and acts everything for you. I must say he acts it most of the time better than you do, but of course he can't play 17-year-old girls so your job is safe.

Nellie dresses up like a gob and sings and dances "Honey Bun" in a Thanksgiving Day GI show. Her partner with the coconuts is Seaman Luther Billis, played by Myron McCormick. McCormick was one of nine people who stayed the entire run of the show, 1,925 performances.

Juanita Hall as Bloody Mary sings "Happy Talk" while Betta St. John as Liat, her daughter, performs for William Tabbert as Lt. Joseph Cable, USMC.

The finale of "Honey Bun": Martin, McCormick, and chorus.

LONG RUNS

Alfred Palca: What happens when you're in a long run is that the show itself loses all meaning. It's the minutia that become important. Who stepped on whose lines. Tonight we skipped three pages. So-and-so has a cold–watch out! Actors talk in anecdotes. How else can they remember?

Alan Hewitt: It's inevitable that in a long run people dry up and forget their lines. It goes through a company like the plague. Suddenly, after you've been playing something for months somebody blows his lines. You're so astonished you can't believe it. And the next day somebody else blows his. And the next day Hewitt, the old reliable, dries up like a prune and can't remember his name. And for the next week everybody is quaking with fright as to who's next. This happens about every four months in the run of a successful play. The way to get out of it is to have the director come around and have rehearsals and either get the actors back to first principles, basic motivations, or find new ways of doing things–change the blocking, line readings, whatever.

Florence Williams: I played Judith Anderson's daughter in *The Old Maid*. We had a small funny scene together. One night, though, she suddenly changed her reading of the lines, and it took me about three days to readjust so that I was getting my laughs. As soon as the laughs were back she changed again, and I had to scramble after her. This went on for two months. When I got the laughs, she'd change her readings. The stage manager kept scolding me for having lost the laughs; he didn't dare talk to her. Finally I couldn't stand it anymore, and I said, "Judith, I'm miserable when you change readings. I'm just not experienced enough to keep up." And she said, "Oh, I'm so sorry, my dear. I thought it would amuse you, too! I get so *bored*." She never did it again.

Broadway Old-Timer: Alfred Drake says that one way to stave off boredom is to try doing your part as someone else would do it. During *Oklahoma!* he caught Howard Da Silva playing Jud as John Barrymore would play it were he playing it like brother Lionel. I may not have the names right but you get the idea.

Seymour Herscher: A long run is when you pay back your investors.

The Time of Your Life 6/20/49
(Westport Country Playhouse)

E. G. Marshall (Kit Carson) and Eddie Dowling (Joe) in William Saroyan's famous comedy, which was written (the author says) in six days. Dowling played Joe in the 1939 Broadway production, which he co-directed with Saroyan.

A Month in the Country 8/2/49
(Westport Country Playhouse)

Ruth Gordon (Natalia, the bored wife of a landowner), E. G. Marshall (a cynical doctor), and Edmon Ryan (Rakitin, a friend of the family) in Emlyn Williams' adaptation of Ivan Turgenev's play about provincial Russian life. Garson Kanin directed.

Amphitryon 38   8/49
(Glen Cove Summer Theater)

Elisabeth Bergner as Alkmena, Amphitryon's faithful wife, whom Jupiter seduces in the guise of her husband. Alfred Lunt and Lynn Fontanne played this Jean Giraudoux comedy on Broadway in 1937. Giraudoux called the play *Amphitryon 38* because he estimated that there had been 37 earlier dramatizations of the myth, the first by Plautus.

148

Good Housekeeping 9/15/49
(Westport Country Playhouse)

Helen Hayes and Mary MacArthur, mother and daughter in real life, play mother and daughter in a William McCleery comedy.

HELEN HAYES: Is that my Mary? It sure doesn't look like her. It's a *bad* picture of Mary. But of course it is . . . But I can hardly recognize her.

Q: I'll tell Fred that and maybe he can do better.

HAYES: Well, he didn't do any others, did he?

Q: Oh, yes. He said he sent you pictures of the production to complete her scrapbook. He said also he remembers that she acted with great intensity and at the same time a wonderful good humor.

HAYES: Yes. She was so good in that play. We were going to bring it in. That was to be her introduction on Broadway. Well, I don't object to it a bit. I'm glad to have it in the book, even if it isn't the very best of photographs of Mary. It startled me at first because of the face she's making: she's speaking, her mouth is pursed. I really didn't recognize her. I do now. I see that the features are all Mary's. I don't mind it one bit.

It was such a blessing that she had that success because when she did *Alice Sit by the Fire* with me several years before this, when she was 16 or 17 . . . She was 19 when she did this; she died right while we were doing it. After Westport. She contracted polio there.

Q: I think this picture was taken just a week before she died.

HAYES: Yes. Yes. She had done *Alice* in the places that we played with this one, and they picked on her a little bit as they will always pick on the young of theater celebrities—as they've done about my son every once in a while. And when we did this play, they took it all back. They said she had made giant strides. Mary would have been a lovely comedienne, a very very good actress.

FRED FEHL: Here's another picture of Helen Hayes and her daughter. I prefer the earlier, but you see the problem: in one picture one person is especially good; in the other, the other.

WALKER EVANS (*said in 1974*): It's really a *law* of the trade. When you make a picture of a person, if he likes it, his wife won't—and vice versa. When you make a picture of *two* people, one of them won't look right.

Q: What happens when you make a picture of three people?

EVANS: It's a landscape.

Lost in the Stars 10/30/49

WILLIAM GREAVES, *who played the villain in the show*: Rouben Mamoulian was for me a kind of idol. He had a unique sense of crowd management. His crowds had shape and personality; they weren't an amorphous mass. Very instructive. For example, to show *fear*, he would place all the people in an aversive slant away from the source of danger. They weren't perpendicular to it; they were at about 75 degrees so that, looked at from a distance, they would almost seem to be starting to run away.

Unfortunately, he was slightly paternalistic. He would say "children" this, "children" that. I will always remember after the opening night he came back and said, "Children, I want to tell you I was deeply moved. And my wife, Zeda, she cried." Zeda was a red-haired woman, dripping in jewels. She wore glasses, not horn-rimmed really but covered with rhinestones. Perhaps, had he not started off with the word "children," my reaction at that moment would not have been negative. But unfortunately in those days a lot of white people had a horrible habit of referring to adult Afro-Americans as Boy, Girl, or Children. The younger members of the cast were too nationalistic to accept that kind of patronizing even though I'm sure Mamoulian meant no harm. Later on he was most helpful in supporting my entry into the production side of the movie business.

Q: Did you feel that Weill's music was "African" enough?

GREAVES: Well, no, the music wasn't African. But when you have someone like Kurt Weill, a genius, he creates his own landscape. In *Madame Butterfly* does Puccini sound Japanese? Nobody who really hears the music asks such a question.

Weill's music was impressionistic and it gives an *impression* of Africa in the way that the abstract art of Picasso and Matisse does, because their eyes had been changed by African sculpture.

Todd Duncan as Stephen Kumalo, a poor South African minister; Julian Mayfield as Absalom, his son; and Inez Matthews as Irina, Absalom's girl, pregnant with his child. Absalom has murdered a white man, has confessed, and will hang. Rev. Kumalo marries Absalom and Irina in prison. This Maxwell Anderson–Kurt Weill musical tragedy was drawn from Alan Paton's *Cry, the Beloved Country*. The most poignant song: "Lost in the Stars." Rouben Mamoulian directed. The Playwrights' Company produced. 281 performances.

The Father 11/16/49

Raymond Massey (a Captain of Cavalry) and Grace Kelly (his daughter) in August Strindberg's searing play. The Captain is driven mad by his wife's suggestion that he is not his daughter's father. This was Kelly's first Broadway role. Massey directed. 69 performances.

That Lady 11/22/49

Katharine Cornell as Ana de Mendoza, Princess of Eboli, in a romantic drama by Kate O'Brien about sixteenth-century Spanish royalty. Ana wears a patch because she lost an eye in a duel. Widowed young, she finds true love with one of the King's advisors, but the King, Philip II, himself tormented with passion for Ana, disapproves. He keeps the lovers apart, in jail or exile, for thirteen years. Their love stays strong, as they do not tire of repeating. 78 performances. Rolf Gérard did the sets and costumes, cribbing from Velásquez and Hollywood. Cornell produced; her husband, Guthrie McClintic, directed. Having panned the play, John Mason Brown added: "It is not pleasant to have to write such words about any production offered by people in whose debt our theatre stands so deeply. We, the non-creative public, are all too apt to forget that artists are entitled to their mistakes. In the arts the wonder is not that lightning does not strike again and again but that it ever strikes." He named some of the productions to which the McClintics had drawn lightning: *Candida, Romeo and Juliet, Saint Joan, The Barretts of Wimpole Street, The Doctor's Dilemma, Antigone, Antony and Cleopatra*.

Gentlemen Prefer Blonds 12/8/49

Carol Channing as Lorelei Lee, the role that made her a star, in the Joseph Fields–Anita Loos–Jule Styne–Leo Robin musical based on Loos' popular comic novel of the 1920s. Channing's big songs: "A Little Girl from Little Rock" and "Diamonds Are a Girl's Best Friend." Herman Levin and Oliver Smith produced. John C. Wilson directed. Costumes by Miles White. 740 performances.

NANETTE FABRAY: I turned down *Gentlemen Prefer Blonds*. What a mistake. Jule Styne was in the lobby of my apartment house crying, "Please, Nan, take it. It's going to be a great show." But I just couldn't see it. You know all of us in show business have stories like that. I've turned down many things that in retrospect you could say, "How could you do that?" Well, who knew?

ANITA LOOS (1973): Lorelei Lee is harder to kill than Rasputin.

The Member of the Wedding 1/5/50

JULIE HARRIS: That was taken during rehearsal, and when I look at that picture I remember how cold the day was. We rehearsed downtown in some dinky theater, and there wasn't much heat. And the play, after all, took place in August, in Georgia—terribly hot. And I had to run around a lot and got overheated and then got cold. I wore those plaid pants and sweater because I wanted to keep warm.

Brandon was so adorable. At that point he was really beginning to act. He had been a little parrot until that time, but he was finally breaking through and really enjoying what he was saying. It seemed to us like a miracle when that happened. And Ethel, of course, was a Stage Mother, taking care of both of us. She was wonderful to work with; I adored her. The rehearsal period was a time of great joy for everybody.

Julie Harris as Frankie, an awkward 12-year-old tomboy; Ethel Waters as Berenice, the family cook; and Brandon de Wilde as John Henry, Frankie's seven-year-old cousin. Carson McCullers did the stage adaptation of her novel without any attempt at conventional drama: "It is an inward play and the conflicts are inward," she said. The part of Frankie made Harris a star. Harold Clurman directed. Robert Whitehead, Oliver Rea, and Stanley Martineau produced. 501 performances.

HAROLD CLURMAN: The kid–who's dead now, died at the age of 28 or so, got killed in an accident–but then he was seven years old and had never acted before. By the time we opened he was technically perfect. He knew exactly what to do. Later I directed him when he was 10 or 12 and he had become self-conscious, and by the time he was 20 he had to take lessons in acting. But at the time of this play he had never even been in a children's show, and yet you could tell him once what to do and he remembered it. For example, during rehearsals there was nobody out front except myself and perhaps the producer. So he wasn't used to hearing any reaction. The first time I called in 14 or 15 people to see the show they, of course, laughed, and he turned around and looked at them because he was surprised. So I said to him, "Now, there will be more people; there will be more laughter. You mustn't turn around and look at the audience. You must keep looking at your partners, Miss Waters and Miss Harris. You must wait until the audience stops laughing." The next day he did wait, but he waited too long–he waited until the last laugh died out. He didn't look out, though. So I said to him, "Now, what you did was right. You did one little thing which you must not do. You waited until the last person stopped laughing. You must wait until you feel the laughter subsiding and then speak so there won't seem to be a break." Next day: perfect. He acted like the most experienced actor in the world. He was steady right through and never lost his spontaneity. Children, when they're good and not spoiled and have some ability, are always spontaneous. It's only when they get too professional that it's very difficult for them to be real.

The Man 1/19/50

Don Hanmer as a psychopathic handyman and Dorothy Gish as a widowed rooming-house owner in Mel Dinelli's melodrama. Martin Ritt directed. 92 performances.

The Devil's Disciple 1/25/50
(New York City Center)   2/21/50 (on Broadway)

Maurice Evans (Dick Dudgeon) and Dennis King (General "Gentlemanly Johnny" Burgoyne) in a revival of Bernard Shaw's lampoon of war (specifically the American Revolution) and heroism. The play was such a hit at the City Center that it moved to Broadway. The move was expensive since the production had to be refinanced to comply with theatrical union rules and new scenery had to be built because City Center scenery wasn't allowed on Broadway. Margaret Webster directed. 127 performances.

ANTA Album 1950   1/29/50

JACK BENNY (1941): What makes people laugh? For years I have made Jack Benny a character who has the weaknesses of many persons—a miser, a braggart, a coward who tries to maintain his dignity with bluster, a would-be Lothario. I exaggerate these qualities, and the exaggerations get laughs. In real life this character causes me many embarrassing moments. I always overtip for fear the persons who serve me will say, "That guy is just as tight as he says he is."

Jack Benny as a fireman in "The Still Alarm," a sketch from the 1929 Howard Dietz–Arthur Schwartz revue *The Little Show*.

Ethel Barrymore as Kate in *The Twelve Pound Look*. She had played the same role on Broadway in 1911. Like many of the *ANTA Album* stars, she returned from the West Coast for this performance.

HAROLD CLURMAN: Ethel Barrymore was like a queen. She was so queenly that there is no queen living today who is as queenly as she was.

MILDRED DUNNOCK: Ethel Barrymore asked me to play with her in James M. Barrie's *Twelve Pound Look* for the ANTA Album. It's too bad you don't have a picture of my dress, because it was gorgeous; some dress house had loaned it to me. This little spinster becomes Cinderella in that dress. To get into it I had to strip absolutely down to my pants. After the performance I was down there pulling off the last of the dress −nobody had anyone to do anything for them−when the door opened and there was Raymond Massey. I was absolutely stripped except for my pants. And maybe that doesn't seem important at this stage in time, but for me at that point! I was absolutely shattered, it was so embarrassing. He fled and I must say I fled too−behind my dress.

JOHN FISCHER: When I knew her, she was old and rather sad. I was Trade Editor at Harper, and we had published the autobiographies of Tallulah Bankhead and Gypsy Rose Lee. She was envious of their success and wanted us to do hers. We would meet in the afternoon to discuss the project over a cocktail. To show how good her book was going to be, she insisted on reading aloud from her journal, which she had kept over the years in a series of school notebooks. As she read she would begin to weep, then excuse herself, asking for an appointment on another day. I told her I would try to get a writer to work with her, but she had hated Gene Fowler's biography of her brother John and didn't trust writers. I offered to read her journal to see whether it could be reworked for publication. She wouldn't let me, saying that she preferred to read it to me. She'd start again, and again she'd weep. Nothing ever came of her book.

WALTER KERR: I was fascinated by folk music, so I did a whole show about American folk music, starting at the beginning and tracking it all the way up. What I did was devise a simple offhand character, Barnaby Goodchild, who was a sort of Johnny Appleseed, except he was a Johnny Appleseed of music. He started back in Puritan times, and he gets thrown out of the community because he was singing and dancing all the time–he was in the stocks for a while. Then he goes down the road by himself, until he finds Virginia, and there, all of a sudden, he's welcomed: it's a different society. So we trace him all the way through, out into the wilderness, the first farm countries and beyond, out to the Gold Rush and back to the Mississippi, through the Civil War, all the way up to the twenties. An obvious formula, but it hadn't been done until that time–certainly not in terms of folk music. So I started reading and digging into folk music. I went down to the Library of Congress–which fortunately was right next door–and talked to B. A. Botkin, who was a considerable authority on folk music and lore.

On Broadway, it almost made it; the notices were 90 percent marvelous. It made Burl Ives. The crazy thing is that in the making of Burl Ives, the show was hurt. Burl was marvelous in the show, but he wasn't the central character who brought music everywhere. Alfred Drake was –except that every place that Alfred arrived, there was Burl Ives. So

Burl Ives sings "The Foggy, Foggy Dew," one of the folk songs he sang in Walter Kerr's 1944 *Sing Out, Sweet Land*.

what's Alfred to do? He's not bringing music anymore. In a sense Burl Ives cut the show in half. We found ourselves using Burl more and more, because he was so good. And the more we used him, the more we reduced Alfred's function. These things can happen almost when you're not looking. And it's only after that you stop and think, "Jeez, what did I do *that* for?"

FREDERICK O'NEAL: I never shall forget what Ethel said the last time I worked with her. It was on the television show *Route 66*. She said, "I used to think I had cancer, I had heart disease, I had everything under the sun, but I found out I didn't have anything a good job wouldn't cure."

Before that, I was with her in the motion picture *Pinky*. John Ford started out directing it, but after two weeks he was taken ill, and Elia Kazan took over. Ford's approach was interesting. But it had nothing to do with the picture. Ford just liked to hear Ethel sing, and he'd stop the whole picture and have her sing and enjoy the hell out of it. He brought in a little combo that played right on the set, played for Ethel. But it had nothing to do with the picture–she didn't sing in it.

Ethel Waters sings "Cabin in the Sky."

MARC CONNELLY: Bobby Clark. Oh! There was nobody like him. He was a complete *master*. He could flick ashes off a cigar, and lead you into Oz. He was such a simple uncomplicated man. When he assured the audience, "I can sing even higher, but my eyes would pop out," you knew he meant it. Oh, God! what a comedian! He was a high comedian, a Molière comedian—one of the greatest artists we had in this century.

Bobby Clark does one of his best-loved revue numbers, "Robert the Roué from Reading, Pa."

The Innocents 2/1/50

Iris Mann as the precocious Flora and Beatrice Straight as Flora's governess, Miss Giddens, in William Archibald's adaptation of the Henry James ghost story *The Turn of the Screw*. The play had a good run, 141 performances, and would have gone longer except that Straight had to withdraw to have a baby. The versatile Archibald was Imogene Coca's dance partner in *Concert Varieties*, seen on page 82. Peter Glenville directed. Peter Cookson produced.

The Bird Cage 2/22/50

Melvyn Douglas (Wally Williams, a Hitleristic nightclub impressario) and Maureen Stapleton (Emily, his gentle wife) in Arthur Laurents' symbolic melodrama. Wally double-crosses one partner, maims another, and when everyone turns against him, sets fire to his club with him in it. Harold Clurman directed. 21 performances.

HAROLD CLURMAN: *The Bird Cage* was not a very good play. But even with the plays I did which were not successful or were not good as plays some wonderful things came out of them. Maureen Stapleton made her first real impression in *The Bird Cage*. As a result, when they were asking me who should play in *The Rose Tattoo*, and were looking for a Magnani, I said, "Why do you have to have an Italian actress? Why don't you get Maureen Stapleton?" And to my surprise they took her.

Q: What would lead one to do a play which wasn't very good?

CLURMAN: It wasn't bad; it wasn't shameful. There are plays which I say are "not very good." And there are plays which are "shameful." I don't think I've ever done a shameful play. But I will say this: I did that particular play because I hadn't had a play to do at all for a long time and I needed a job. Suddenly, at the same time, along came *The Member of the Wedding* and it took precedence. But since I'd promised to do *The Bird Cage*, I wasn't going to say, "Well, now I have a big success . . .," although many directors, quite rightly from a box office and professional standpoint, say, "Oh, now that I'm a big success, I'd better accept plays which I'm sure are going to be hits."

MELVYN DOUGLAS: *The Bird Cage* was a tremendous success in Philadelphia and a complete failure in New York, but it did provide me the opportunity of working with Harold Clurman, who is one of the most stimulating and articulate theater persons of our time. The play was set in a jazz nightclub, and one morning Harold began to talk about jazz. At the end of somewhat more than an hour I realized that I had been listening to a brilliant essay.

Traveller's Joy 8/7/50
(Westport Country Playhouse)

Gertrude Lawrence (Beatrice "Bumble" Pelham) in a "farcical comedy" by Arthur Macrae. The co-star was Dennis King.

The Amazing Adele 9/11/50
(Westport Country Playhouse)

RUTH GORDON (1976): I don't know the problem with being pretentious if you can follow it up with something.

Ruth Gordon (Adele) in Pierre Barillet and Jean-Pierre Gredy's comedy, adapted and directed by Garson Kanin.

Call Me Madam 10/12/50

Ethel Merman as Mrs. Sally Adams, U.S. Ambassador to Lichtenburg, and Paul Lukas as Cosmo Constantine, Lichtenburg's prime minister. The Irving Berlin–Howard Lindsay–Russel Crouse musical borrowed from the career of Perle Mesta, the famous Washington party giver whom President Truman named Ambassador to Luxemburg. Leland Hayward produced.

THE PLAYBILL: Neither the character of Mrs. Sally Adams nor Miss Ethel Merman resembles any other person, alive or dead.

WALTER KERR: When they do a show out of town Ethel will go right along. She plays the game; she takes instruction, does what she's told and does it just as well as she possibly can. Then comes a point, about a week before you're to come to New York, when that's it. It's customary to freeze the show that way, but not everybody does it. Sometimes they keep tinkering, tinkering, tinkering, right till the opening night in New York. Somebody came up to her on the last Friday before the opening with a new piece of paper and a couple of little lines, and she said, "Kid, you can call me 'Birdseye Merman'–this show is frozen." She'd been cooperative all through, but she wouldn't make another change. She's that kind of person.

Merman describes Sally Adams in a Berlin song: "The Hostess with the Mostes' on the Ball." The show had a strong start and a weak finish, so in Boston the song that was working best, "You're Not Sick You're Just in Love," was moved from act one to near the end of act two. Result: 644 performances—a big hit.

The Tower beyond Tragedy 11/26/50

Judith Anderson (Clytemnestra) in
Robinson Jeffers' reworking of the
Oresteia. The bodies on the stage indi-
cate that Clytemnestra's revenge has
started. When playing tragic heroines,
Anderson was heard to make her en-
trances muttering, "Death, death."
ANTA produced, in its new theater
(formerly the Guild). Robert Ross directed. 32 performances.

Twentieth Century 12/24/50

José Ferrer (Oscar Jaffe), Robert Strauss (Owen O'Malley), Gloria Swanson (Lily Garland), Donald Foster (Oliver Webb), and William Lynn (Matthew Clark) in an ANTA revival of Ben Hecht and Charles MacArthur's affectionate farce about life in the theater, based on an earlier play by Bruce Millholland. The scene: a car of the Twentieth Century Limited en route from Chicago to New York. The plot: Oscar is trying to con the great star Lily Garland back from Hollywood to Broadway and his production of *Everyman*. Matthew is a rich lunatic who may finance the play. This revival, scheduled for two weeks at the ANTA Playhouse, was so popular that it moved to Broadway and was running strong in June when Ferrer left for Hollywood. He was replaced by the movie actor Robert Preston, appearing in his first Broadway role. 218 performances.

Ferrer starred and directed and, when the revival moved to Broadway, produced. In the memorable 1934 movie of *Twentieth Century*, Oscar Jaffe was played by John Barrymore, Lily Garland by Carole Lombard.

King Lear 12/25/50

Louis Calhern as Lear in the least often done of Shakespeare's major tragedies. With a strong cast, staging by John Houseman, and music by Marc Blitzstein, this production lasted 48 performances, a meager run but Broadway's longest *Lear* in this century. Robert Joseph and Alexander Cohen produced.

LEE J. COBB (1958): I would do *Lear* if they asked me. They did ask me a few years ago when Louis Calhern, may his soul rest in peace, did it in New York. I turned it down then, because I'd been playing Lear for two years—in *Death of a Salesman*.

Darkness at Noon 1/13/51

Claude Rains as Rubashov, an old Bolshevik being purged by the new order in Sidney Kingsley's dramatization of the Arthur Koestler novel. Kingsley directed. The Playwrights' Company produced. 186 performances.

THE PLAYBILL: Walter J. Palance (*Gletkin*). Pennsylvania coal miner, professional prize-fighter, railroad maintenance worker, radio repair man, Army soldier and Air Force B-24 pilot—all these careers are background for Walter J. Palance who is playing his first featured role in *Darkness at Noon*. He was born in Lattimer Mines, a whistle-stop of the Lehigh Valley Railroad, in northeastern Pennsylvania, and got his impressive physique by backbreaking work in the coal mines. He was a heavyweight boxer until Pearl Harbor, when he joined the Army. He hunted submarines as a heavy-bomber pilot attached to a Hawaiian Islands unit until a bad crash grounded him in 1944. Then he went back to school and was graduated from Stanford University in 1946.

EDWARD G. ROBINSON (1951): I never thought I would get stage fright. I didn't in my younger days when I was starring on Broadway. But I am so anxious about this play because, aside from entertainment value, it concerns a major problem of our time, the individual versus the totalitarian state.

I believe in what it has to say so much, I know that when I give the first performance before an audience I will get over being nervous about returning to the theater.

On the Broadway stage, I never played but one gangster role and that was the one that got me into the movies. That was when I played the gunman wearing a yellow camel's hair overcoat in the play about the Chicago underworld, *The Racket*, in 1927.

People seem to forget that I had also played in such classics as *Peer Gynt*, *The Brothers Karamazov* and as Caesar in *Androcles and the Lion*. That's why I'm coming back to the stage in *Darkness at Noon*. In the part of Rubashov I'll still be in prison, but it won't be because I'm supposed to be a gangster.

Rains and Jack Palance (Gletkin, the
brutal interrogator). The role brought
Palance stardom.

Edward G. Robinson (Rubashov) and
Leo Gordon (Gletkin) in the road
company production, which premiered September 28, 1951, at Prince-
ton's McCarter Theater.

Peer Gynt 1/28/51

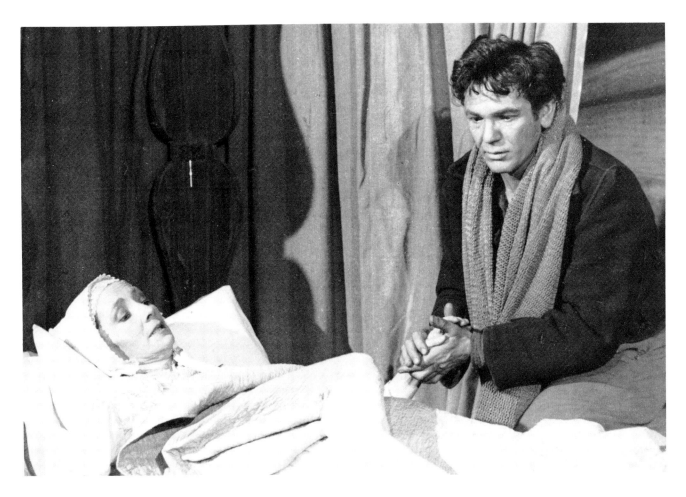

MILDRED DUNNOCK: It's sad for me to see this picture. That's a marvelous part, a small jewel of a part. Lee Strasberg directed the play. It's hard for me to talk about things unless I say complimentary things, and I can't say complimentary things about that production. Lee spoke brilliantly about the play for three days, and then never said anything else. And that's very difficult. I shall never forget what he did say to me because it threw me into such a state. When Aase gets up from the bed, when she's going to her death, he said, "I'd like you to do this the way Duse died in such-and-such film." Well, there's just one thing you do not tell anybody, and that is to do it the way one of the greatest actresses in the world did it. And it just stumped me. You cannot do it any other way except the way *you* can do it. . . . That's a perfectly beautiful picture, though, isn't it? I never saw that picture before.

Mildred Dunnock (Aase) and John Garfield (Peer Gynt) in Paul Green's "American version" of Ibsen's vast poetic play. Cheryl Crawford and Robert Stevens produced. 32 performances.

The King and I 3/29/51

Gertrude Lawrence (Anna) and Yul Brynner (the King of Siam). Rodgers and Hammerstein's hit musical launched Brynner as an international star. John van Druten directed; Jerome Robbins choreographed. 1,246 performances.

YUL BRYNNER: The things that were wrong with *The King and I* when we first opened in New Haven became absolutely evident on the very first performance with an audience. There was no love story between the King and Anna—none. There was nothing but conflict. So after the show, which lasted about five hours and was obviously a flop, I took Gertrude Lawrence to supper, alone, and I said, "Darling, from now on, from the moment you come into my palace, from the moment we are together on stage, we are going to play a great love story, through conflict, through everything." So she said, "Well, we'll try. I don't see how, but we'll try." In Boston, Hammerstein, who had an extraordinary eye, caught what Gertrude Lawrence and I were doing. And out of that came his writing of the whole section that surrounds "Shall We Dance?" She finds the King reading poetry; he tells her what nonsense the English poets write about "love, etcetera, etcetera, etcetra." And that leads to "Shall We Dance?" which is really as close to being a love scene be-

Page 182, Yul Brynner.

Page 183, Gertrude Lawrence.

tween them as anything can be. It was marvelous to see how these things happen, how Rodgers could write "Shall We Dance?" in something like three or four minutes. That's the length of time it takes to play it–and that's how fast he wrote it. Hammerstein laboriously worked out the words–merciless with himself, not accepting easy solutions to anything, torturing himself.

I've never had such an experience with a costume designer as I had with Irene Sharaff. Every costume she designed revealed another aspect of the scene I was going to do in that costume, an aspect I had not imagined. She's the one who suggested that I shave my hair, and she was absolutely right. That was what was needed for the character. It was needed for her costumes. It was needed for the whole conception. And, in fact, it was needed for me, because it gave me a certain kind of liberation. It was like shedding old vanities in a funny way. Shaving my head, I suddenly was free of all that nonsense of young actors–you know, of being concerned with my looks. And I've never been concerned with my looks since, frankly. I knew the name of the game was something else.

Nobody knew that Gertrude was ill. I don't think that *she* knew that much–I think she simply thought she had some problem. She'd been on vacation, in fact she'd just come back from six weeks on Cape Cod, come back in wonderful shape and wonderful spirits. She had asked me, before she left, not to take my vacation immediately upon her return. This would give her two weeks to get back into the swing of the show; she could then do it with my understudy while I went off for a week.

Two weeks after she came back–it was the middle of August–I went off on a friend's boat after playing the Saturday night show and was steaming toward Cape Cod when we were contacted by ship-to-shore communication with the message that I must turn back to New York, that there was an emergency, that Gertrude Lawrence was taken to the hospital. I came back and found out that she was gravely ill. I went back into the show, and she died four weeks later. She lost consciousness, I believe, two weeks after she was taken to the hospital and never regained it. Just died. It was cancer of the liver.

Apparently–the way I understood it at the time–she had been on a USO tour, and they were given anti-malarial shots and the whole company got hepatitis, or something similar to it, from this shot. As a result she developed cirrhosis of the liver, though she was not a drinking person–she was anything but that! It was a terrible, terrible loss.

A Tree Grows in Brooklyn 4/19/51

Shirley Booth and Nathaniel Frey in the Betty Smith–George Abbott–Arthur Schwartz–Dorothy Fields musical based on Smith's autobiographical novel about her girlhood. Booth was Aunt Cissy, who never learns to say no, and Frey was one of her many suitors. Among the songs: "Make the Man Love Me," "Look Who's Dancing," "Love Is the Reason for It." Abbott produced and directed. 267 performances.

WALTER KERR: I always remember Nat Frey. He was a marvelous actor. Jean and I used him twice and would have used him anytime we ever could. In *Goldilocks* we'd thrown new comedy material to the three or four supporting people and put it in the show that night to try it out. And okay–fine–we got four new laughs out of one piece of paper. But I remember the next day Nat coming in to Jean so apologetic, so humiliated, so humble, and he said, "I'm ashamed, I'm so sorry, I didn't get that laugh last night." And she said, "What laugh didn't you get?" And he said, "I got some of it, I tried . . . I could not get it." He pointed to the script and she looked at it. "Nat," she said, "that is the straight line." He was trying to get them even on straight lines, and felt crushed when he couldn't.

I remember when we did *Touch and Go,* he could get laughs that other people couldn't get. If somebody else didn't get a laugh, we just turned the same lines over to Nat and he'd have it the next night. He was like that. No temperament whatsoever; just eagerness to help, to do, to get what you wanted. George Abbott had been using him for a long time, mainly in the chorus for a bass baritone. George put us on to him. He said: "You'll like to have that guy around. He's not a star or anything like that. You'll like to have him around." And I can remember sitting in an apartment in New York, which we briefly rented during rehearsals for *Touch and Go,* desperately trying to write a new lyric for a song for Nat. I wanted to give him a spot "in one," all by himself, you know. I never got it finished. We opened out of town, there were other things to do, I never got it done. But I always wanted to do it.

The Little Blue Light 4/29/51

Arlene Francis (Judith Brock) and Melvyn Douglas (Frank, her husband, a crusading journalist) in Edmund Wilson's play about liberalism and totalitarianism in America, secret weapons, infidelity, homosexuality, and the Wandering Jew. Brooks Atkinson said: *"The Little Blue Light* is a valiant attack on the theatre by a man with a hatful of ideas. The theatre's defenses are formidable." Albert Marre directed. 16 performances.

MELVYN DOUGLAS: It was a difficult play to begin with, but there was the added problem of an author, Edmund Wilson, who cherished every last one of his words. The play needed cutting badly; everyone realized this. But he would have none of it. The director took us aside one day and confided he was going to take the responsibility of making certain discreet cuts in the text. Wilson got wind of this, came to rehearsal next day, sat with the script in his lap, and restored every *if*, *and*, and *but*.

ANTA Album 1951   5/6/51

Tallulah Bankhead, who was a "Mistress of Ceremony."

WALTER KERR: Kazan had a terrible fight with Bankhead in *Skin of Our Teeth*. It was finally a question of who was going to rule the roost, who was going to dominate. And Gadge said, "By God, it's going to be me because I'm the director or I'm through." So he locked himself in his hotel room after he'd issued an ultimatum to Bankhead. This all had to do with whether she'd come off the stage or go down into a little tent for the seduction scene in Atlantic City. She didn't want to go down some steps; she thought she'd break her neck on "those goddam stairs" and so forth. Gadge was going to have it, that's all, and he finally just absented himself from rehearsals, cut off the phone, locked the door, and waited until Bankhead was ready. Finally she gave in. He won the fight.

Pat Rooney sings and dances to "The Daughter of Rosie O'Grady." He had introduced the song, his hallmark, in 1919.

Above, Mary Boland and Philip Tonge in a scene from *Meet the Wife*, Lynn Starling's 1923 comedy.

Below, Todd Duncan (Porgy) and Muriel Rahn (Bess) sing "Bess, You Is My Woman Now" from *Porgy and Bess*, the immortal George Gershwin–DuBose Heyward–Ira Gershwin opera. Duncan played Porgy in the original, 1935 production.

Above, Lawrence Tibbett, blackened up, in the prayer solo from Louis Gruenberg's operatic version of Eugene O'Neill's *The Emperor Jones*. Tibbett had played Jones in the opera's premiere, at the Met in 1933, because grand opera was considered beyond the competence of Negro singers.

Below, Barry Gray, Phil Baker, Joseph Santley, and Jack Carter in "If Men Played Cards as Women Do," a George S. Kaufman sketch from the 1923 *Third Music Box Revue*.

GROUCHO MARX (1941): What makes people laugh? With Americans, sympathy is important. In *Go West*, the character I play starts out as a wise guy bent on fleecing suckers. In the original script I cheated Harpo and Chico out of scads of money. In rehearsals of our stage version it looked funny, but it just didn't go with the public. We rewrote that whole act. I lose money on every sale and wind up broke. The slicker is slicked. The audience howled.

Groucho Marx puts in an unexpected appearance. He waits for the applause to die down.

Two on the Aisle 7/19/51

Bert Lahr as Siegfried and Dolores Gray as Brünnhilde in a takeoff on Wagnerian opera, the first act finale in this Betty Comden–Adolph Green–Jule Styne revue directed by Abe Burrows. 281 performances.

Gray and Lahr, the latter declaring his
affection.

BROADWAY OLD-TIMER: In the trade Bert was nearly as famous as a
worrier as he was as a comedian. When he was doing the revival of *Burlesque*, the press agent set him up with some reporters. Bert was supposed to say how great the show was, naturally. Well, one reporter happened to ask him how much the show cost. And Bert said, "Jesus
Christ, *too* much! $65,000. You know, boys, when this show was done
21 years ago it cost $12,000. And maybe the show isn't as good now."

BERT LAHR (1941): What makes people laugh? Injured dignity is funny,
but it takes a funny man to put it across. Some people are just naturally
funny. Conversely, of course, some are not.

Island Fling 8/6/51
(Westport Country Playhouse)

Claudette Colbert (Lady Alexandra Shotter) in a Noël Coward comedy that never made it to Broadway. Colbert was returning to the theater after 21 years in films.

PROGRAM ANNOUNCEMENT:

TEA WILL BE SERVED

after every Wednesday and Friday matinee, in the patio at the right of the theatre. You are cordially invited to be the guest of the Management and meet the Playhouse personalities of the week.

The Fourposter 10/24/51

JESSICA TANDY: *The Fourposter* had a long history of trial and error.

HUME CRONYN: Yes. It's odd that you should come up with these photographs on *The Fourposter* just as we are doing *The Gin Game*, the only other two-character play we've ever done in our lives. Two-character plays, needless to say, are very difficult. They require an enormous amount of concentration from the actors performing them. We bought both plays with a view to trying them out somewhere and seeing how they worked. And that's what you've caught us at here at the Long Wharf right now.

We started *The Fourposter* in the summer of 1951, and it was almost immediately obvious that we had a bear by the tail. It was tremendously popular with audiences. However, we started off doing every scene Jan de Hartog had written, and he had done two versions of the play. We had seven scenes, one more than either version. He was tremendously attached, at least intellectually, to the final scene of the play, which showed utter disaster and tragedy. The audience loved the first six scenes and totally rejected the last one. And eventually he was persuaded to drop it.

We got him over here after *great* difficulty. He was Dutch and had been in Holland hiding from the Nazis during the war. State Department regulations said that anybody who had been in occupied territory during the war, regardless of where his sentiments lay, had to have a letter from the mayor and the chief of police in his town swearing that he was not a Nazi. Jan was a bit casual about all this and never managed to get the right papers. We had to pull wires furiously to get him here and hire planes to meet him at La Guardia and get him up to Skowhegan, Maine, where we were giving the last performance of a ten-week run.

I frankly don't think he was terribly anxious to come because the play had been a dismal failure in England: one review referred to it as "piffle and balderdash." Not wanting to come, he told us he had had a diving accident and broke a leg–he was an avid diver. So I reserved two aisle seats for this last performance–one on the right in case it should be his left leg, and one on the left in case it should be his right. And he came leaping out of the taxi after he'd been picked up and didn't even have the courtesy to limp! There was nothing wrong with his leg whatsoever.

Once here, he did a wonderful job of rewriting. Then we got Joe Ferrer to take over as director, and we took it out all over again before going to Broadway. And here we are going through the very same thing *again*, how many years later?

TANDY: Oh, I don't know–we have never learned wisdom obviously.

Q: Is it fair to ask if it is trying on a marriage to be working together?

TANDY: Everything is trying on a marriage. *Life* is trying on a marriage.

Jessica Tandy and Hume Cronyn as Agnes and Michael in Jan de Hartog's hit two-character play about a marriage from wedding night to old age. The Cronyns remained in the Broadway production till June 1952, then turned it over to Betty Field and Burgess Meredith, and took the play on tour around the United States; John Chapman remarked, "Mr. and Mrs. Cronyn seem to be about the only actors in Equity who are eager to tour." *The Fourposter* ran 632 performances, the longest run of any two-character play to its time. In 1966 Mary Martin and Robert Preston did a musical version, *I Do! I Do!* adapted by Tom Jones and Harvey Schmidt.

Returning home from a party, Agnes has just told Michael he's a swine and a hack writer.

Michael and Agnes: the years advance.

CRONYN: We were playing in Chicago, and playing a very funny scene. I was aware–you're acutely aware of what goes on in an audience, I mean I can tell, actors can tell, "That woman in the fourth row on the aisle has that goddam paper bag out again. I wish she'd put it under her seat." Or, "This man over here in the ninth row has got a terrible cold. Didn't anyone ever teach him to use a handkerchief?" Well, I was aware that somebody got up in a row of the orchestra during this performance and tried to get out, and then, halfway down the row, pitched headlong. There were small muffled exclamations of alarm and people stood up around him. Then people in the balcony stood up to look down, because suddenly you had this terrifying feeling that somebody had died. The man couldn't be moved because he'd gotten lodged between the seats. I had to stop the performance, and I said, I remember, as I stepped down, "There's a gentleman in trouble. Perhaps some of the ushers would come down. We need the houselights." And they carried him out. The audience was shaking. And I had to say, "I think we should go back and start this again." Well, we went back and did it again and let me tell you it wasn't very funny.

When we finished the performance, a man came back to our dressing rooms and said, "Mr. Cronyn, I thought you'd like to know that that gentleman who fell was not seriously hurt. As a matter of fact," he said, "it was rather amusing. I am a doctor and when I got out to the lobby to see what I could do, I saw a man in his late sixties, sitting on the ground, his back against the wall, and a woman stuffing chocolates into his mouth. And I said, 'Madam, excuse me, but would you mind telling me why you are doing that?' And she said, 'I am a doctor; this is diabetic shock and I am giving him sugar.' And I said, 'Well, would you mind if I examine him? I am also a doctor.' At which point the man opened his eyes and said, 'I'm a doctor, too!'" At the age of 65 or so he had had the chickenpox.

TANDY: Mumps!

CRONYN: Mumps! Mumps. I knew it was a childhood disease. He'd recovered and was convalescing.

TANDY: It was his first night out and he wasn't going to let the tickets go.

CRONYN: He wasn't going to let the tickets go because they were just about impossible to get.

TANDY: This must have been a very early photograph. This must have been in the summer, because you see what I'm wearing here is my own coat, which was eventually changed to something else. I remember that coat had a neutria front.

Gigi 11/24/51

Audrey Hepburn made a triumphant Broadway debut as Gigi in Anita Loos' play based on the Colette novel. In this scene Gigi, dressed in her aunt's chiffon negligee, wonders whether becoming a courtesan, as her mother, grandmother, and aunt want, is something *she* wants. She decides not. Gilbert Miller produced. Raymond Rouleau directed. Raymond Sovey did sets and costumes. 219 performances.

ANITA LOOS (1973): The people I'm furious at are the women's liberationists. They keep getting on soapboxes and claiming that women are brighter than men. That's true, but it should be kept very quiet or it ruins the whole racket.

Point of No Return 12/13/51

HENRY FONDA (1976): The harder change is going from film back to theater. In films the camera and the microphone do all your work for you. Acting is just being as natural as can be. But on the stage you have to project, and when you come from film you feel you're overacting. So I make the change gradually. As rehearsals go on and I get comfortable in a part, I project more.

Bartlett Robinson (Roger Blakesley), Henry Fonda (Charles Gray), and Frank Conroy (Anthony Burton) in Paul Osborn's adaptation of the John Marquand novel about getting to the top in banking. Roger and Charles are assistant vice-presidents competing for Burton's approval. Despite Roger's tricks, Charles gets the promotion and saves his integrity. H. C. Potter directed. Leland Hayward produced. 364 performances.

The Wild Duck 12/26/51

Mildred Dunnock as Gina Ekdal, Maurice Evans as Hjalmar, her dreamy husband, and Diana Lynn as Hedvig, their daughter, in a City Center revival of Ibsen's tragedy about the destructiveness of "truth telling." Morton Da Costa directed.

Anna Christie 1/9/52

Celeste Holm as Anna, the prostitute redeemed by love, in a City Center revival of the Eugene O'Neill play. Michael Gordon directed.

The Shrike 1/15/52

José Ferrer as Jim Downs and Judith Evelyn as Ann, his estranged wife, in Joseph Kramm's melodrama about a sweetly vicious woman who dupes hospital psychiatrists into giving her control over her husband. The patient at left is played by Will Lee. Ferrer produced and directed, as he had done with *Stalag 17* eight months before. With *The Fourposter* he had three hits on Broadway simultaneously and won Tony awards as Best Director and Best Actor. 161 performances.

HELEN HAYES: There was a time when we thought it would be mandatory they rename 48th Street "Ferrer" Street, because he had about three or four plays running on that street at the same time. The Ethel Barrymore, the Cort—well, he had plays going in all of them.

Come of Age 1/23/52

Judith Anderson (A Woman) and Marian Seldes (A Close Friend) in a City Center revival of Clemence Dane's poetical fantasy with music by Richard Addinsell. Anderson played the same part in the 1934 production, which ran only 35 performances but which, many people believed, could have had a longer run. The revival lasted 30 performances. Guthrie McClintic directed.

VARIETY (2/20/34): *Come of Age*, which Delos Chappell closed at the Elliott after a month in the red, went out with the final day's figures indicating that it might have gotten across had the engagement been continued. Takings for the day (Saturday, 10) amounted to $2,200. Show was accorded 17 curtain calls at the finale performance and 10 curtains at the matinee.

ALAN HEWITT: The closing night of a flop can frequently be a hell of a performance because the audience—friends of the actors, the sentimental public—will go there to try to tell the actors how much they love them, how much they appreciate them, and what a shame this marvelous play is closing. Of course nobody came near it earlier in the week. Now they pack in on Friday and Saturday for the final three performances, and the actors have the sweet illusion, "Oh, my God, we could have stayed open! We could have made a fight for it." Not a chance.

Mrs. McThing 2/20/52

Helen Hayes, as the ludicrously rich Mrs. Howard V. Larue III, orders a dentist to come to her estate and check her son's teeth–and bring his dentist's chair. She makes him promise not to hurt the boy, Howard IV, called "Howay." In her right hand she holds a toy railroad car like a highball glass. Mary Chase's fantasy was written to please children–she had tried it out on her growing sons–and, despite the enormous success of her 1944 *Harvey*, was scheduled for just a two-week run. It scored an instant hit. Joseph Buloff directed. Robert Whitehead produced for ANTA. 350 performances.

BETHEL LESLIE: I remember somebody asking Helen Hayes what she was doing at a certain point on stage, and she replied, "I wouldn't presume to answer that. It's a secret between me and the audience."

Hayes, Mildred Chandler, Marga Ann Deighton, Enid Markey, and Brandon de Wilde as a changeling Howay. Mrs. Larue doesn't know it yet but Mrs. McThing, the Witch of the Blue Mountains, has substituted a stick for her son. That's why he's so polite and doesn't eat candy before meals and lets the old ladies kiss him.

HELEN HAYES: Mary Chase's plays are always comforting. Do you realize they always soothe the heart? This one says to mothers: "Consider yourself blessed if your child is a handful." Remember? Because when he became too good he became the stick and his mother was horrified. She loathed having him around then.

Oh, those marvelous lines Mary Chase wrote! Great things. "My father always said to me"–what was it?–"'If you can't be clever, be pleasant.'" Oh, that's so nice. It's changed my whole life, that line.

HAYES: Isn't Brandon delightful to look at! He made the cover of *Life* in that play.

De Wilde as the real Howay and Jules Munshin as the gangster Poison Eddie Schellenbach in Poison Eddie's hangout, the Shantyland Pool Hall Lunchroom. Chase put gangsters in the play when she found her sons less interested in an early draft of it than in newspaper accounts of a jailbreak from the state penitentiary.

A stick has replaced Mrs. Larue at her estate, so she joins Howay in the Shantyland. Despite her pleading, he wants to stay with his new, disreputable friends. The Larues get home again, but it takes a little magic and an end to Mother's snobbery.

Golden Boy 3/12/52

Art Smith (Tom Moody), Bette Grayson (Lorna Moon), Rudy Bond (Roxy Gottlieb), John Garfield (Joe Bonaparte), and Joseph Wiseman (Eddie Fuseli). Joe is torn between being a champion boxer or the best violinist in the city; the others are pushing him into the ring. Clifford Odets directed this ANTA revival of his popular tragedy. 55 performances. Both Garfield and Smith had played different parts in the original, 1937 Group Theatre production, directed by Harold Clurman.

HAROLD CLURMAN: Garfield was Odets' first choice for Joe Bonaparte, but he was wrong for it. He was wonderful as Siggy, the taxi driver in the original *Golden Boy*. He was immense in that because it was just right for him. I remember Spencer Tracy raving over that performance as "so macho, so New York, so off the streets." Garfield got his jobs in Hollywood through it. But he wasn't really a tragic actor. He was charmingly wistful when he played in *Johnny Johnson*, but he didn't have the inner torment for Joe Bonaparte.

Joe pleads with Lorna to give in to her love for him and promises he will box for her. Grayson was Mrs. Clifford Odets. Joe Bonaparte was Garfield's last role; a month after *Golden Boy* closed he died of a heart attack, age 39.

ODETS

William Gibson: I met Clifford in 1950, '51. He had come back from the Coast, and he announced in the *Times* that he would lead a playwrights' workshop at the Actors' Studio. He invited people to send in scripts. He got two or three hundred, and he picked out 16. He wrote me a note about mine, saying he wasn't going to include me in the class. And I wrote back, "Why not?" or something like that, and he wrote back, "You know how to write a play." The script I sent him was *A Cry of Players*. He really just didn't like it. I never had the feeling in all my life that Clifford liked my work, any part of it. I wrote him back saying I would very much like to be in the class because I thought I could learn a lot from the theatrical thinking he represented—the Group Theatre, the Stanislavski tradition, and so on. So he let me in.

He taught it two afternoons a week, four hours a session, from fall to spring. It was marvelous, just marvelous, and I never learned so much in my life. I was at that point where I was just about to discover certain things, maybe by myself, and Odets was pointing them out, so every word out of his mouth was a revelation to me.

He influenced me tremendously. I'm just finishing a book which examines the structure of Shakespeare's plays, and although I've elaborated, the book is basically what I heard Clifford say. I'm enormously indebted to him because it was from him that I learned such things as what a scene was. He would go through our scripts line by line—we'd read the script out in class—and he wouldn't let anything go by. It was shotgun stuff: sometimes he was talking about large structural points, sometimes he was talking about veracity, verisimilitude. Other subjects, too. He'd suddenly get interested in music, and he'd talk for an hour or two about music. He was fascinating, one of the best talkers I ever heard. He could tell you the gospel story and it would absolutely be like the first time you ever heard it. He was a genius, he had genius.

We became friends. He got in the habit of calling us up. He liked the idea of me and my wife–Margaret was pregnant with our first kid, and he liked the whole family sense. It was something he had missed out on because his marriages were both disasters. He would call up 11:30 at night and talk long distance for an hour or two. I'd get tired, I'd go to sleep, my wife would stay up talking to him. It was his pattern of life: he was a night bird; he'd sleep until 1 or 2 in the afternoon and then he'd get up and begin living.

Writers are sort of like automobiles: they have a certain period and then they go into obsolescence. And Clifford had become obsolete. In practical terms. If the theater had been less expensive, if it were a place where he could have experimented, had failures without feeling like a failure . . .

But he had been spoiled. Clifford was famous when he was 28, internationally famous. He was more than a playwright: he was a charismatic figure, the apostle of the whole new world that was going to come in after the revolution, you know, and all that was part of his life. The war came, 1939, and broke up that whole domestic scene, his *Night Music* flopped, the Group Theatre fell apart. And Clifford was now in the normal position of a writer vis-à-vis the professional theater–naked, without the Group Theatre as a vehicle, a bridge. And his earlier message–that was what had become obsolete: that the working class was going to save the world. It didn't seem quite as convincing after the Second World War.

But Clifford was a very creative person. What he needed was a form, a literary form in which he could explore the new things that were happening in himself. He never found it. He was sort of stuck. He was a writer who could write nothing except for actors on the stage or the screen–Bill Inge was the same way. And this is a trap. In the cruel context of the commercial theater, the capacity of a writer to use other forms is vital to his survival and to his self-respect. That's something else Clifford taught me–*showed* me.

In January 1955 he went out to the Coast. I had just come back–*The Cobweb* had been made into a movie–and we met Clifford in New York. He had signed a contract to do *Joseph and His Brothers* for Harry Cohn, and he was going to be out there for a few months, three or four months he thought, and then he'd be back. But he never came back. He stayed out there for 10 years and died, and never wrote anything else for the theater.

The week he was dying, I didn't know he was dying. It was sudden. Clifford had invited Jean and Dido Renoir over for dinner on Bastille Day. A couple of days after that he went into the hospital to see what was causing these stomach pains. Three weeks later he was dead. They found him riddled with a cancer so extensive that I think they drugged him and let him die.

There were a half dozen people he asked to come out and see him before he died, because he sort of knew he was dying; it was like a last request. But on the other hand he didn't act as though he were dying, so it was ambiguous. Margaret and I were on that list, and Lee Strasberg was calling people. And Kazan went out, and Clurman went out, and Strasberg couldn't get hold of us. We were down here swimming, and this is an unlisted phone. Finally Strasberg got the message to us, about a week after he'd started. So I called Lee in Clifford's house out there, and he said, "Clifford's dying." And I said, "What?" I had just written him; I knew he had some stomach trouble, so I said, "Is it cancer?" And he said, "I don't want to say, I don't know who's listening." He didn't know if the daughter was listening–they were keeping it from her.

I said, "Shall I come out?" And he said, "Well, he's unconscious. He's sedated." And I said, "I'll come out." I went off looking for my wife, who was off with the kids in the bay, and I had trouble finding her. I remember I wound up shouting to her, "Clifford's dying!" It was a dreadful day, a nightmarish kind of day. I got on a plane that night. I had told Strasberg, "Lee, if I come in it may be four o'clock in the morning." He said, "So?" "I don't know where I'll stay." He said, "Stay here." I said, "I'll wake everybody up." He said, "So you wake everybody up."

I got there, and Paula Strasberg opened the door for me. There was a big poodle barking like hell, and Clifford was in the hospital. I stayed there a week, and half way through that week Clifford died. He never came out of the drugs. I was at the hospital several times. Jean Renoir and his wife would just sit there in the corridor. Jean was strange to see. You know he looks like a loaf of French bread all the time. And he just sat there in the corridor, with his cap. Just sitting there. Nothing could happen, you know. But he was in attendance at a death. We were all like that.

Clifford had maintained an apartment in New York all the years he was out on the Coast. People used it as a love nest, and anybody who came from the Coast put up in it for a week. It was a shambles, it was like a campground. But there were all Clifford's things: books, a couple of hundred albums of 78 records. And the next fall Paula and Lee were selling stuff off trying to raise money for the estate. And one thing they couldn't do anything with was an old table. Paula said, "I hate to throw this out." It used to be in the communal apartment the Group had downtown–they called it Groupstroy, after Dnieperstroy, a show-place Soviet city. She said, "It was in the kitchen down there, and Clifford wrote *Awake and Sing* on it." And I said, "We'll take the table."

We kept it on our porch in Stockbridge all winter. And the next spring we brought it down here and I put it in my studio. The first thing I wrote on it was the musical book of *Golden Boy*, the year after Clifford died. It's a very Odetsian table.

JOHN CHAPMAN (1952)

The New York theater season means the American theater season, for all practical and most artistic purposes.

The Male Animal 4/30/52

Martha Scott as Ellen Turner finds herself drawn to Robert Preston as Joe Ferguson, an old flame. This City Center revival was so popular that it transferred to Broadway for a nine-month run. Michael Gordon directed.

Elliott Nugent, reappearing as Tommy Tucker, gives John Gerstad, as Michael Barnes, a boozy demonstration of how he's going to fight Joe to keep his wife, Ellen.

Tommy. Let us say that the tiger wakes up one morning and finds that the wolf has come down on the fold. What does he–? Before I tell you what he does, I will tell you what he does not do.
Michael. Yes, sir.
Tommy. He does not expose everyone to a humiliating intellectual analysis. He comes out of his corner like this–[*Rises, assuming an awkward fighting pose, fists up, then sits quickly again.*] The bull elephant in him is aroused.
Michael (plaintively). Can't you stick to one animal?
Tommy. No, that's my point. All animals are the same, including the human being. We are male animals, too. Even the penguin. [*His voice shows some emotion as he thinks of the penguin.*] He stands for no monkey business where his mate is concerned.

New Faces of 1952   5/16/52

Eartha Kitt, the hit of this hit revue, does her big number, ''Monotonous'' –music by Arthur Siegel, words by June Carroll. Leonard Sillman produced. John Murray Anderson and John Beal directed. Thomas Becher did the costumes. 365 performances.

Sunday Breakfast 5/28/52

Cloris Leachman plays the hot-tempered daughter of an unhappy household in a play directed by Stella Adler. 16 performances.

An Evening with Bea Lillie 10/2/52

Bea Lillie. 276 performances. Edward Duryea Dowling produced and directed.

BROADWAY OLD-TIMER: Bea's husband was a peer of the realm; she's Lady Peel. And to me her title always seemed something of a joke—you know, "peals" of laughter, that sort of thing—because she was the most *unpremeditated* person I ever saw on stage. It was literally as though she were making her part up as she went along. You felt she didn't have a haughty bone in her body.

There's a story that once in Chicago she was having her hair done by the man who did Mrs. Swift's or Mrs. Armour's hair. And Mrs. Swift or Mrs. Armour came in, without an appointment, and wanted the man to give her a quick comb. Bea sat up in her chair and said to the hairdresser: "Lady Peel hasn't finished with you. Tell the butcher woman that!" The title was good for something.

THE PLAYBILL (1952)

In the event of an air raid alarm remain in your seats and obey the instructions of the management. – Arthur H. Wallander, Director of Civil Defense.

Dial "M" for Murder 10/29/52

Maurice Evans as Tony Wendice and Gusti Huber as Margot, his wife, look at the dead would-be murderer, Captain Lesgate, played by Anthony Dawson. Tony Wendice hired Lesgate to do in Margot; Lesgate bungled the job. The popular melodrama was by Frederick Knott. Reginald Denham directed. James Sherwood produced. 552 performances.

GUSTI HUBER: One evening Anthony Dawson, who played the murderer, *really* nearly choked me to death and I could hardly get any choking noises out. It sounds crazy, but in order to make choking noises, you have to have a lot of breath. The scene was not so effective as on other nights—besides which he scared me very much, of course. From then on the stage manager and I had a signal: I would wave one hand in a certain way if Tony got carried away again. Then the curtain would quickly be let down in order to rescue me. But after a good talking-to he did not repeat his carelessness.

Time Out for Ginger 11/26/52

Melvyn Douglas (Howard Carol) defends his daughter's right to be different in the Ronald Alexander comedy. Shepard Traube produced and directed. 248 performances.

MELVYN DOUGLAS: This play occupied me much longer than I would have anticipated when we tried it out in summer theater. We ran for a season on Broadway, toured it around the country, including one-night stands and a nine-month run in Chicago; and I finally played in and directed it in Australia with an all-Australian cast.

"Ginger" was a typical American teenager who was determined to play football on the local high school team. But, no! The principal and the entire Board of Education were against it. However, I, the father of three girls and no son, was all for it. This was the crux of the play. The subject matter is probably more timely now, with NOW, than it was then.

The Australian Ginger spoke English with an extremely cultivated British elocution school accent and behaved as though playing Gwendolyn in *The Importance of Being Earnest*. The role of the small town banker, which that lovable actor Philip Loeb had played in New York, was done by a Czechoslovakian refugee actor whose English was indecipherable. My wife in the play had a delicious Australian cockney accent. Nevertheless, all the reviewers said that the play as we'd done it was typically American.

At center, Agnes Carol, Howard's wife (played by Polly Rowles), with the Carol girls: Joan (Mary Hartig), Jeannie (Lois Smith), and, on the cover of *Life* magazine, Ginger (Nancy Malone). At the end of the play Ginger surrenders to femininity.

See the Jaguar 12/3/52

James Dean and Arthur Kennedy in N. Richard Nash's portentous allegory. Michael Gordon directed. Five performances.

MARGARET BARKER: I played Jimmy Dean's mother, a crazy old witch that kept him shut away from the world, in a cave, I believe, since he was a "wild thing," more animal than boy, and I "feared" for him. They thought me too young for the role, but I proved zany enough and died in my first five minutes (exciting ones) on stage. So I never really acted with Jimmy Dean, who as yet had not put in his appearance. But his dressing room was next to mine in the try-out in Hartford (I think), and he was practising the saxophone or clarinet. He loved music and dancing. I find the time before a play starts one in which I like quiet and concentration and so admonished Jimmy, perhaps a bit too harshly, requesting that he shut up for the rest of our sakes. He took it pleasantly, as I remember, and acquiesced immediately. He was just wonderful in the part and had that extra *numinosity* that stars must have. The play did not go, but it certainly helped Jimmy get to Hollywood. Alas, there all destructive values are magnified, and for a kid from his background to sky-rocket that fast was bad and sad and certain as to its end. (Just this last year we have had another such, haven't we? Prinze.) Jimmy would have resented my saying it, but there was an endearing sweetness about him.

The Love of Four Colonels 1/15/53

In Peter Ustinov's playful satire on the four powers occupying postwar Germany, colonels of the allied countries–Britain, France, the U.S., the USSR–try to win their nation's ideal Sleeping Beauty (played by Lilli Palmer). One by one the colonels fail, despite meddlesome help from a Wicked Fairy (Rex Harrison). Harrison directed. The Theatre Guild produced. 141 performances.

The French ideal: Beauty (Palmer) as an eighteenth-century coquette with a gouty old husband (Harrison).

The Russian ideal: Beauty as a bored Chekhovian romantic with a dotty uncle.

The American ideal: Beauty as a 1930s gun moll with her escaped-convict boyfriend.

The Crucible 1/22/53

Witchcraft in Salem: evil spirits possess the court. Madeleine Sherwood (Abigail Williams, the slut whose vengeance keeps the trial going), another of the possessed girls, Don McHenry (Ezekiel Cheever, the court clerk), Walter Hampden (Deputy Governor Danforth, the judge superior), Fred Stewart (the fanatical Rev. Samuel Parris), Jenny Egan (timid Mary Warren), Philip Coolidge (Judge Hathorne), and E. G. Marshall (the tormented Rev. John Hale). Arthur Miller's controversial tragedy of conscience was understood as an attack on "witchhunting" congressional committees of the Joseph McCarthy era. Jed Harris directed. Kermit Bloomgarden produced. In the middle of the run Miller redirected the play, adding a scene. 197 performances.

Overheard on a Train Bound for a Wilmington Try-out of the Play, January 1953

ARTHUR MILLER: Salem was only a part of the whole, general world picture–France, Spain, Sweden, England, Germany, the Inquisition. Except in Europe it was worse. In Salem they had hung only sixteen persons. In Europe they burned thousands.

JED HARRIS: In Andover they hanged a dog. The dog said, "I'm not even a human." They said, "That's what you say," and they hanged the dog.

MILLER: The idea came to me a long time ago. I became fascinated with it because altogether these people of Massachusetts were quite ordinary people, and it is rare in history or in life that you get such a complete heroic tragedy occurring in reality.

Theocracy ruled in Massachusetts. The government and the church were practically one. It is generally taken as a fact that, due in great part to what happened in Salem–the heroic revolt–the power of the church was broken and Massachusetts developed into a democratic government.

Of course, in itself it does not account for the development of the American democracy, but it was one of the acts that created a legend–a resistance to tyranny which became part of the experience of the people so that they had a precedent to go by. It became part of their wisdom, although the detail faded from memory. It was a warning that nobody could pull that again, nobody could try to do that for a long time, because they learned a lesson from it. It was an event that shook the mind of the time.

Yes, there may be repercussions on this play. There may be those who will think that it was deliberately written because of the present period through which we are living. But that doesn't matter. I have had repercussions before. My own attitude is that others have a right to their opinion and I have a right to mine.

I don't worry about attacks from left or from right. The Communists criticized *Death of a Salesman*. They would have done the same to *All My Sons* had it come out eight months earlier. *All My Sons* showed a factory owner in a bad light and the Communist line at the time I was writing that play was that you couldn't do this because it would hurt the war effort. I didn't feel it would, if it were true, and I knew it was true. What good is freedom unless you are willing to use freedom. If a man can't speak his heart he is robbing his art.

HARRIS: Art–schmart. That this should have to be said is a symbol of the times we are living in. Everybody says this is a great age we live in–the great new media of communications. It is really one of the saddest things in the world. Because what it has done is to give the greatest possible distribution to the most grotesque lies or to the stupidity of conventionally held opinion.

What gives me a pain is this conception of Arthur as a big social thinker, a man sitting like a sort of Brooklyn Ibsen, thinking about the ills of society. I never knew him until the past summer, and I have spent a lot of time with him since then. I feel about him as I feel about myself: pretty damn good operator. If this play is any good it can only be good for one reason: as a theatrical experience.

BROADWAY OLD-TIMER: This was my generation's *Waiting for Lefty*. It wasn't upbeat like the Odets play. It didn't tell us "Strike! Strike! Strike!" It said, "Suffer, suffer"—and we said, "Yeah, baby! Hit me again." We went to it *avidly*—oh, God, yes—because Miller was on the right side.

He had trouble with Jed Harris, and the production wasn't in the same league with the ones Kazan had given him. We liked it *better* because of that: it wasn't tainted by Kazan's genius, you see. [*Laughs.*] Because Kazan named names to the Un-American Activities Committee. Miller wouldn't work with him.

Q: Was there much blacklisting on Broadway?

OLD-TIMER: Not compared with the Blacklist in Hollywood and TV. The audience was too radical—or they had been; some of the producers too. But I say that and I remember the actor who committed suicide, he was a Broadway actor.

Q: Philip Loeb?

OLD-TIMER: Yeah. Very funny actor. He played Gertrude Berg's husband on *The Goldbergs*; when he was attacked as a Communist, she bought out his contract to get him off the show. After that he did one or two things on Broadway . . . The air was poisoned. People selling out their old friends. You're going to run into this. Ask some people about ——— ——— or ——— ———, for instance, and they'll say, "That rat. That fink."

Q: That's happened to us already.

OLD-TIMER: How're you going to handle it?

Q: In the book? Leave it out. It's not that kind of book.

OLD-TIMER: You're not willing to name names, eh? [*Laughs.*]

Q: It's not that kind of book.

The Fifth Season 1/23/53

John Griggs, second from right, plays a millionaire buyer appraising Richard Whorf's new line of clothes in Sylvia Regan's crowd-pleasing farce about shenanigans in the garment industry. The principal model, third from left, is Phyllis Hill. Gregory Ratoff directed. George Kardolf produced. 654 performances.

Hazel Flagg 2/11/53

Helen Gallagher (Hazel Flagg) and John Brascia (Willie) whoop it up in "You're Gonna Dance with Me, Willie," the big dance number at the Roseland Ballroom. Hazel is taking advantage of everyone's belief that she has only a few weeks to live (actually her doctor read the wrong X-ray). This Jule Styne–Ben Hecht–Bob Hilliard musical was based on the 1937 Carole Lombard film *Nothing Sacred*. Its hit songs: "Every Street's a Boulevard in Old New York" and "How Do You Speak to an Angel." Robert Alton and David Alexander directed. 190 performances. *Hazel Flagg* was reworked into the 1954 Dean Martin–Jerry Lewis film *Living It Up*; Lewis played the Hazel Flagg role.

My Three Angels 3/11/53

Walter Slezak and Jerome Cowan as two trustworthy murderers on leave from Devil's Island salute the Ducotel family, played by Joan Chandler, Carmen Mathews, and Will Kuluva in this popular comedy about good people's need of evil. Sam and Bella Spewack adapted the play from a French original. José Ferrer directed. Boris Aronson did the set. 344 performances.

Hamlet on the Hallmark
Hall of Fame 4/26/53

Maurice Evans (Hamlet), Joseph Schildkraut (Claudius), and Ruth Chatterton (Gertrude). This was Evans' TV debut and his 778th performance as Hamlet. The production was live, began at 3:30 Sunday afternoon (New York time), and ran two hours. Hallmark announced that it was given to commemorate the 398th anniversary of Shakespeare's christening. Evans told the press that he did the show with "a hundred hours rehearsal, sandwiched in at such hours as I was not deep in uxoricide in *Dial 'M' for Murder*." In a line cut from this production Hamlet speaks of a play which "pleased not the million; 'twas caviare to the general." This *Hamlet* had an audience of 16 million.

A LIVE TELEVISION STORY

Hume Cronyn: I'll never forget one of the *Omnibus* productions. I was playing John Adams, if you please, with, oh, that very famous Columbia historian—

Jessica Tandy: Nevins.

Cronyn: Allan Nevins was the sort of supervisor of the program. And every word we spoke was the language of the people themselves; it was all historically accurate.

Tandy: Was it Quincy or John?

Cronyn: I don't know. Maybe John Adams or John Quincy Adams—I can't remember. It was one of them. And I was addressing Congress. Well, this program had been changed every single day right up until air time. There was no question of learning it; you had to have teleprompters. They'd cut out this piece and they'd put in that, and they'd jam in this, and the teleprompter man was pasting things together with bits of Scotch Tape. Well, I'm in the middle of the speech, addressing the Congress, and of course I'm reading from the teleprompter. And suddenly the teleprompter rolls and there's nothing there. They have neglected to include a speech. And I find myself saying, "Gentlemen, I am at a loss for words." Boy, no word was ever truer. And at this point everything becomes hysterical and the teleprompter suddenly goes br-r-r-r-.

Tandy: Trying to find it.

Cronyn: Trying to find it, and then backward, br-r-r-r, trying to find it, and I'm going, "Ab, blub, blub, blub, blub." At which point a stage manager hurls himself to the floor, under the teleprompter, and holds up a manuscript, like this. Well, I tell you, I'm as far as from here to you: I can hardly see the page, let alone the words. I mean, that was a nightmare. I have to, as it happens, grey my hair for this part, but I'm surprised that it's not genuine.

Can-Can 5/7/53

Lilo, touted as "the French Ethel Merman," plays La Mome Pistache, mistress of a disreputable Paris dance hall, and Peter Cookson plays the Judge who comes to see what she is up to. Inevitably they fall in love. Here they sing "C'est Magnifique." The Cole Porter–Abe Burrows musical, with dances by Michael Kidd, was produced by Cy Feuer and Ernest Martin. The reviewers didn't love it; everyone else did. 892 performances.

ABE BURROWS (1953): Last summer I was standing in front of the Beverly Hills Hotel contemplating the lawn, which was all covered with beautiful late-blooming Hydromatics, when, suddenly, Feuer and Martin come driving up in a Jaguar. Feuer and Martin are the two kinetic bolts of energy who involved me in *Guys and Dolls* (a very nice involvement).

These two guys are very difficult to say no to on foot, but in a Jaguar they are just about irresistible. They landed the Jaguar at my feet, reached out, grabbed me by my lapels (I wear lapels out there so people will know I'm a New Yorker) and said the following: "*Can-Can* with Cole Porter and you."

This is actually true. It may sound like a breezy thing I made up in order to get a gay start to this article, but that's the way these fellows talk. They come right to the point: "*Can-Can* with Cole Porter and you." Inasmuch as I'm used to them, I didn't take it to mean that they wanted Cole and me to do a can-can dance. Ernie and Cy "felt" a show.

I am writing this piece in Philadelphia. *Can-Can* and I have been here almost six weeks. We were quite lucky. Most shows have to cut their out-of-town tryouts pretty short because you can lose a bundle out-of-town. But Philadelphia was wonderful to us. With true brotherly love they bought all our tickets, so we were able to extend our run here for additional polishing.

Vive la Philadelphia. Vive la France. Vive la Box-Office.

NEW YORK POST (4/29/53): Abe Burrows rewrote the entire second act of *Can-Can* in Philly.

Hans Conried as Boris Adzinidzin-adze, a sculptor, complains that Gwen Verdon as Claudine really doesn't love him or she would stop interrupting his art with her palaver about wanting to be a dancer. Verdon's was a secondary part, reduced on the road at Lilo's behest. Verdon still stole the show.

CHARLES ADAMS BAKER: I don't think *Can-Can* could have succeeded without her: it was Gwen, the one song "I Love Paris," and Michael's dances. Gwen had that marvelous experience which happens once in a while. She was the new girl in town—which they then used as the title for her Anna Christie musical. You couldn't go to dinner anywhere without having to talk about Gwen Verdon. It's curious: one show every year becomes *the* thing to see. And you can't go out without having seen it or else you're just going to be strapped there without any conversation because everyone else is talking about it—even if it isn't any good.

Verdon in an Apache dance with Ralph Beaumont.

Verdon does the can-can.

Q: In *Celebrity Register* they quote you as saying that in your next incarnation you want to be a musical comedy actress.

MILDRED DUNNOCK: Yes. My. Who says that? Do they say that? That's true, I would. I'd like to extend myself further. I'd like to be able to use my body better and I'd like to be able to move to music, and I'd like to have something which is more abstract, perhaps—I don't know what that means. I say it lightly and humorously; I don't mean it to be quoted.

Me and Juliet 5/28/53

The prime movers in putting on this musical about putting on a musical. *Back row*: George Abbott, director; Richard Rodgers, music, co-producer; Oscar Hammerstein II, book and lyrics, co-producer; Robert Alton, choreography; Jo Mielziner, scenery and lighting. *First row*: Joan McCracken (Betty, the Principal Dancer); Ray Walston (Mac, the Stage Manager); Isabel Bigley (Jeanie, a Chorus Singer); Bill Hayes (Larry, the Assistant Stage Manager); Irene Sharaff, costumes; Jackie Kelk (Herbie, the Candy Counter Boy). *Front*: Mark Dawson (Bob, an Electrician). The hit song: "No Other Love." Note how intently each actor catches the camera's eye; the nonperformers are more diffident. 358 performances.

The Teahouse of the August Moon 10/15/53

John Forsythe (Captain Frisby), David Wayne (Sakini), and Paul Ford (Col. Wainwright Purdy III) in John Patrick's whimsical comedy about the U.S. Army's occupation of Okinawa. The play suggested that democracy must be allowed to have a local flavor. A tremendous hit, it achieved the feat –rare for a work that isn't "serious" –of winning both the Critics' Circle and Pulitzer awards. Robert Lewis directed. Maurice Evans produced. 1,027 performances.

The Solid Gold Cadillac 11/5/53

Reynolds Evans, Wendell Phillips, Josephine Hull, Henry Jones, and Geoffrey Lamb in Howard Teichmann and George S. Kaufman's fairy tale about a little old lady who asks such impertinent questions at stockholders' meetings that the corporation hires her to shut her up. The lady was Hull, who has just discovered that she's to be the head of the firm. Max Gordon produced. Kaufman directed. 526 performances.

HERBERT GREENE: George Kaufman and I were sitting in the theater, rehearsing *Silk Stockings* – somebody was doing something onstage. I used to feed straight lines to him whenever I got the chance. I'd sit down next to him, say something, and just wait for a line to come back. And, sooner or later, it would come. He knew what I was doing, of course. One day he was kind of – he seemed to be ill-at-ease – so I asked, "George, what's the matter with you?" He said, "I don't know. I guess just life." I said, "Well, what more could you ask? You've had success, you've had fame, been one of the world's great lovers, what more could you want?" He looked at me for a bit and said, "More." He was 69. Two years later he was dead.

Madam, Will You Walk 12/1/53

Hume Cronyn (Dr. Brightlee, the Devil in thin disguise) and Jessica Tandy (Mary Doyle, a rich recluse). Brightlee takes Mary out on the town and bring her back to life, in Sidney Howard's comedy, revised by Robert Sherwood. The play was the first production at the Phoenix Theatre. 42 performances.

Kismet 12/3/53

Joan Diener (Lalume) and Alfred Drake (Hajj) in a "musical Arabian Nights" with a potpourri book by Charles Lederer and Luther Davis, based on an Edward Knoblock play, music adapted from Aleksandr Borodin, and lyrics by Robert Wright and George Forrest. The song hits: "Stranger in Paradise," "And This Is My Beloved," "Baubles, Bangles and Beads." Lederer produced. Albert Marre directed. Lemuel Ayers did sets and costumes. 583 performances.

SEYMOUR HERSCHER: *Kismet* was the one musical that opened during the newspaper strike and, because it wasn't reviewed, became a hit. People saw it and liked it.

Mademoiselle Colombe 1/6/54

Julie Harris as Colombe in Jean Anouilh's dark comedy about theater life and immorality in turn-of-the-century Paris. It was Anouilh's fifth Broadway failure in a row. Louis Kronenberger adapted, Harold Clurman directed. 61 performances.

HAROLD CLURMAN: The audience really didn't like it, not because of any casting problems, but because it's cynical and bitter–"no nice people in this play" is the way they put it. Brooks Atkinson said, "Superior theater work, but it's tired." Well, it's tired in the sense that Anouilh kept on writing these cynical plays, one right after another. He's still writing them! Full of hatred for everybody, including himself, I guess –but very deftly. As a matter of fact, the truth is it's a joke on me really: when I saw it in Paris, I felt more or less as the New York critics did. I did it anyhow, because I liked working with Julie Harris. But when they said the same things I'd said about it when I'd seen it in Paris, I got sore.

The Burning Glass 3/4/54

Walter Matthau as Tony Lack, a British scientist, and Maria Riva as Mary Terriford, his partner's wife, in a drama about the ethical implications of a new source of power, a device that concentrates the sun's rays. Lack blabs about the ur-laser, and "the Enemy" learns of it. At the end of the play, to prevent further security leaks, Lack does the noble thing: he takes poison. Matthau had a remarkable string of Broadway flops; this was number seven. 28 performances.

THE PLAYBILL: Walter Matthau made his acting debut in *Anne of the Thousand Days*. In that play, the 28-year-old Matthau played an 80-year-old character and understudied a number of parts whose stage ages totaled 350 years. To get the small role of the Courier to the Earl of Northumberland in that production he blandly lied to the director and informed him that he was English and cut his theatrical teeth on Shakespearean drama.

ERIC BENTLEY (1953): Any producer with a sure flop on his hands should hire Mr. Matthau, for he has the ability to ignore the rubbish around him and establish on stage the fact of his own ingratiating manner and strong personality; he has become Broadway's leading stopgap.

By the Beautiful Sea 4/8/54

Shirley Booth as Lottie Gibson, a former vaudevillian who runs a boarding house for actors on Coney Island in the early 1900s. Booth carried the musical and was the reason for its respectable run: 268 performances. Book by Herbert and Dorothy Fields, music by Arthur Schwartz, lyrics by Dorothy Fields, sets by Jo Mielziner, and costumes by Irene Sharaff. Robert Fryer and Lawrence Carr produced. Marshall Jamison directed.

MARC CONNELLY, *speaking of Shirley Booth*: I saw her in *The Queen of the Beach* playing a girl who worked maybe for Woolworth's and has the afternoon off. She knows she's glamorous, a Recamier. She's the Queen of the Riposte–there isn't a phrase that comes to her lips that she doesn't realize has something pretty magical and golden about it. And when she turned to a young man and said, ''Don't be an Airedale,'' her satisfaction was something really devastating. She just *knew* nothing could top her, and you celebrated it in your heart because here was a little thing who had about two cents worth of brain, who imagined herself competent to meet the great world of social contact. It was one of the most poignantly funny things I think I've ever seen. Of course, good comedy–anything in the theater–is always best by implication. Statement ruins implication, incandescence, and Shirley was nothing less than incandescent. She sat there on the sand, ready to be admired and ready to meet rapier points, you know. Of course, she had nothing but a piece of salami with which to fight . . . God! And then, in *Come Back, Little Sheba*, well, she was just a superb artist.

Mae Barnes as Ruby Monk, Lottie's worldy-wise maid in ''Hang Up,'' the number that opened the second act. Barnes had the show's best-remembered song, ''Happy Habit.''

GEORGE JEAN NATHAN (1954): The show is largely of the kind that tries to boost itself into some life by periodically bringing on the routine chubby Negress singer who while rendering the routine saucy ditties pumps her avoirdupois up and down like a tureen of demented meringue to an accompaniment of the usual dental and ocular exuberance and that further purveys the usual cute little colored boy in dance steps with the leading lady.

Sabrina 4/54

Audrey Hepburn and William Holden.

Billy Wilder and Hepburn.

FRED FEHL: I had photographed Audrey Hepburn in *Gigi* and I was much interested when I heard she was making a picture in New York. I asked to take some pictures, not for the film company, just for the fun of it. There were three locations: Wall Street, a dock in the Hudson River, and an estate in Westchester on the Sound. It was supposed to be summer but it was very cool. In the Westchester scene poor Audrey had a short dress and goosebumps.

Humphrey Bogart.

THE NEW YORKER (8/1/77): *Sabrina* (1954)–Audrey Hepburn is forced to overdo her gamine charm in this horrible concoction about a Cinderella among the Long Island rich. She's the chauffeur's daughter who's in love with the playboy son (William Holden) of her father's employer (Walter Hampden). There's also an older son–an earnest magnate–and Humphrey Bogart got trapped in the role. Billy Wilder directed, and he had a hand in adapting the Samuel Taylor play (*Sabrina Fair*), though Bogart is said to have accused Wilder's three-year-old offspring of being responsible for the script.

The Sea Gull 5/11/54

Montgomery Clift as Constantin, a sensitive aspiring writer, is briefly reconciled with his self-centered mother, Irina Arkadina, played by Judith Evelyn. At the end of the play, cheated of his hopes, Constantin commits suicide. For this revival, the Chekhov tragedy was adapted by Clift and two other cast members, Mira Rostova and Kevin McCarthy. The Phoenix Theatre produced. Norris Houghton directed. A limited engagement: 40 performances.

The Pajama Game 5/13/54

At center Janis Paige (Babe Williams, a labor organizer) and John Raitt (Sid Sorokin, a factory manager) in the George Abbott–Richard Bissell–Richard Adler–Jerry Ross musical smash concerning a strike for 7 1/2 cents hourly raise in a small-town pajama factory. The dancers at left are Marilyn Gennaro and Eric Kristen; at right, Marion Colby. Abbott co-directed with Jerome Robbins. Frederick Brisson, Robert Griffith, and Harold Prince produced. Bob Fosse choreographed. Among the hit songs: "Hey There," "Steam Heat," "Hernando's Hideaway." 1,061 performances.

HAROLD PRINCE: Shirley MacLaine was in the chorus and became Carol Haney's understudy. She wasn't the original understudy, but she wanted to be. After the show opened, she cut her hair to look like Carol Haney, and one night when we were looking at Shirley, we suddenly realized everybody was confusing her with Carol. You saw the resemblance immediately. That's where we got the idea of assigning her as Carol's understudy. And that's what got her started. Carol hurt her ankle: Shirley went on–and there were offers of two movies from her first performance.

Carol Haney as Gladys, the fickle secretary, leads the "Once a Year Day" number at the company picnic. This was Haney's memorable Broadway debut. Previously, with Gwen Verdon, she had been an assistant to Gene Kelly in Hollywood (she dubbed the sloshing sound effects to his "Singin' in the Rain" dance). The chorus girl at left is Shirley MacLaine.

250

On top, Haney; *on bottom*, MacLaine.

ALFRED PALCA: I made a film about the Harlem Globetrotters—this is so typical. And Dick Adler, I ran into him on Sixth Avenue one day, and he said, "What are you doing?" and I told him about the movie and I said, "I need a song." And he said, "This is my partner, Jerry Ross. Jerry and I, we write songs. Let us write the song!" And I said, "Dick, I want someone who can really write songs, not you fellows." And so some nobody wrote a song for me that was just nothing, and of course the next week Dick Adler and Jerry Ross' *Pajama Game* opened on Broadway. Ow! "Don't bother me," I was saying.

Candle-Light 7/12/54
(Westport Country Playhouse)

Eva Gabor and Richard Kiley in a
Siegfried Geyer comedy adapted by
P. G. Wodehouse.

Darling, Darling 8/16/54
(Westport Country Playhouse)

Gypsy Rose Lee and Tom Tryon in an Anita Loos comedy. The program referred to Lee as actress, writer, painter, and ecdysiast.

JOHN FISCHER: I was the editor of her autobiography—a book which, incidentally, tells nearly all the truth. We'd meet to discuss chapters at her house in New York at 11:30 A.M., when she had just gotten out of bed. She wore an old bathrobe and had a stocking tied around her head; she didn't care how she looked when she wasn't in public. Her house was enormous, and every room had dozens of photos, sketches, and paintings of her. Evidently she got all her friends to do them. In some pictures she was dressed; in others she wasn't. The most conspicuous thing in the living room was a life-sized oil painting of her, naked.

She was a pleasure to work with—intelligent, well organized and diligent. She needed no help with her writing, and very little editing.

On Your Toes 10/11/54

Vera Zorina as the Strip Tease Girl in "Slaughter on Tenth Avenue," the landmark jazz ballet. Richard Rodgers and Lorenz Hart's musical, a hit in 1936, failed in this revival, though George Abbott returned as director and George Balanchine as choreographer. The critics felt that everything except "Slaughter on Tenth Avenue" had dated. 64 performances. *On Your Toes* was the first of four Rodgers and Hart musicals for which Balanchine did the dances in the 1930s.

RICHARD RODGERS, *on Balanchine as a musical comedy choreographer* (1960): I expected fiery temperament. He had bushy black hair, gleaming eyes and an aquiline profile. He was Russian, artistic, a genius. I was scared stiff of him. I asked him how he worked. Did he make the steps first and have music written to fit them, or what? He answered, in the thick Russian accent he had then, "You write. I put on." For me, that was marvelous. I went ahead and wrote the score, and I never had to change or cut a note of it as far as he was concerned.

Q: You don't do musical comedy any longer?

GEORGE BALANCHINE: No. I finished. I can't do it any more. It's not any more the same, you see. It's new type dances, people–also the way they speak differently. The music is not the same. You know, all the guitars–the way they rock 'n roll. This is not my life. I don't understand *absolutely* one word they say, ABSOLUTELY don't know what they say. I understand *the words*, but I don't know what they mean. There is no sense, that's all. It looks like they repeat the same thing all the time. I don't know. It's not my type. I'm just old, I can't do it. I'm not interested. To me Larry Hart and Rodgers and Gershwin–I worked with them, Irving Berlin, all of these people–Schwartz, Dietz–wonderful, beautiful words, music and I understood, I *learned*. You see, I am Russian; you see, it took me a long time before I start to speak English. So finally I got that, but *then* it's different world, see? But they are all Americans, they all look like they are people live on earth, but it's absolutely from another planet. But we're going away . . . I couldn't do it. I wouldn't know how to. It's young people. Ballet? Yes. I still can do it. But that's my . . . you see I was born that way.

HOLLYWOOD STORY

Variety (1/5/55): Alfred Lunt and Lynn Fontanne made only one Hollywood film, *The Guardsman*. Good, too, but they were not satisfied. Miss Fontanne was the first to see the early rushes of the film. She sped back to the Beverly Hills Hotel, burst into their suite, where her husband was reading, and broke into tears. "Alfred . . . Alfred," she wailed, "I've seen the rushes–and we're ruined. Ruined! You photograph without lips, and I come out old and haggard and ugly and my tongue is thick and I lisp and fall against the furniture. I look like I don't know my lines, and my feet are big and my clothes hang to me like from a clothesrack and . . ." But she couldn't go on, so great were her tears. Lunt pondered a moment and then muttered: "No lips, eh?"

The Bad Seed 12/8/54

Patty McCormack as Rhoda Penmark, the eight-year-old murderer in Maxwell Anderson's melodrama about hereditary evil, adapted from William March's novel. Rhoda pushes an old woman down the stairs, drowns a school chum, sets fire to a sleeping handyman, and finally shoots her mother. In the play her deeds go unpunished; in the later film version she is electrocuted by a convenient bolt of lightning. The Playwrights' Company produced. Reginald Denham directed. 334 performances.

The Master Builder 3/1/55

Joan Tetzel (Hilda Wangel) and Oscar Homolka (Halvard Solness) in this Phoenix Theatre revival of Ibsen's tragedy about an architect driven by the dreams of a young woman to attempt what is beyond his powers. Homolka directed. 38 performances.

Bus Stop 3/2/55

Kim Stanley as Cherie, the Kansas City nightclub "chanteuse," belts out her specialty, "That Old Black Magic," for the enjoyment of her snow-bound busmates. The one who looks on in the background is the alcoholic professor Gerald Lyman, played by Anthony Ross. Harold Clurman directed the William Inge comedy. Robert Whitehead and Roger Stevens produced. 478 performances. Ross, who played the original Gentleman Caller in *The Glass Menagerie*, died during the run of this show. In the film *Bus Stop*, Marilyn Monroe played Cherie, the best role of her career.

VARIETY (3/7/56): Louis Cline, manager of the Colonial Theater (Boston), had "Bus Stop" on the marquee of his theatre for the past few weeks heralding the engagement of the William Inge comedy, which started yesterday. He was kept busy by out-of-towners who took the billing literally. In desperation, he finally put up a sign explaining, "This is not a bus stop, but the play 'Bus Stop' opens here Mar. 5."

Cat on a Hot Tin Roof 3/24/55

Ben Gazzara (Brick) and Barbara Bel Geddes (Maggie the Cat, his wife) in Tennessee Williams' oddly hopeful domestic tragedy, his favorite among his plays. Brick has injured himself in a drunken fall and won't sleep with Maggie. The Playwrights' Company produced. Elia Kazan directed. 694 performances.

MILDRED DUNNOCK: I wanted very badly to be in a play by Tennessee directed by Kazan. And I said to Kazan, "Isn't there anything for me in *Cat?*" And he said, "No, Milly, there really isn't." And I said, "There must be one *older* woman in it." And he said, "Yeah, but . . . all right," he said, "read the description of the older woman." And I read the description of Big Mama: "Short, fat woman with big feet looking like a boxer dog or a Japanese wrestler." And I said, "You're not going to find anybody in the theater that looks like that; one spends one's life trying not to look like that."

Well, they couldn't get what they wanted, and, of course, I am Southern. They asked me to come and read for it, so I went. I had had a school chum whose mother had had what was called, in my day, a "whiskey voice." I suppose she had nodes on her vocal chord; she talked with this big deep rasp. And I thought, "That's what I'll do." So I did this strange voice for Big Mama. People used to come backstage—

Danny Kaye and other performers—and say, "How did you get that voice?" Well, I just did it. And I got it in rehearsal so I didn't destroy my vocal chord. Then I went down in the middle of the show because I'd agreed to do it to play in *Baby Doll*, the movie. *Cat* sent for me to come back to play the Christmas rush, and I returned and lost my voice totally because I'd tried to use the whiskey voice too quickly, and you can't come to such use without gradual preparation. I had to get out of the show temporarily.

I loved doing that play and the part of Big Mama. I think that speech of Big Mama's in which she says, "Time moves by so fast, nothing can outrun it," is one of the most beautiful speeches I've ever read.

Mildred Dunnock and Burl Ives as Big Mama and Big Daddy, Brick's parents. Big Daddy is dying of cancer. His Mississippi dominion, "twenty-eight thousand acres of the richest land this side of the Valley Nile," won't go to Brick and Maggie because they don't have children.

DUNNOCK: Burl was the way he was because he'd never acted on stage. He'd performed, but never acted. And he was like Santa Claus. He could say or do anything and you couldn't help but love him because of that extraordinary presence. Gadge put him stage center, and there he was in his element. It can be difficult working with nonexperienced actors, but when you have a person like Kazan, he finds ways.

Maggie tells Big Daddy she is carrying Brick's child. Big Daddy looks her over, palpitates her, and announces, "This girl has life in her body, that's no lie!" It is a lie, but Brick, impressed by Maggie's tenacious will, agrees to sleep with her.

Inherit the Wind 4/21/55

Ed Begley, Tony Randall, and Paul Muni, the three principals in Jerome Lawrence and Robert E. Lee's popular dramatization of the 1925 Scopes "monkey trial" in which the state of Tennessee prosecuted a public school science teacher for telling his classes about Darwin's theory of evolution.

Begley's role (Matthew Harrison Brady) was based on William Jennings Bryan, who sought to have Scopes convicted for violating the word of God. Muni (Henry Drummond) was Clarence Darrow, who defended Scopes and his right to free speech. Randall (E. K. Hornbeck) played a

cynical journalist reminiscent of H. L. Mencken, who covered the event. Much of the dialogue in the play's second act came from the actual transcript of the trial. Louis Hector, *at right*, was the Judge. Herman Shumlin produced and directed. 806 performances.

BETHEL LESLIE: It was always difficult for Muni to learn lines because as a kid he had been in the Yiddish theater and in the Yiddish theater nobody ever learned lines because they played so fast they didn't have time to learn them; they had prompters. And Muni used a prompter. On opening night in Philadelphia everybody knew he didn't know the second-act courtroom scene, and he waited to be prompted because all he needed was one word and he'd know the rest of the speech. He was prompted all the way through it, and it was one of the most exciting performances I've ever seen in my life.

Bethel Leslie, who played the fiancée of the man on trial, and Randall. He tells her he may be rancid butter but he's on her side of the bread.

TONY RANDALL: This picture with Bethel Leslie and the apple proves conclusively how bad I was at that moment.

I did the usual research on Mencken. Shumlin rejected it all. In many photos of Mencken there was his partner, George Jean Nathan, so I tried to dress like him. This sort of thing is very important to the actor but to no one else.

Muni rests during the trial.

At the end of the play Muni as Drummond weighs the Bible in one hand against Darwin's *Origin of Species* in the other. Then he puts them side by side in his briefcase.

FLORENCE WILLIAMS: On, that second act! It was the trial, the heart of the play, and *wonderful* for the audience. But on stage it was Tennessee in the depths of August, only worse. The lights made it about 90 degrees, and those of us in the crowd—I replaced Muriel Kirkland as Ed Begley's wife—had nothing to do but sit there and look attentive. The women could fan themselves—that was in character—and we did it not so much to get cool, because you couldn't, as to stay awake. When all else failed I carried a hatpin to jab myself with.

Paul Muni had left the show to have an eye removed for cancer. When he came back, it was very touching: the lights in the second act were so pitiless that he had to rest his good eye from them. He'd close the eye and turn that side of his face upstage, leaving the glass eye open. And he'd play on, play on, as fiercely as though it were opening night.

264

ADVICE

Frederick O'Neal: At one time I wanted to go into medicine, and my father said, "I'll help you do anything you want to do, as long as you make the best you can of yourself in whatever field you choose." And then he said something that I'll never forget as long as I live; he said, "And if you're not successful, it's not because you're a Negro; it's because you didn't take advantage of every opportunity. You remember that." He knew that I knew that color would be a problem–this was Mississippi and Vardaman was governor–but what he was saying in effect was, "Color's a crutch, boy, and if you've got it, you'll use it. So throw it away."

What he said was very true, because I've seen crutches used so often. I had a girl come into my office with a wonderful idea for television animation. She kept saying, "You know, I could get much further with this if I was white; if I was white I could do so and so; but, you know whitey ain't gonna let me do this, that and the other." And I said, "Just a minute. I want to say this to you. I don't know whether you realize it or not, but you are defeating yourself. What you should be saying is, 'I'm going to do this. I don't care what whitey, blackey, grayey, or anybody else says. I'm going to do it.'" Two weeks later she called me and said, "Nobody ever said that to me before. I'm doing all right now."

We are always wanting to put the blame on somebody else. I've heard girls say, "She didn't give me good marks because she doesn't like the clothes I wear." What the hell have clothes got to do with her achievement? She didn't get good marks because she didn't earn good marks. She didn't want to face that fact. We won't be honest with ourselves. "To thine own self be true"–there never was a better piece of advice than that little line. Because 98 percent of us will not be true to ourselves, own up to our crutches, admit our biases. It's very difficult to face up to them, but unless you do, I don't think you can really *build*.

For instance, the other day Andy Young said Ford and Nixon were racists, and he was criticized for it. But it's true, no question about it. Not "racist" in the sense that we use that word now, but in the sense that they weren't aware that they had that bias. Every last one of us has a bias in one way or another, whether it's racial, religious, national, social–whatever it is, we got some of it in us. I have some of it in me, and I say to myself, "I'm going to try to get rid of it. Every single day I'm going to try to get rid of it, as much as I can."

If you do not admit to the fact that you do have certain prejudices, you really don't have control over them. You have to be consciously working against them. When you admit you have those shortcomings and work to overcome them, you're building on solid ground. But if you say, "I don't have any," you're building on sand. And this is what Andy was trying to say. We have prejudices, but we can get rid of them. It's the things we don't understand about ourselves that keep us distant from the truth and ourselves.

Damn Yankees 5/5/55

Gwen Verdon (Lola) sings "Whatever Lola Wants, Lola Gets." This George Abbott–Douglass Wallop–Richard Adler–Jerry Ross musical derived from Wallop's comic novel *The Year the Yankees Lost the Pennant*. Abbott directed. Harold Prince co-produced. Bob Fosse choreographed. The show's other hit song was "Heart." 1,019 performances. This was the last Adler-Ross musical. Ross died later that year of a lung ailment; he was 29.

266

The original poster.

The replacement poster.

HAROLD PRINCE: Fred's picture made a difference. There was an earlier studio photograph someone else took of Gwen in a baseball uniform and cap, looking over her shoulder with a glove and a ball in her hand. We used it on posters and in all our ads, but the show wasn't moving; they weren't selling any tickets at the box office. And we decided that baseball was anathema as musical comedy material. So we junked the original photograph and put in this one, from "Whatever Lola Wants," and the show took off. We always thought that the ad did it. The ad plus word-of-mouth.

You see, the problem was *Damn Yankees* meant "Civil War" to people, and then the baseball picture meant baseball. And neither thing interested anyone. Fred's picture showed people what the show was like and they came to see it.

Verdon and Ray Walston. Walston played the devil; Verdon, his delicious bait.

Julius Caesar 7/12/55
(Stratford, Connecticut)

Raymond Massey (Brutus) stands over Hurd Hatfield (the slain Caesar) as the other conspirators flee. Jack Palance (Cassius) is visible behind Massey's shoulder. Denis Carey directed. Horace Armistead did the sets, Robert Fletcher the costumes. This was the inaugural production of the American Shakespeare Festival at Stratford. The Festival's founder was Lawrence Langner, who, 36 years earlier, had been one of the founders of the Theatre Guild.

The Tempest 7/26/55
(Stratford, Connecticut)

Raymond Massey (Prospero) supervises Roddy McDowall (Ariel) as he approaches Joan Chandler (the sleeping Miranda). The American Shakespeare Festival, unable to raise money for another season, closed its doors in 1977.

WALTER KERR: We don't have enough thrust houses. The Beaumont is a compromise house, and compromise houses are never the answer. And Stratford, Connecticut–really a proscenium house. I think that's one of the things that killed it, you know. They sort of took it out of the on-going mainstream for Shakespearean houses and pushed it back into an old scenic nineteenth-century stage, where what you're looking at are pretty-pretty productions of *Midsummer Night's Dream*–a lot of gauze. Well, we've had that.

A View from the Bridge 9/29/55

On the ground Van Heflin as Eddie Carbone, the Brooklyn longshoreman who violates the code of blood in Arthur Miller's tragedy. Looking at Eddie with hatred, horror, and compassion are Jack Warden (Marco, his wife's cousin), Gloria Marlowe (Catherine, his niece), Eileen Heckart (Beatrice, his wife), and Richard Davalos (Rudolpho, another cousin). Marco and Rudolpho are illegal aliens from Sicily. Eddie has reported them to the authorities because he is tormented by an incestuous passion for Catherine and cannot stand to have her marry Rudolpho. At play's end Marco kills Eddie. In this production the death weapon was Eddie's knife; in many later productions it has been his longshoreman's hook. Martin Ritt directed. Kermit Bloomgarden, Robert Whitehead, and Robert Stevens produced. 149 performances.

The Diary of Anne Frank 10/5/55

GUSTI HUBER: The *Diary* was a "once in a lifetime." There was a special star over it. The thing I remember best was a rehearsal in the Cort Theater where we later opened. In one scene someone says, "It's raining outside," and at that moment it started to pour. On another occasion, the church bells in the back of the theater started to ring a moment before Anne has to say, "It's the Westertoren"–a church in Amsterdam. It became quite spooky. I went to Frances Hackett, who together with her husband, Albert, had written the play, and I said, "If the spirit of Anne could instigate anything, would all these happenings not be exactly what she would do?" I felt a little silly saying it, but Frances said, "It's not as crazy as you think. When we were at a dead end with the play, out of nowhere came the missing piece–at one time in a letter from Hong Kong!"

Dennie Moore (Mrs. Van Daan), David Levin (Peter Van Daan), Susan Strasberg (Anne Frank), Jack Gilford (Mr. Dussel), Lou Jacobi (Mr. Van Daan), Eva Rubenstein (Margot Frank), Joseph Schildkraut (Mr. Frank), and Gusti Huber (Mrs. Frank) in Frances Goodrich and Albert Hackett's play based on the diary 13-year-old Anne Frank began in July 1942 while her family and four other Jews were hiding from the Nazis in a warehouse attic in Amsterdam. The people of the play have just learned of the Allies' landing at Normandy on June 6, 1944. They have celebrated and now Mrs. Frank weeps and asks forgiveness for having upbraided Mr. Van Daan for stealing bread from their common larder. Kermit Bloomgarden produced; Garson Kanin directed. 717 performances.

Mr. Frank comforts Anne, who has had a nightmare that the Gestapo, the Green Police, were coming to get them. Strasberg was 17; this was her first Broadway role and her warm, restless performance made her a star. Schildkraut, a star for more than 30 years, was making his last Broadway appearance. After the dress rehearsal, he decided to shave part of his hair to make him look more like the actual Mr. Frank.

Mrs. Frank encourages Anne to curb her high spirits. Anne, puberty come upon her, considers what it will be like to be grown up.

Peter Van Daan has knocked over a lamp while a thief was downstairs in the warehouse. Mrs. Van Daan says a thief will never report them to the police. Mr. Dussel says, "I think he will. I think some day he'll be caught and then he'll make a bargain with the Green Police. If they'll let him off, he'll tell them where some Jews are hiding." In the summer of 1944, apparently on a tip from a thief, the Gestapo broke into the attic and took the eight Jews off to concentration camp. All but Mr. Frank died. Anne Frank died at Bergen-Belsen in March 1945, two months before the war ended. She was 15.

A Roomful of Roses 10/17/55

Patricia Neal and Darryl Richard as mother and son in Edith Sommer's uneasy comedy about divorce and childhood deprivation. Guthrie McClintic produced and directed. 88 performances.

No Time for Sergeants 10/20/55

Myron McCormick (Sergeant King), Andy Griffith (Will Stockdale), and Roddy McDowall (Ben Whitledge) in Ira Levin's comedy hit adapted from the novel by Mac Hyman. Will and Ben are cheering up Sergeant King, who has just been transferred with them from the Air Force to the Infantry where they can go on being buddies. Will, a lovable rube, overturns the military way of doing things with his innocent good humor. Morton Da Costa directed. Maurice Evans produced. The comic strip sets were by Peter Larkin. 796 performances.

A Quiet Place 11/55
(Shubert Theater, New Haven)

Tyrone Power in a drama that closed out of town.

Pipe Dream 11/30/55

HAROLD CLURMAN: Many people wanted to invest in it, but I kept on saying, "Don't do it. Rodgers and Hammerstein also have their failures." They believed Rodgers and Hammerstein couldn't fail, even though their last musical, *Me and Juliet*, had been an *enormous* flop. It was so bad that Hammerstein said to me, "Don't go to see it." But *Pipe Dream* sold $2 million worth of tickets in advance; out of this failure the director could make more money than out of a success.

Traubel was no longer a great singer. I can say it now that she's dead and I can't offend her. She had ruined her voice. In the best days she must have had a tremendous voice, so Rodgers and Hammerstein thought, "Well . . ." And she looked good. But she couldn't sing anymore, not really. And you know, it was her fault, because she wanted to be in the opera and also sing in nightclubs. And Bing said, "You can't do that. It's too much." She insisted, so he fired her. He was absolutely right.

Judy Tyler was determined to make it and when she sang—she had a good voice—she *belted*. She'd sung in a lot of nightclubs where you have to shut the people up to be heard. I said to her, "Don't belt." I said it to her the first time I heard her sing. "Very nice, but don't belt. Don't try to prove the power of your voice." I never could get her to overcome it.

Her determination was so strong that it made her seem hard and that took away from the sympathy of the character. Oscar Hammerstein and I talked with Dick Rodgers about it, but he was overwhelmed by her. We said, "Doesn't that belting disturb you?" He said, "She's so pretty I can't even think about that."

William Johnson (Doc, a reclusive marine biologist), Judy Tyler (Suzy, an almost fallen woman), and Helen Traubel (Fauna, a big-hearted whorehouse madam) in Rodgers and Hammerstein's musical based on John Steinbeck's novel *Sweet Thursday*. A friend has broken Doc's arm with a baseball bat, hoping thus to promote Suzy's affection for him. The popular songs: "Everybody's Got a Home But Me," "All at Once You Love Her." Traubel was a dramatic soprano famed for Wagnerian roles. Johnson, a musical comedy actor, had built his reputation in London. Tyler had played Princess Summer-Fall-Winter-Spring on *The Howdy Doody Show*. Harold Clurman directed. 246 performances. Within a year of the show's closing, Johnson died of a heart attack and Tyler in a car accident.

Fallen Angels 1/17/56

Nancy Walker and Margaret Phillips play two wealthy golf widows who get uproariously drunk while waiting for a Frenchman to whom each means to give herself. Noël Coward updated his 1925 comedy and changed its locale to New York. Charles Bowden directed and co-produced. 239 performances. Tallulah Bankhead played Walker's role in the original, London production.

A BRITISH REVIEWER (1925): An author is doing a bad service to morality when, in presenting "Fallen Angels," he fails to suggest, by introducing other types, that there are angels who have not fallen. He also sins against the canons of his art in populating his fancy world with only one, or at most, two, classes of people. Further, in making the great point of a play a business so painful and repulsive as female drunkenness he offends against mere good manners.

My Fair Lady 3/15/56

A musical based on Bernard Shaw's *Pygmalion*, with book and lyrics by Alan Jay Lerner and music by Frederick Loewe. Producer Herman Levin, director Moss Hart, choreographer Hanya Holm, sets Oliver Smith, costumes Cecil Beaton. Of *My Fair Lady*, the biggest hit of the decade, Broadway's longest-run musical to its day (2,717 performances), Lerner said later: "The time was ripe for something gay and theatrical, something that was not two lonely people finding each other in a dark alley. *My Fair Lady* filled the bill."

Julie Andrews as Eliza Doolittle, a Cockney flower girl, sings "Wouldn't It Be Loverly" about the comforts of the lower middle class.

Rex Harrison as Professor Henry Higgins assures Eliza that her life will be better if she allows him to teach her proper English.

Higgins. Think of it, Eliza. Think of chocolates, and taxis, and gold, and diamonds.
Eliza. No! I don't want no gold and no diamonds. I'm a good girl I am.

Eliza does it! She says "the rain in Spain stays mainly on the plain" with the correct vowel sounds. Colonel Pickering, Higgins' colleague (played by Robert Coote), Eliza, and Higgins sing and dance the triumphal tango "The Rain in Spain."

Eliza tries out her fine pronunciation at the Ascot races. Higgins, Freddy Eynsford-Hill (Michael King), and Mrs. Higgins, Henry Higgins' mother (Cathleen Nesbitt), listen with varying degrees of astonishment.

Eliza (*darkly*). My aunt died of influenza, so they said. But it's my be-lief they done the old woman in. Why should she die of influenza when she come through diphtheria right enough the year before? Fairly blue with it she was. They all thought she was dead; but my father, he kept ladling gin down her throat. Then she came to so sudden that she bit the bowl off the spoon. Now, what call would a woman with that strength in her have to die of influenza, and what become of her new straw hat that should have come to me? Somebody pinched it. And what I say is, them as pinched it, done her in.

BERNARD SHAW, *in a 1948 letter to a Royal Air Force soldier whose friends wanted to put "Pygmalion" to music*: I absolutely forbid any such outrage. If *Pygmalion* is not good enough for your friends with its own verbal music, their talent must be altogether extraordinary.

Overheard at the Lambs Club, early fall 1942: "You are Alan Jay Lerner? You write good lyrics? I am Frederick Loewe. I would like to talk to you."

Harrison and Stanley Holloway as Alfred P. Doolittle, a dustman and Eliza's father. Doolittle has come to beg five pounds from his daughter's benefactor. He says he knows Higgins' intentions are honorable or he would have demanded fifty.

Doolittle has a last fling with his low-life cohorts before he is delivered into the "hands of middle-class morality." He's finally going to marry his wife. They sing "Get Me to the Church on Time."

Higgins ponders what he will do now that Eliza has left him. He sings the show's finale, "I've Grown Accustomed to Her Face."

WALTER KERR: Rex Harrison brought intelligence and the skill of a light comedian to the musical. But I don't know that he was all *that* much of an advance. Because he also brought the "talk" song–you know, the star who doesn't sing–or who *sings*, but can't sing. That got to be quite a vice for a while when you were training actors to get through a song by hitting four notes out of the melody and talking the rest. I personally don't know how much of that you want in a musical.

Mr. Wonderful 3/22/56

Sammy Davis, Jr., sang, danced, improvised, impersonated, mugged, played trumpet and drums, and did a full nightclub act in this Joseph Stein–Will Glickman musical about a small-town boy who makes it big as a Miami Beach entertainer. A reviewer observed, "We're lucky it wasn't called *Mr. Very Wonderful*." Jerry Bock, Larry Holofcener, and George Weiss did the songs, which included "Mr. Wonderful," "Too Close for Comfort," and "Without You I'm Nothing." The idea for the show was Jule Styne's, who produced with George Gilbert and Lester Osterman, Jr. Jack Donahue directed. 383 performances.

BROADWAY OLD-TIMER: Davis would interrupt the play to tell the audience who was speaking at the Democratic Convention or the score of the All Star Game. He'd say, "They don't do this for you in *My Fair Lady*."

Separate Tables 10/25/56

Margaret Leighton and Eric Portman each had two widely contrasting roles in Terence Rattigan's duet of plays set in a run-down British resort hotel.

Above, Leighton is Anne Shankland, a chic divorcée reduced to modeling and drugs and terrified of growing old, and Portman is John Malcolm,

Anne's first husband, once a tough Labour politician, now an alcoholic journalist. Anne ruined his life; she begs him to take her back; he does.

286

Here, Portman is Major Pollock, a pathetic fraud cashiered from the Army—he was only a lieutenant—for molesting women in the cinema, and Leighton is Sybil Railton-Bell, a timid spinster entirely under her mother's thumb. Mummy tells her to drop Mr. Pollock. Pollock tells her, "We're both of us frightened of people, and yet we've somehow managed to forget our fright when we've been in each other's company. Speaking for myself, I'm grateful and always will be." Sybil disobeys Mummy and sticks with Pollock. Peter Glenville directed. 332 performances.

GERALDINE PAGE, *who replaced Leighton in this play* (1964): Eric Portman is anti-Method, at least that's what he says, but I never knew where he was going to be onstage. He had the greatest freedom of movement.

The Sleeping Prince 11/1/56

Barbara Bel Geddes as a fetching American chorus girl in London and Michael Redgrave as the fetched Prince Regent of Carpathia. Redgrave directed. 60 performances. This "occasional fairy tale" by Terence Rattigan had originally been produced in London for the 1953 Coronation Season; playing the leads were Laurence Olivier and Vivien Leigh.

Bells Are Ringing 11/29/56

Sydney Chaplin as a playwright and Judy Holliday as Ella, a meddlesome answering-service operator who falls in love with his voice. Ella's company, Susanswerphone, is a front for a race-track bookie; the complications are endless. This long-running musical had book and lyrics by Betty Comden and Adolph Green, music by Jule Styne, and staging by Jerome Robbins. The Theatre Guild produced. Herbert Greene did the vocal arrangements. The hit song: "Just in Time." 924 performances.

HERBERT GREENE: Comden and Green asked me to teach Judy Holliday how to sing. That was an experience–a one of a kind. She was sure she would never be able to sing. "Well, if you're right about that," I told her, "we'll learn about it in about four days. And then you can quit." In about four days she could see that there were possibilities. She was very musical. But she always kept saying, "It's not going to work, it's not going to work." After about six weeks, I said, "Well, it's not enough to do it in the studio. I invited Betty and Adolph and Jule up here today."

"I'm not going to . . . you did not!"

I said, "Yes, I did."

She said, "How could you do that to me?"

"Because you're going to have to do it in front of sixteen hundred people every night."

Well, Betty and Adolph and Jule came to the studio, and Judy turned white.

"Okay, let's start with 'The Party's Over, da da da . . .'"

"I don't want, I don't want to sing it in front of these people."

"Come on, Judy."

"Well, all right." She walked to a corner of the room and faced the wall.

I looked at this and thought, "She's a strange dame in many ways, but very bright. Frightened." So I said, "Okay, try it like that." I pretended I was going to sit down at the piano. Instead I walked right over to her, grabbed her, spun her around, and zipped to the piano. I yelled, "Now!" [*Snaps fingers.*] And she started to sing. It worked.

Lap dissolve. Opening night in New Haven, Judy was in the wings, ready to make her entrance. I was standing next to her. I was conducting *Happy Fella* at the time and took a day off to go out to New Haven for the opening. She turned to me, and she said, "I'm not going to go out there."

I said, "It's your career. You'll have egg on your face, you'll be a jackass, you'll be sued for breaking your contract." I said, "What the hell has it got to do with me? If you don't want to go out there, *don't* go out there."

She looked like a child, like, "How dare I not care."

I heard her musical cue, put my hands on her shoulders, and *threw* her out. She stumbled a bit–but she was on stage.

At the end of the show she said, "You know, it's a good thing that you're the kind of son-of-a-bitch who's really a son-of-a-bitch. That's why it worked." [*Laughs.*]

She just was star. Absolute star. Star, star, star.

Candide 12/1/56

Robert Rounseville (Candide) and Barbara Cook (Cunegonde) in a memorable lost cause: Voltaire's satire on optimism redone as a parodic operetta. Splendid music by Leonard Bernstein; bright lyrics by Richard Wilbur, John LaTouche, Dorothy Parker, and Bernstein; libretto by Lillian Hellman. Ethel Linder Reiner and Lester Osterman, Jr., produced. Tyrone Guthrie directed. 73 performances. In 1974, its book rewritten by Hugh Wheeler, *Candide* became a bit hit.

RICHARD WILBUR (1977): We asked Tyrone Guthrie to direct because he looked like Charles de Gaulle, and we thought he would give us orders. But he didn't and we continued our squabbles.

CHARLES ADAMS BAKER: The 1974 production solved a tremendously important problem. I think it was Hal Prince's doing, and I give him all credit. The production went *young* with the two leads. Their idiocy was acceptable because they looked like they were 15 years old. In the original Barbara Cook, even though young, was a woman, and Robert Rounseville was a middle-aged man. So when they were doing those dumb things, it wasn't amusing, it was tiresome. The revival's performers weren't as good–I mean not a patch on Barbara Cook–but they were so young that their stupidity didn't irritate you.

Happy Hunting 12/6/56

WALTER KERR: She's never nervous on opening night. One of the actors backstage one opening night–I don't know what show but they were all in a tizzy and she was not–asked her, "Miss Merman, why? Why aren't you nervous tonight?" She said, "Why should I be nervous? If they could do it as good as me, they'd be up here." That's what she means; she really believes it.

Ethel Merman (Liz Livingstone, a capricious Philadelphia matron) cuts loose in the title song of this Howard Lindsay–Russel Crouse–Harold Karr–Matt Dubey musical. The big number: "Mutual Admiration Society." Abe Burrows directed. Jo Mielziner produced. 412 performances.

Merman and Fernando Lamas (the Duke of Granada, a titled available bachelor). Because her daughter wasn't invited to the Grace Kelly–Prince Rainier wedding in Monaco, Liz decides to stage a countermarriage in Philadelphia between her daughter and the Duke. The daughter discovers that she doesn't love the Duke, the mother that she does.

Visit to a Small Planet 2/7/57

Cyril Ritchard as Kreton, an interloper from the future, comes to help the world wage bigger, bloodier wars. He intended to have the South win the Civil War, whence his costume, but muddled his dates; his UFO arrives in suburban Virginia in the midst of the Cold War, the destructive possibilities of which he finds delicious. Appalled by him are Sibyl Bowan, Eddie Maye- hoff as the blowhard Maj. Gen. Tom Powers, Philip Coolidge, Sarah Marshall, and Conrad Janis. Gore Vidal's satire was an expansion of a TV script. George Axelrod and Clinton Wilder produced. 388 performances.

Ritchard and Rosemary.

GORE VIDAL: Cyril is not an animal lover and regarded the cat (Rosemary in the play) with a neutrality that bordered on suspicion. He never knew when the cat would pick up her cues and answer him. In heat, she never did. The cat replaced a scene with the head of the UN–a nice scene but far too sharp for the '50's. The Kreton-Rosemary scene was added not in New Haven but, next stop, in Boston–where Fehl photographed it (I assume). Perhaps he got the pictures in N.Y. Since the play was expected to fold, no programs were made in advance. When they were put together, Cyril and Rosemary were on the cover.

P.S. Rosemary in real life was a granddaughter of Pyewacket, star of *Bell, Book and Candle*.

The Tunnel of Love 2/13/57

Tom Ewell as Angie Poole tries to comfort Nancy Olson as his wife, Isolde, in Joseph Fields and Peter DeVries' adaptation of the latter's satirical novel. Angie and Isolde, wanting to adopt a baby, meet with a social worker whom Angie seduces and impregnates. He spends the rest of the play worrying whether the offspring, whom he and Isolde plan to adopt, will look so much like him that Isolde will suspect what's happened. He grows a moustache. Critic Louis Kronenberger remarked, "Whether or not motherhood is sacred, it cannot very happily be, for three long acts, profaned." Audiences loved it. Fields directed. The Theatre Guild produced. 417 performances.

Ziegfeld Follies 3/1/57

Beatrice Lillie as a geisha girl who gets bad news in this last edition of the legendary revue. Critics found the follies part of the evening—the semi-nude girls with gardens in their hair—dismal, but Lillie as fresh as ever. Ten people did the songs, five the sketches. John Kennedy directed. 123 performances.

HELEN HAYES: I went up for the opening of *An Evening with Bea Lillie* in Falmouth and sat with Gertie Lawrence. We laughed so hard that Gertie fell over onto the row in front of us and hit the back of the seat. She was begging me at the entr'acte, "Would you look at my forehead? Is there a lump there?" You laughed so hard at a performance of Beatrice Lillie that you injured yourself.

Shinbone Alley 4/13/57

Eartha Kitt as mehitabel, the *toujours gai* free-living cat, and Eddie Bracken as archy, the cockroach and lower-case poet who loves her, in a musical drawn from the famous sketches by Don Marquis. 49 performances.

PRESS RELEASE:
FROM: PRESS DEPT.
WILLIAM MORRIS AGENCY, INC.
  FOR IMMEDIATE RELEASE

APRIL 8, 1957

As of April 4, Norman Lloyd has withdrawn as director of "Shinbone Alley." The reason for this withdrawal is that a great difference of opinion regarding the approach to the show has occurred between Mr. Lloyd and the producer, Peter Lawrence, and the writers, Joe Darion and Mel Brooks. The director requested that his name be removed from the billing. It will not be necessary to engage another director, according to Mr. Lawrence.

New Girl in Town 5/14/57

Gwen Verdon as Anna, the fallen woman trying to reform, in the George Abbott–Bob Merrill musical based on Eugene O'Neill's *Anna Christie*. Abbott moved the setting from 1921 to 1900 because, he said, "the clothes were prettier then. They had the ugliest clothes in the world in 1921. In 1900, too, woman's place was so much more inferior that her problems were greater. Women could vote by 1921; there was considerable emancipation by then." Abbott directed; Bob Fosse choreographed. The hit song: "It's Good to Be Alive." 431 performances.

GWEN VERDON (1957): I was crippled when I was little and I wore special black shoes. I could see people look at me and think I'm pretty but still think I'm crippled. And even after I was able to take those shoes off, I was afraid something would stick out and give me away. For Anna, I think, "I'm trying to be a lady but now people look at me and still think I'm a prostitute. Something gives me away."

BROADWAY OLD-TIMER: The Cathouse Ballet was very shocking for its time—very gamy.

VERDON, *asked whether people were shocked by "New Girl in Town" (1977):* They've been shocked by everything I've done.

The start and the finish of the Cathouse Ballet, which showed Anna's becoming a prostitute and her life in the trade.

Show Time 8/19/57
(Westport Country Playhouse)

Comedian George Jessel and singer Toni Carroll in a summer stock revival of the 1942 Broadway vaudeville show Jessel headlined with Jack Haley and Ella Logan. That show, produced by Fred F. Finklehoffe, ran 342 performances, longer than any other vaudeville bill. Jessel's routines were ones he had perfected over the years in burlesque and vaudeville. Carroll was the latest recording star at MGM Records.

BURLESQUE STORY

Red Buttons: The immortal drama "Who's Got the Pocket?"—a beautiful thing. As a matter of fact, I'll never forget the mad dash we made for the patrol wagon. I mean, no one likes to stand riding downtown. I'll give you an idea of how dirty this sketch was. When we got to the courtroom, the judge made us do the sketch, right? And when it was over, he had the jury arrested for watching an obscene performance.

West Side Story 9/26/57

Carol Lawrence and Larry Kert as the lovers Maria and Tony in the balcony scene of this landmark musical, which translated *Romeo and Juliet*'s Montagues and Capulets into feuding New York City street gangs, the (Anglo) Jets and the (Puerto Rican) Sharks. It was Jerome Robbins' idea; he directed and, with Peter Gennaro, choreographed. Music by Leonard Bernstein, book by Arthur Laurents, lyrics by Stephen Sondheim. Among the songs, "Maria," "Tonight," "I Feel Pretty," "Somewhere." Produced by Robert Griffith, Harold Prince, and Roger Stevens. Sets by Oliver Smith, costumes by Irene Sharaff. 732 performances.

302

The Jets sing, ''Gee, Officer Krupke'' in mockery of the various explanations that adults give for juvenile delinquency.

The rumble. Thomas Hasson (Riff) lunges at George Marcy (Bernardo). Hasson and Marcy replaced Mickey Calin and Ken LeRoy, who originated the roles. Fred Fehl rephotographed this show whenever there were important cast changes.

CHARLES ADAMS BAKER: I handled the leading man and the leading lady: Larry Kert and Carol Lawrence. We always thought Carol got the role of Maria because she followed our advice. I had a very clever woman who worked for me, Phyllis Rab, and she'd read the script and realized what they'd be looking for. Carol was a beautiful girl and a wonderful dancer and a pretty good singer, but Phyllis told her, ''You're going to have to look *plain*.'' And she picked out of Carol's wardrobe a simple cotton dress. It was a pink shirtwaist, with buttons down the front. Carol wore it and right away she caught Jerry's eye. They were having endless callbacks because they were working with unknowns, giving them leads in a Broadway musical. So we established a rule that every time Carol went back, which was like twice a week and 40 times before she got the part, she always wore that dress. Once you make a favorable impression, you don't jar them by changing your act. She had to take it off and wash it every time she wore it to an audition so it would be ready for the next one. But it worked. They began referring to her as ''the girl in the pink dress.'' She got the part.

Q: It's strange because didn't I read that Jerome Robbins said she originally came all bejangled and done up, trying to look like a Puerto Rican Juliet?

BAKER: That's true. That was her idea of the part. [*Laughs*.] And Jerry told her to go home and wash her face. And she came back as a plain girl in this little pink dress looking sweet.

Chita Rivera, whom one critic compared to a bonfire center stage, leads the Shark girls in ''America.''

GWEN VERDON (1977): *West Side Story* was not funky junky Spanish; it was elegant Spanish.

The dance at the gym. The Sharks and Jets show their stuff. *At center* Chita Rivera as Anita, the girl of the Shark leader, Bernardo, played by Ken LeRoy (*back to camera*). *At right* Lee Becker as Anybodys, the tomboy who wants to be a Jet.

STEPHEN SONDHEIM (1974): *West Side Story* is about the theater. It's not about people. It's a way to tell a story. What was best was its theatricality and its approach to telling a story in musical terms. I had always claimed that it would date very quickly. Not because of the subject matter, but because of the lack of characters. When it was done in revival at Lincoln Center, the critics were disappointed and blamed it on the production. Well, the production was at fault but what the critics didn't realize—and they never realize anything—is that the show isn't very good. By which I mean, in terms of individual ingredients it has a lot of very severe flaws: overwriting, purpleness in the writing and in the songs, and because the characters are necessarily one-dimensional. They're not people. What lasts in the theater is character, and there are no characters in *West Side*.

Copper and Brass 10/17/57

Dick Williams and Nancy Walker in a musical that lasted 36 performances. Walker played Katey O'Shea, a bone-headed cop with a knack for sniffing out trouble and falling into it.

Time Remembered 11/12/57

Helen Hayes as the eccentric Duchess of Pont-au-Bronc who tries to keep her nephew from suicide by hiring a milliner to impersonate his late, beloved Léocadia, a haughty ballerina who strangled while making a gesture with her scarf. Jean Anouilh's ethereal comedy played 248 performances, his best Broadway run. The Playwrights' Company produced. Albert Marre directed. Miles White did the costumes.

Q: There are a host of anecdotes connected with you in this role; for instance, that handsome revelation about hearing some harpsichord music.

HELEN HAYES: Yes. I was sitting up in my room in Boston. It was—what *was* the name of that instrument?—it was a radio program. I kept listening because I didn't know what the instrument was when they said they were going to play some things on it. We could say harpsichord, just to make it easier. It was a tinkling but extremely elegant and very proud sound—*regal* is the word. And so unimportant, too, that sound, really. The combination of tinkling and regal together was kind of weird and wonderful and was that woman. And I was so grateful when I heard that sound because I knew that's how it had to be.

Hayes and Susan Strasberg as the milliner Amanda in training to be the divine Léocadia.

HAYES: That girl was the most beautiful thing when she was doing that part. Oh, so beautiful! Look at that neck. That is a real swan's neck, isn't it?

Richard Burton (Prince Albert, the Duchess' nephew) and Strasberg at the Viennese restaurant where Albert dined with Léocadia. The Duchess had the restaurant rebuilt stone by stone on her estate. Albert learns that he never should have loved Léocadia; Amanda is a much more substantial person.

The Dark at the Top of the Stairs 12/5/57

Judith Robinson as shy Reenie Flood meets Timmy Everett as Sammy Goldenbaum, her blind date for the big dance. The scene is an Oklahoma town in the 1920s, where Sammy, a Jew at military school, is an outsider. Nevertheless, he puts Reenie at her ease. She leaves him at the dance, not wanting him to see that other boys won't ask to dance with her; later that night he commits suicide. William Inge's drama about the fears that people have to overcome was produced by Elia Kazan and Saint Subber, and directed by Kazan. 468 performances.

At the end of the play Pat Hingle and Teresa Wright, as Rubin and Cora Flood, Reenie's parents, are reconciled to their imperfections and acknowledge their deep love.

William Gibson: I knew Inge well – that is, I knew him over a long period of time. I knew him in Kansas, before he came East, before he was a playwright. My wife trained at Menninger's and we met him. He was drinking a little too much then, and when we came East – my wife came to Austen Riggs from Menninger's in 1948 – Bill wrote a letter asking us if we could get him into Riggs as a patient to "solve this problem," of, I presume, the alcohol. Then another letter came saying, "Never mind. Something good has happened. Westport is going to do a play of mine." It was *Come Back, Little Sheba*. So he didn't come to Riggs then. *Sheba* was the first of four successes: *Bus Stop, Picnic, The Dark at the Top of the Stairs*. Every couple of years Bill had a success and that was what gave him a feeling of self-worth.

He was very restless; he would never stay put anywhere. He'd go to the theater and he couldn't sit for more than an act; he'd go to a movie and leave in the middle; at parties he'd come for an hour and wander away. I don't know where he went, but wherever he was he wanted to be somewhere else. He kept putting deposits down on houses, kept thinking he'd like to live here, like to live there. He wanted to live in Great Barrington and put like a $1,000 deposit on a house and walked away from it. And he did that all over the country: Florida, Kansas.

He eventually did come to Riggs, and I met him in the workshop there. I was surprised to see him because he hadn't let us know he was coming. And then he would come over to the house. I well remember – I wrote about this after he died – on a Sunday there was a big ad in the *Times*, one of those first ads for a new show: "THE DARK AT THE TOP OF THE STAIRS, WILLIAM INGE" – big type. The same Sunday that that ad appeared, which seemed the height of success – every writer in America, every playwright in New York who read that ad said, "Oh, if only I were Inge now!" – that day he called, as he did on many such Sundays, and said, "Can I come over and watch Perry Como with you tonight?" And he'd come over and we'd sit and look at Perry Como or Dinah Shore, these shows that I'd never look at but which he loved. And that was his social life in Stockbridge: coming over and looking at television with us.

After *Dark at the Top of the Stairs* he had four flops in a row. They left him with no footing at all. He went out to the Coast and tried to write screenplays. After *Splendor in the Grass* they were not successful. Then he was teaching for a while, and he holed up, he holed up.

Then he wrote me. I was one of the people who started something called the Berkshire Theater Festival, which was an attempt to take the Stockbridge Summer Theater and convert it to an all American new plays operation. It was one of the great mistakes of my life, although I had some good times with it. In the course of that we had two full-length plays by Bill Inge that I kept trying to get people to produce. They were not very good, and people just wouldn't do them. He couldn't even get a summer stock production, as it were, from these plays. This is a guy who was named with Williams and Miller as one of the three "giants" of our postwar theater.

And Bill wrote me at that time a phrase that I misread. He wrote, "I guess it's curtains for me, since my beloved theater doesn't want me."

I thought he meant by curtains that it was the end of his stage career. He meant something else.

He would call up once in a while from the Coast, or we'd send a note; we didn't keep in very close touch. But there was a Saturday night when he called, and he wanted to know whether he could be admitted to Riggs. My wife was out of town for the week, and I said, "Do you want me to pursue this, or do you want to wait till Margaret gets back?" He said, "No, you pursue it." His voice was very thick with sedation. I said, "I'll see what I can do. I'll have to track people down. And I'll call you. Are you alone out there?" He said, "No, my sister is here." I said, "I'll call you back as soon as I have information."

I then spent a couple of hours tracking everybody in that Institute down, at parties and movies. Everybody was gone Saturday night, and I couldn't find out if there was a bed or if there was a therapist available. Finally some guy said, "Such-and-such a person will be back in town in the morning," and he thought there was a bed. He wasn't sure there was a therapist, but I couldn't be positive about either point until the morning when I would talk to so-and-so. This was midnight here, nine o'clock out there, so I called Bill back.

This time his voice sounded much better; the sedation had worn off. And I told him what I had found out. He had rewritten *Picnic* a little bit, called it *Summer Brave*, and we were supposed to do it that summer, in stock—we no longer had the new plays program. And Bill was supposed to come East for it. I said, "We're going to see you in a couple of weeks." And he said, "Yes, it's nice they're doing my play."

And I remember the last thing I said. I said, "Have a good night's sleep." He said, "What?" I said, "Have a good night's sleep, if you can." So he said, "Thank you, Bill, for all you've done"–something like that. I said, "I'll call you tomorrow morning."

I got up at nine o'clock, but it's six o'clock out there. I was waiting till like noon to call at a decent hour, and my son came and said, "Bill Inge is dead. Somebody called you to tell you, from the theater. Bill Inge is dead. He killed himself." He had killed himself not long after my phone call–sometime during that night. He was found the next morning. He had gone out in the garage and turned on the motor.

Q: Had he lost touch with Kazan? Had Kazan been somebody who'd been able to encourage him and make him believe in what he was doing?

Gibson: You see, directors are interested in successes, right? Like everybody else in the theater. I mean, a director doesn't want to direct a play if he thinks it's going to be a flop. Bill Inge's work changed: he was no longer able to write that kind of Midwest idyll, with a touch of sex under it, you know, so that it was a sort of tainted idyll. *Picnic, Sheba, The Dark at the Top of the Stairs*–the Midwest family in the Midwest house. *Bus Stop* was beginning to break away from it. *Dark at the Top of the Stairs*, which followed it, was actually an earlier play. It was one of his first plays, which he rewrote. But then he sort of moved out of the Midwest and started writing big city life. Do you know those later plays? *Natural Affection, A Loss of Roses*–they were all flops. And a certain kind of sickly sexuality had come into them. For Bill, I think this meant being "modern" and right on the forefront of everything. But he had trouble getting directors for them.

You see, I imagine if he took *A Loss of Roses* to Kazan, Kazan would look at it and say, "I can't make a success out of this. I don't want to be associated with it." And that's always the case. That happens with my scripts. I take it for granted. There's no sense of personal loyalty in the theater, that one guy is willing to let his talent go down the drain to serve another guy's talent. I've never seen that happen.

Now when there was a Group Theatre, there was a group morality which permitted much more of that, although even there when Clifford wrote a play called *The Silent Partner*, which was never produced, a big strike play and not a very good one, Clurman said to him, "The Group Theatre will produce this play, but it's going to cost us $40,000." So Clifford said, "What could I do? I withdrew the play." But at least there was that framework, and they were waiting for plays by Clifford, desperate for them. But in the business world of commercial productions, the kind of loyalty that you're speaking about hardly exists.

It exists *socially*. I mean Kazan did go out to Clifford's bedside when he was dying. But he wouldn't direct a play of Clifford's and he wouldn't make a movie—Clifford the last years of his life was hanging on possible movie deals where he would write the screenplay and Kazan would direct, because Kazan was a big shot in movies at that time. Clifford was hanging on this, and it never happened.

That's not part of the morality of the theater. There *is* a morality in this dollars and cents operation. And it is: no bullshit. I mean, I never once saw a producer get his mistress to play an important part in a play. Because it costs money! You don't do it if it costs money! There is a morality there. In the world of poetry, there is no morality. Poets review each other's books; they suck around magazines to get the right to review each other's books. It's completely amoral. That kind of sycophancy doesn't exist in a hard-cash operation like the theater.

The Music Man 12/19/57

CHARLES ADAMS BAKER: We were at Kermit's apartment one day and we were reading through the lyrics of I think it was "Trouble" and Meredith had a new song he was demonstrating, and all I could hear was Bob Preston's voice. Bob's whole attack toward acting suggests musicals to me; I mean he's a little broader than life. If you see him in a straight play, there's so much energy that it's almost as if the guy were going to get up and sing or dance or do *something*. And the minute I said, "Bob Preston," everybody said, "Oh, God, yes! He'd be *marvelous*."

Then he had to audition 5,000 times to get the part. Terrible. Terrible. Terrible. You wonder why anybody wants to get in that business.

HERBERT GREENE: Everybody's always tried to take credit for getting Robert Preston. So why shouldn't I join the game? The *true* story is *I* got Robert Preston. Everybody opposed it. They all wanted Ray Bolger or Danny Kaye. Since I was one of the producers of *The Music Man*, I had an official voice, and I said, "Over my dead body. I *don't* want a song-and-dance man doing a song-and-dance part. That's as obvious as the nose on your face. I want somebody that I can train." I worked with Preston for nine months.

Preston was always known as the heavy, Francis Macomber–the coward Hemingway created–or the guy who chickened out in the submarine or the guy who betrayed everybody in the Royal Mounted Police. Whatever the hell he was, he had the face and he had the character that people always associated with the bad guy. Which is precisely what I wanted. Because as soon as he turned around onstage and began to sing [*claps*], "Well, you got trouble. Right here in River City"–we were in. All I had to do was to get him to imitate that he was singing. And all Onna White, the choreographer, had to do was to get him to imitate that he was dancing, and we were away, home and free. Because here is this big coward, rat, no-good from the movies suddenly singing and dancing! He can't sing and he can't dance! But he's a good actor. And he created the illusion of doing both. An actor's job.

When you get first-class singers doing musical comedy, you lose an important element. Because the theater taxes an audience. In a straight play, there's a single taxation. That is to say, the audience watches the people onstage, and they're asked to believe that the situation is real and that the lines the actors are saying are their own. In a musical you have a double taxation; not only must you do the same thing as in a straight play, but on top of that [*sings*], "I love you, my darling . . ." you've got to believe the song just as much as a line. If the singing is too straight, too good, the tax is too high.

Page 314, Robert Preston took Broadway by storm as Harold Hill, the con-man who sells band instruments, in Meredith Willson's romping musical about Iowa, 1912. In his 20 years of show business Preston had never sung or danced before. Here he does the hit number "Seventy-Six Trombones." Morton Da Costa directed. Kermit Bloomgarden and Herbert Greene produced. The costumes were by Raoul Pène du Bois. 1,375 performances.

ANN BURK, *the interviewer*: How about working with children? Did that pose—

GREENE: That was a pain in the ass.

BURK: Yeah. I sorta wondered.

GREENE: But little Eddie Hodges was a well-behaved kid. The other kids came equipped with their stage mamas. I passed them to the stage manager.

Barbara Cook (Marian the librarian), Eddie Hodges (Winthrop, her brother), and Preston. Marian has set her standards higher than a common *salesman*.

At the show's finale Marian and Harold Hill declare their love in the song "Till There Was You."

GREENE: By staying with what we had and not giving an inch to any of the smart asses who were talking about how corny it was and how old-fashioned it was, we preserved its charm. I made one ghastly error, but fortunately the error didn't cost. There was one song in that show that I loathed. I fought and fought and fought until I got Meredith to shake hands with me that that song would go out of the show in Philadelphia, after we got all the other bugs out. Came opening night, and the song was "There were bells, on the—"

BURK: Oh, no! [*Laughs.*]

GREENE: [*Laughs.*] There was dead silence after that song was sung, no applause, nothing. But it was the silence of an audience being *totally* enraptured. Meredith kept his word. "Well, I've made you a promise about that song."

"Are you kidding? I eat my words, every last one. That song works like magic." God, how it worked. I humbly apologized, ever ever so humbly.

The Infernal Machine 2/3/58

John Kerr (Oedipus) and June Havoc (Jocasta) in Jean Cocteau's reworking of the Greek myth. Herbert Berghof directed. A Phoenix Theatre production. 40 performances.

Oh Captain! 2/4/58

Tony Randall, as Capt. Henry St. James, is shocked to find Jacquelyn McKeever as his proper British wife, Maud, misbehaving in a Paris night spot. That, he thought, was *his* prerogative. The Al Morgan–José Ferrer–Jay Livingston–Ray Evans musical was based on the Alec Guinness film *The Captain's Paradise*. Howard Merrill and the Theatre Corp. of America produced. Ferrer directed. James Starbuck choreographed. 192 performances.

TONY RANDALL: This picture is from a ballet cut after opening night in Philadelphia. It was done just once—about $50,000 in costumes.

RANDALL: The *Mr. Peepers* show, which was live, ran three years. And during that time I did three Broadway plays. I went one period of 365 days without a day off. I did jury duty! And I wasn't sick a moment–felt great. You can do that when you're young.

RANDALL: The ballet with Danilova was the best thing in the show. Seven minutes, that's all she had. But she would stand in the wings watching the rest of the show, her eyes gleaming. All the other dancers were bored to tears with the show. Nothing has been heard of any one of them.

Randall and the ballerina Alexandra Danilova.

A Touch of the Poet 10/2/58

Eric Portman, Kim Stanley, and Helen Hayes as the self-tormenting Melody family in the first American production of Eugene O'Neill's last play. Cornelius Melody (Portman) is a low-born Irishman who was a major to the Duke of Wellington in the Napoleonic Wars. Dismissed from the army for dueling, he has brought Nora, his loyal wife (Hayes), and their hot-headed daughter, Sara (Stanley), to America in the 1820s, where he expects to be treated as an aristocrat. Instead, he is tricked into buying a failing tavern, the only clients of which are poor Irish, whom he scorns and who scorn him and his airs. Harold Clurman directed. Robert Whitehead produced. 284 performances.

WALTER KERR: Kim was kind of in one of her moods, and she was going through the stage left wall. Eric Portman was in one of *his* moods, and he was going through the stage right wall, leaving stage center vacant with only Helen Hayes to fill it. Which she proceeded to do by doing everything she possibly could to keep the audience awake. And then some people criticized her for it, which I thought was insane. They complained she was practically doing vaudeville, but what was anybody going to do with those two people back to back? Good actors, good performers both of them, but not playing with anybody: Kim with her nose stuck to this wall, Portman with his nose stuck to that wall. Helen Hayes comes in center, what's she going to do?–practically a tap dance. It had to be. She was heroic.

Sara, who has been nursing the injured son of a rich Yankee merchant, tells Nora that they are in love. She has discovered that Nora was right: a woman in love has no pride. "It's love's slaves we are, Mother, not men's—and wouldn't it shame their boasting and vanity if we ever let them know our secret?"

HAROLD CLURMAN: Kim Stanley has a curious nature: she hates to act; it disturbs her. The same thing is true of Marlon. There's a certain resistance to acting. Because they work from their gut, and their gut is easily upset.

322

Dressed in his old uniform, Con Melody went to fight the Yankee merchant to avenge a slight. The Yankee disdained him; the Yankee's servants and the police beat him up. Melody is a man broken and reborn, all his genteel pretenses stripped away.

Melody. Sure, it'd take more than a few clubs on the head to darken my wits long. Me brains, if I have any, is clear as a bell. And I'm not puttin' on brogue to tormint you, me darlint. Nor play-actin', Sara. That was the Major's game. It's quare, surely, for the two av ye to object when I talk in me natural tongue, and yours, and don't put on airs loike the late lamented auld liar and lunatic, Major Cornelius Melody, av His Majesty's Seventh Dragoons, used to do. He's dead now, and his last bit av lyin' pride is murthered and stinkin'.

Henceforth, Con Melody will have the vulgarity and cynicism to do well in the New World.

CLURMAN: I don't think Mr. Portman ever learned his lines accurately, but he was a very good actor. Opening night I almost collapsed because he was talking gibberish half the time. I said I didn't mind if he spoke in what seemed like Chinese if he would only speak O'Neill's lines in Chinese. Then I could say, "At least they're O'Neill's lines." Everybody said, "Do you want to fire him?" And I said, "No." And they said, "Why not? He's giving you trouble, he's anti-Semitic; he's anti-Ameri-can; he's anti-human"–he wasn't–"and he drinks." I answered, "Because he has enormous authority on stage." He served the play in a way that almost no one else could.

Goldilocks 10/12/58

WALTER KERR: We had book problems, fundamentally, to begin with. And we made one curious mistake, and I think it's an easy mistake if you're of a certain turn of mind. We were in trouble out of town; we knew it right away–the writing on the wall was absolutely clear. But what we tried to do, what we put our energies to, was trying to make it funnier. As a matter of fact, if we'd only stood back for about three seconds and looked at it and kind of clocked the laughs that were already there, we would have realized that that wasn't what we needed. We had enough laughs really. And we still had when we opened to bad notices in New York; we were still getting laughs–big laughs, lots of them. What we should have done was forget all about working for any more comedy whatsoever, and straighten out the emotional line instead. I mean, make something real seem to happen between the principals, emotionally. And that we didn't do. It would have been a lot easier to do than invent additional comedy. But we didn't do it; it never occurred to us. We were thinking more laughs, more laughs.

The Walter and Jean Kerr–Leroy Anderson musical spoofing the early days of movie making in suburban New York. The scene is Egypt on the pyramids, but it's snowing in Fort Lee. The woman in white is Elaine Stritch. Walter Kerr directed. Robert Whitehead produced. 161 performances.

The Man in the Dog Suit 10/30/58

JESSICA TANDY: That was another of our babies. We tried to nurse it along for two summers, working hard to make it right.

HUME CRONYN: It was a very popular play. I remember David Merrick coming to see me and saying, "We would like to bring it on to Broadway." But *we* felt that the play was not yet right, and despite the fact that we were doing extraordinary business around the country, we decided not to bring it into New York but to wait another full season and do more work on it. Which is what we did, and it failed. And I must tell you that I think the intervening year in which we labored, the authors labored, long and hard to make it better, I don't think we helped it at all.

We had such a big investment of time and energy in it that I've never really forgotten it. The play was about breaking out of conformity and it was a popular subject at the time—Sloan Wilson had handled it in *The Man in the Grey Flannel Suit*. The play treated the theme very lightly, but it had a serious core. Brooks Atkinson, when he reviewed it, ended with a line something like, "Why do Mr. and Mrs. Cronyn waste their talents on such dreary nonsense?" And *I was hysterical*. For the first and only time in my life I wrote a letter of protest. I had great respect for Brooks; he was a damn fine critic—he is a damn fine critic—there are few like that around. But I wrote him. The night after we opened *Man in the Dog Suit* he reviewed something called *Marriage-Go-Round* that *I* thought was dreary nonsense. That got quite a good review.

TANDY: It was very successful.

CRONYN: It was very successful. And I was [*laughs*] livid. And I wrote him a letter. I must say I wrote a polite letter. I said I didn't understand his standards and values and didn't agree with them. And I got an equally polite letter back, saying, you know, it was a matter of individual taste.

Hume Cronyn as Oliver Walling, an unhappy bank employee, and Jessica Tandy as Martha, his wife, whose family owns the bank. Oliver revolts against his secure stuffy life by donning a dog suit he once wore to a costume party. Albert Beich and William H. Wright adapted this comedy from a novel by Edwin Corle. Ralph Nelson directed. 36 performances.

Flower Drum Song 12/1/58

Pat Suzuki belts out "Grant Avenue," a song celebrating the variety of life in San Francisco's Chinatown. The Rodgers and Hammerstein–Joseph Fields musical, based on the novel by C. Y. Lee, treated the conflict between Oriental parents and their Americanized young. Gene Kelly directed. Carol Haney choreographed. 600 performances.

The Cold Wind and the Warm 12/8/58

HAROLD CLURMAN: Timmy Everett was excellent as the young Sam Behrman. First we tried two actors: a boy of seven and a 22-year-old. It didn't work, so we got Everett and he could play both. But he never did anything important after that. He opened a nightclub, a discotheque.

Q: He recently died.

CLURMAN: Did he die?

Q: About five weeks ago.

CLURMAN: You know, it must have been a terrible thing for this young man who started off very well with Kazan, playing the Jewish boy in *The Dark at the Top of the Stairs*, and then coming into my play and being very nice in it, to have had so little luck on stage after that.

Q: He won an award for the Inge play.

CLURMAN: Did he? I'd forgotten. An award is good for three months –except in the memory of the man who receives it. For the public the award business is a commercial thing. And it's a fake. All awards are fakes. All our prizes are fakes–even when they're deserved. How do you judge between Mozart and Beethoven? Who's better, Picasso or Matisse? That's all nonsense. That's not what the arts are about.

But after *Cold Wind and the Warm*, poor man, he never got jobs for one reason or another. He was a very special type. He wasn't too effeminate, but he was slightly effeminate. He was a young man who would never seem to get older, yet he would get older and not be young enough. So he went into the discotheque business.

Timmy Everett as the boy Tobey, who grows up to be a composer because of the encouragement given by his brilliant, passionate older friend Willie. S. N. Behrman's comedy was drawn from sketches he'd written about his Worcester, Massachusetts, childhood. Harold Clurman directed. Robert Whitehead produced. 120 performances.

Suzanne Pleshette (Leah) and Eli Wallach (Willie). Leah loves Willie. Willie, who only loves what's unattainable, loves a self-centered actress. Leah bears Willie's child. When he learns this, Willie, to everyone's disbelief, kills himself.

Redhead 2/5/59

Opposite, Gwen Verdon gets up as a raffish cockney character for "Erbie Fitch's Twitch" in a Herbert and Dorothy Fields–Sidney Sheldon–David Smith–Albert Hague musical about a Victorian waxworks museum. Verdon, with Bob Fosse's peppy dances and direction, made the show go 452 performances. Robert Fryer and Lawrence Carr produced.

BROADWAY OLD-TIMER: You know you asked for Gwen Verdon stories.

Q: Yes?

OLD-TIMER: I don't know that there are any. There are Shirley Booth stories, Kim Stanley stories, Ethel Merman stories by the dozen. But no Gwen Verdon. People admire her, they like her, but they don't gossip about her. It's like Sandy Koufax–remember him? No one has a Sandy Koufax story. He'd just come on and strike everybody out.

Q: Well, with Koufax you have his sore hand and his pitching despite the pain to keep the Dodgers in the race.

OLD-TIMER: Ah! Pagliacci. "The show must go on." In fact, you have that with Gwen in *Chicago*, singing and dancing while her heart is breaking. She and director Bob Fosse are bringing the show in, while she and husband Fosse are getting a divorce. But there's no *story* to it. When Ethel Merman divorced Ernest Borgnine, she said, "I made a mistake. People make mistakes. That's why they put erasers on pencils." Gwen didn't have a quip for the press.

Look after Lulu 3/3/59

Tammy Grimes as Lulu, a Parisian cocotte, with Roddy McDowall and Kurt Kasznar as two of her many lovers. Noël Coward's farce was an adaptation of Georges Feydeau's *Occupe-toi d'Amelie*. Cyril Ritchard directed. 39 performances.

Juno 3/9/59

Melvyn Douglas ("Captain" Jack Boyle) and Jack MacGowran ("Joxer" Daly) in the Joseph Stein–Marc Blitzstein musical adaptation of Sean O'Casey's *Juno and the Paycock*. José Ferrer directed. Agnes de Mille choreographed. 16 performances.

MELVYN DOUGLAS: I had never done a musical–and probably never should have–but it gave me great pleasure to work with Agnes de Mille and the dancers. And I mean *work*. Compared with dancers, we actors don't know what work is.

Sweet Bird of Youth 3/10/59

Opposite, Geraldine Page in her greatest role, the Princess Kosmonopolis, alias Alexandra Del Lago, a frowsy Hollywood has-been, and Paul Newman as Chance Wayne, the Princess' kept man, in the Tennessee Williams melodrama about sinning and feeling good, the South, venereal disease, castration, art, time, and politics. Elia Kazan directed as though it were an opera. Cheryl Crawford produced. 375 performances.

The Princess wakes to find Chance in her bed. She can't remember him.

Princess. Your voice sounds young. Are you young?
Chance. My age is 29 years.
Princess. That's young for anyone but an Arab. Are you very good-looking?
Chance. I used to be the best-looking boy in this town.
Princess. How large is the town?
Chance. Fair-sized.
[*She motions him to come near and touches his bare chest with her finger tips.*]
Princess. Well, I may have done better but God knows I've done worse.
Chance. You do that like you were feeling a piece of goods to see if it was genuine silk or phony.
Princess. It feels like silk. Genuine!

GERALDINE PAGE, *of her understudy, M'el Dowd* (1959): Poor girl, she'll never get to play the part.

KENNETH TYNAN (1959): There is only one trend in the Broadway theatre, and its name is Kazan.

PAGE (1964): Kazan's vision of things is very strong and forceful. Every time I'd get shy, he'd push me. For example, I didn't want to go downstage and talk right to the audience. During rehearsal I'd get frightened and Kazan would say, "What's the matter?" and I'd say, "They'll hate me." And he'd say, "Every time you go down there and you get scared, get louder and nastier." Even in performance, I used to frighten myself; but every time I did what he said the audience loved it.

The Princess does an aside to the audience.

WILLIAMS, *an aside*

Virginia Spencer Carr: A few weeks ago I saw Tennessee in New York City, where we met for cocktails at the Monkey Bar of the Hotel Elysee and immediately launched into reminiscences of earlier meetings. We recalled the time he had gone to the hospital to visit my brother Jack Spencer, who was gravely ill in an intensive-care unit and could have visitors only from the immediate family. Williams had seen Jack only once before, but he had been struck by his gentle manner and courageous spirit. Williams does not like to go to hospitals, for visiting the sick depresses him, but Jack had no family in New Orleans and I could not be there, so he presented himself to the hospital staff as a cousin. Jack was thrilled.

I was in New Orleans several times the following year to visit my ailing brother and then to see Williams when our visits to the city coincided, for I was deep into Carson McCullers research at the time and needed all the help he could give me. When Jack was back in the hospital for the last time, it was a Christmas week. My other brother, Melville, was there, and Williams was, too. One night he suggested that we have lunch together the next day, then go visit Jack. But the next morning I had to call him on the phone and tell him that Jack had died during the night. Obviously shaken by the news, Williams expressed his sympathy, then said gently: "Virginia, although we can't be with Jack today as we had planned, we can have a wake of sorts that he would have liked. Why don't you come over to my place this evening with Melville, and we can talk and drink a little sherry, and walk down Dumaine Street to a restaurant that Jack was fond of."

The evening was a joyous one. Williams encouraged Melville and me to talk about some of the crazy things we had all done together as siblings and enjoyed with us the memories of our youth in south Florida that Jack's death had brought into sharp focus.

At the end of the evening Melville said: "Tenn, come with us to Palm Beach to bury Jack."

"Oh, no, I couldn't do that. I never go to funerals. I've only been to one in my life, and that was my father's. I didn't even go to Carson's."

"Well, it won't be a regular funeral," Mel explained. Jack, who had been a sea captain and loved the sea, was to be cremated and his ashes dispersed in the Gulf Stream.

"But I get seasick. I never go out in a boat," Williams countered, his stomach obviously getting queasy at the very thought of it.

"It'll be a good-sized boat," said Mel. "And the family will go out early in the morning with Jack's ashes."

"I guess I am sort of a member of the family," smiled Williams. "All right—I'll go. Just call me two hours before plane time and pick me up on the way to the airport."

Alas, we were delayed two days beyond our scheduled departure by having to close up Jack's house, and Williams could not wait for us. He was due in New York for the cast's first reading of the play he was getting ready to open off Broadway, the play he called *Small Craft Warnings*.

We buried Jack at sea the next morning, but it was not a sad farewell. It was an exhilarating occasion, quiet save for the pounding of the surf and the 12-foot-high waves tossing our boat about. It was the kind of sea Jack loved, and he could not have asked for a more fitting or adventurous last voyage. The wind whistled through the riggings and whipped his ashes about our faces and flung them high, then down into the churning Gulf Stream.

Although Tennessee was in New York that morning, he was very much with us at sea. Small craft warning flags were flying everywhere.

Triple Play 4/15/59

Jessica Tandy as Angela Nightingale, a frolicsome strumpet, and Hume Cronyn as John Jo Mulligan, her sanctimonious customer, in Sean O'Casey's "Bedtime Story." Angela won't leave Mulligan's flat until her services are handsomely recompensed. *Triple Play* included two other one-acts, O'Casey's "A Pound on Demand" and Tennessee Williams' "Portrait of a Madonna," and Anton Chekhov's monologue, "Some Comments on the Harmful Effects of Tobacco." Cronyn directed. 37 performances.

HUME CRONYN: It suffered the fate of a lot of bills of one-act plays—they're hard to sell and are not commercially successful.

JESSICA TANDY: However, it was fun to do.

CRONYN: Yes, that's something I'm glad we did. I mean sometimes one has great affection for things that have not been wildly successful—they were thoroughly worth doing.

Gypsy 5/21/59

Ethel Merman as Rose, the fiercely ambitious stage mother of girls who would grow up to be June Havoc and Gypsy Rose Lee, placates Jack Klugman as Herbie, their long-suffering agent, by assuring him "You'll Never Get Away from Me." Arthur Laurents drew the libretto of the musical from Lee's autobiography. Jule Styne wrote the songs and Stephen Sondheim the lyrics. Their hits: "Small World," "Together," "Everything's Coming up Roses." Jerome Robbins directed and choreographed. David Merrick and Leland Hayward produced. 702 performances.

Much Ado about Nothing 9/17/59

John Gielgud and Margaret Leighton as Benedick and Beatrice, Shake- speare's wittiest lovers. Gielgud directed. 58 performances.

The Gang's All Here 10/1/59

MELVYN DOUGLAS: We came to Broadway with a big advance sale—theater parties and benefits. We got fine reviews and settled in for a long run, but when the advance and the theater parties were used up, the bottom fell out. One night Howard Lindsay came back after the show, full of praise, but puzzled because we weren't doing better business. Finally he said that he and Russel Crouse had decided many years before that "no matter how good a play we wrote, no matter how good the reviews, unless the main character was one with whom the audience could sympathize, even if he was a bastard, the play wouldn't go." The main character of *The Gang's All Here* was Warren Harding under another name, and Warren Harding was neither a hero nor a bastard. He was just a handsome slob. The audience was interested, titillated, perhaps even somewhat touched, but they weren't deeply sympathetic.

Fred Stewart, Bernard Lenrow, Bert Wheeler, E. G. Marshall, Melvyn Douglas, Paul McGrath, and Howard Smith. Douglas was President Griffith P. Hastings, a dissolute weakling; the others, his cronies. Smith as Higgy, a minor New Jersey politico, interrupts the camaraderie of the poker table by threatening to expose their corruption. Jerome Lawrence and Robert E. Lee wrote the play. George Roy Hill directed. Kermit Bloomgarden produced. 132 performances—not enough to break even.

The Miracle Worker 10/19/59

WILLIAM GIBSON: When I was a kid in the seventh or eighth grade we had to read Helen Keller's *Story of My Life*. That and Julius Caesar were the two textbooks that year. And it always stuck with me.

In Topeka, Kansas, when I was first immersing myself in theater at the Topeka Civil Theater, I worked as an actor and stage manager and I started writing plays. I thought I'd like to write a one-act play about Helen Keller, using the lights of the stage and the darkness of the stage for blindness and stuff like that, and this idea turned around in my head for a while. Later when I was leading a drama group at Austen Riggs Center, I thought it would be good to have an evening of one-acts. They had a dance teacher there and I thought, "Maybe I can get her to do a dance about Helen Keller if I provide her a commentary." That's when I went back to get Helen's book and found, instead of the edition that I had had in public school, the 1903–I think it is–Doubleday edition, of which her account is one third, the middle third is a description by John Macy of her education as Annie Sullivan had told it to him later, and the last third is the letters Annie wrote to people at Perkins from Tuscumbia. She was writing two or three letters a week and they give in the greatest detail an account of the whole education of Helen Keller. There in the letters was the play. Out of those letters I did the dance commentary–the girl never did the dance.

Then when I needed dough Arthur Penn was directing television and I said, "I think I have an idea that might make a 'teleplay.'" And he said, "What is it?" So I gave him these 12 pages of dance commentary. And he said, "Marvelous. I can sell it instantly. When can you put in ten days to write it?" I said, "You have to tell me what a television play is." We didn't own a television set; this was 1957. We spent a day talking about what a television play is and in effect laying out the action of *The Miracle Worker* for television. My second child got born in the middle of those ten days–which became six weeks actually, I was only working part time on it.

The writing went very easily; I never thought it was much of a play. But when I read it to people, I was astounded; they all fell apart. I knew it was a damn good story or it wouldn't have hung around in my head for that long, but I didn't know it would do to people what it did. So it went out on television. And Bill Inge said to me, "Why don't you turn it into a stage play?"

Anne Bancroft (Annie Sullivan, the "miracle worker"), Patty Duke (the six-year-old Helen Keller), Torin Thatcher (Captain Keller, Helen's father), and Patricia Neal (Kate Keller, her mother). Helen has been blind, deaf, and mute since she had a severe illness at the age of 19 months. Now, like a desperate animal, she gropes about her world, trying to understand and control it. Annie Sullivan, 20, partially blind herself, a graduate of the Perkins Institution for the Blind, has come as Helen's tutor. William Gibson's play had memorable performances by Bancroft and Duke. Arthur Penn directed. Fred Coe produced. 719 performances.

GIBSON: By the time we did *The Miracle Worker* on stage, I had had enough of life in the theater, and I said to Fred Coe, "The only thing is, I'm not going to live with this the way I lived with *Two for the Seesaw*. I can't go through that again. So I want you to book it in Hartford and Boston—any place I can commute from Stockbridge." He came back and said, "I can't get Hartford. They haven't had a show in there for 20 years. But Philadelphia and Boston." I said, "All right, but I'm not going to live with it."

Because if you live with it, everything else ceases to exist and you become vulnerable to every little wisp of anxiety that drifts across the scene. Everyone goes around shaking with anxiety, because they're locked up in what I called "the spaceship" in *The Seesaw Log*. Nothing else has any reality. So that's what I did. I didn't go to rehearsals in New York very much. I went down once a week to see what was going on.

I went to opening night in Philadelphia, and opening night we got about 13 curtain calls. Every act they were stopping the show with applause, like an opera with arias. It was altogether hysterical, so we had no worries from the beginning. But the next day we got together to discuss the set. We had seen it in model, but when we saw it on stage, it was a monster. Somehow this nice little model had become an enormous apartment house which was drowning everything. We sat there for an hour or two saying how we could take this piece off or that piece off. At the end of that hour we were so depressed by that set that we acted as though we had a total flop on our hands. And I said, "This is insane, because don't we remember last night we had all those curtain calls—with *this* set?"

I went to Philadelphia twice to visit the show; I went twice to Boston; I went three times to New York. I kept really aloof. It would have been a better play if I hadn't—if I'd rewritten it more. But I just couldn't do it again.

Because no one can communicate with her, Helen has been indulged, placated with candy, allowed to run wild. Annie changes all this. In the play's most powerful scene, which usually runs eight minutes without a word spoken, she gets Helen to obey her will. Helen pinches; Annie slaps her back; the two wrestle on the floor; Helen throws food, plates, and utensils; but finally Annie forces her to eat properly, while seated at table and with a spoon.

Annie's goal is to teach Helen a language, and throughout the play she spells words in her hand, trusting that Helen eventually will see that words stand for things. Here, having spelled "water," she holds Helen's hand in a tumbler of it. A precocious child, Helen had begun to talk at the age of six months, her first word being "wahwah" for "water."

Opposite, in the play's last scene the miracle happens. Helen is filling a pitcher at the pump and suddenly realizes that the water that spills on her hand and the letters spelled in her other hand mean the same thing.

Helen. Wah. Wah. [*And again, with great effort*] Wah. Wah.

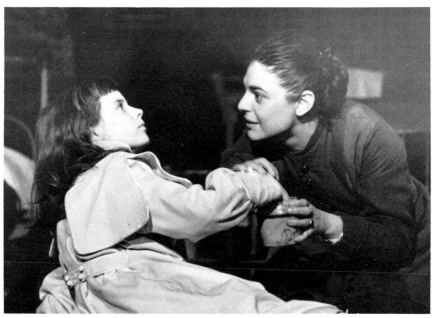

The Warm Peninsula 10/20/59

June Havoc as a worldly actress and Julie Harris as a simple working girl. Their love lives are contrasted in Joe Masteroff's play, which had a modest run (86 performances) on Broadway and a big success touring. Manning Gurian produced. Warren Enters directed.

The Sound of Music 11/16/59

Mary Martin as Maria, governess to the Von Trapp children, cheers their spirits during a thunderstorm by getting them to sing "The Lonely Goatherd." The children are Mary Susan Locke, Evanna Lien, Marilyn Rogers, and Kathy Dunn. This last Rodgers and Hammerstein musical had a book by Howard Lindsay and Russel Crouse. Among the songs: "My Favorite Things," "Do Re Mi," "Climb Every Mountain." Vincent Donehue directed. A blockbuster on Broadway, *The Sound of Music*, with Julie Andrews as Maria, became one of the all-time top-gross movies. 1,443 performances.

JOHN RAITT: Mary Martin has the quality to make you feel, as an audience, that you could never possibly love her as much as she loves you.

Fiorello 11/23/59

Tom Bosley as Fiorello LaGuardia tells sweatshop garment workers that, if they're going to strike, they've got to shout about it: "Unfair!" A few women echo him. "Louder," he says, "unfair!" More speak up. "Again," he says, "*unfair!*" They all yell, and a big number begins. Jerome Weidman and George Abbott did the book, Jerry Bock the music, and Sheldon Harnick the lyrics. Bosley was about to quit show business when he landed his role. 796 performances.

Five Finger Exercise 12/2/59

Roland Culver as Stanley Harrington, a furniture manufacturer, and Jessica Tandy as Louise, his selfish wife, in Peter Shaffer's drawing-room tragedy. The Harringtons take in a young German tutor who is rebelling against his Nazi father. The tutor discovers that people who aren't Nazis can be nasty, too. With the exception of Tandy, the cast that came to Broadway had done the show in London. 337 performances.

Director John Gielgud, Tandy, Shaffer, and Culver.

Greenwillow 3/8/60

Ian Tucker, Anthony Perkins, Bruce MacKay, Brenda Harris, Pert Kelton, Lynn Brinker, and John Megna as a big happy family sing one of many anthems to country living in this Frank Loesser–Lesser Samuels musical drawn from B. J. Chute's novel.

Perkins played a young man unwilling to marry because afraid of his own wanderlust. The quainty-quaint rurality of the show made the critics grind their teeth. George Roy Hill directed. 97 performances.

Bye Bye Birdie 4/14/60

"What's the story, Morning Glory?" "What's the word, Mocking Bird?" The telephone grapevine passes the news. This bright Michael Stewart–Charles Strouse–Lee Adams musical twitted Elvis Presley, his teenage fanatics, and suburban America. The song hit: "Put on a Happy Face." Gower Champion directed and choreographed. 607 performances.

SHARON LERIT, *14, one of the kids in the telephone grapevine* (1960): Last Saturday afternoon I was standing on top and I flopped off. I hurt a couple of ribs so I watched the evening performance from out front. It was fun to see the show for the first time. But I wouldn't want to do it that way again.

KARIN WOLFE, *16, who played the "girl who doesn't smile"* (1960): My most embarrassing moment was kicking off a shoe during the "Happy Face" number. When I got backstage they gave me another one, but by the time the number was over I had lost it, too. Boy, it practically ended up in the orchestra pit.

Dick Van Dyke (Albert) and Chita Rivera (Rose). Albert manages a rock star. Rose wants Albert to go back to teaching English.

The musical's high point: Rose disrupts a roomful of tipsy Shriners and leads them a Keystone chase.

Duel of Angels 4/19/60

Vivien Leigh (the corrupt Paola) and Mary Ure (the pure Lucile). Jean Giraudoux's sardonic comedy, a reworking of the myth of Lucrece, suggests that virtue is more pernicious than vice, and less secure.

Paola [*to Lucile*]. You're one of the women who never get used to being a woman. Your reserve, and apparent modesty, come from this inability to take your sex for granted. You're curious about the woman you are, and at the same time rather frightened. You look at her in the mirror without ever getting to know her. You move anxiously towards her when you're in bed. This game of virtue you play is nothing but affectation, to cover up the alarm you feel.

Christopher Fry translated and adapted. The British dancer Robert Helpmann directed. 51 performances.

No Concern of Mine 7/4/60
(Westport Country Playhouse)

Jane Fonda in a play by
Jeremy Kingston.

BROADWAY OLD-TIMER: I saw Jane Fonda in her professional debut.
It was in 1956 at the Dennis Playhouse on the Cape. She played the
ingenue in *The Male Animal*–her father was the lead–and she was quite
ordinary. Her face still had its baby fat, her shoulders were tense, and
she seemed short and dowdy. I remember her movements had a *tenta-
tiveness* that was wrong for the part but that showed you how "well"
she'd been brought up.

She has overcome a great deal. Her shoulders are still tense.

Susan and God 8/22/60
(Westport Country Playhouse)

Joan Fontaine as Susan Trexel, a wealthy woman who joins a new religious cult, converts her husband, and saves him from drink. Rachel Crothers' upper-class comedy had a successful 1937–38 Broadway run with Gertrude Lawrence in the lead role.

The Hostage 9/20/60

Glynn Edwards ("Monsewer," owner of a disreputable Dublin boarding house), Celia Salkeld (Teresa, a country girl working as a char), and Alfred Lynch (Leslie, a British soldier kept hostage by the Irish Republican Army) in Brendan Behan's uproarious, and suddenly touching, comedy. Joan Littlewood directed. 127 performances.

BROADWAY OLD-TIMER: Joan Littlewood had the cast come an hour early to dance and sing and warm up. When we got to our seats we heard them behind the curtain, and I remember my wife saying, "Oh, *no*. What now?" She thought it was going to be more pretentiousness. But it wasn't; it just put them in the mood. The audience was light-headed from drink and freedom (this was Saturday night), and the cast was light-headed from jumping about and hyperventilating. When the curtain went up, they were doing a clog dance, but immediately they stopped, and the old lame cynic center stage said, "Well, thank God that's over!" The audience sort of gasped, and then we howled and beat our hands. From then on the cast would do their outrageous things, and we'd follow them every step with laughter. I've wondered why other comedies don't use the Littlewood warm-up. I've wondered, too, whether it works on a *Monday* night.

The Wall 10/11/60

George C. Scott as the loner Dolek Berson and Yvonne Mitchell as Rachel Apt, the underground worker through whom he finds love and a mission. Millard Lampell's play about the Jews of the Warsaw Ghetto was based on John Hersey's documentary novel. Kermit Bloomgarden and Billy Rose produced. Morton Da Costa directed. Despite a campaign to keep it running longer, it closed after 167 performances, a financial failure. It fared better abroad.

MILLARD LAMPELL (1960): The Jews of the Warsaw ghetto were obsessed by the thought that they might be wiped off the face of the earth and no one would ever know what happened. They left behind them an immense cache of diaries, letters, notes, shopping lists, children's poems, concert programs, photographs, collections of private jokes (their code name for Hitler was Horowitz).

THE NEW YORK TIMES (1/7/62): *The Wall* is a solid hit in Munich. The actor who plays the rabbi in the play was a Jew who had spent five years in various concentration camps. Terror robbed him of his speech. His voice has slowly returned during the last few years and, Mr. Lampell says, he speaks with a hoarse rasp that is very strong, and theatrically hypnotic. Ursula Lingen, who plays Rachel, is half-Jewish–the daughter of Bertolt Brecht's first wife.

The remainder of the cast is German, and includes a number who were in the Wehrmacht. Most of them grew up during the Hitler period knowing nothing about Jews except what they read in the Nazi papers. They prepared for their roles by reading every book about Jews and the Warsaw Ghetto they could get their hands on, playing Yiddish music and holding seminars on the culture and the event itself. They did not, Mr. Lampell says, expect success and now are somewhat baffled by the proportions of their hit. One member of the cast asked, ''Why do they come? This is schwarz Deutschland (black Germany) full of Nazis. There must be Nazis in the audience. Why do they come?'' Mr. Lampell, groping for an answer, replied, ''Why does Raskolnikov keep seeking out a policeman?''

The Unsinkable Molly Brown 11/3/60

Harve Presnell as Johnny "Leadville" Brown, a miner who strikes it rich, and Tammy Grimes as Molly, his illiterate irrepressible wife, in Meredith Willson and Richard Morris' musical based on the actual career of a turn-of-the-century Irish hoyden from Hannibal, Missouri. Molly takes Johnny from Leadville to Denver to England to Monte Carlo. He goes back to Leadville; she follows later—on the *Titanic*, which she survives. Dore Schary directed and Peter Gennaro choreographed, but it was Grimes who did most to keep the show afloat. 532 performances.

Big Fish, Little Fish, 3/15/61

HUME CRONYN: Of all the plays I've ever been in, this probably had the finest cast throughout. It played less than 100 performances.

Martin Gabel, Hume Cronyn, Jason Robards, Ruth White, and George Grizzard. Robards played William Baker, a compassionate loser who spends his life protecting friends less strong than he. Hugh Wheeler's play was directed by John Gielgud. Lewis Allen and Ben Edwards produced, in association with Joseph I. Levine.

Mandingo 5/22/61

Brooke Hayward as Blanche Maxwell, Dennis Hopper as Hammond, her husband, and Franchot Tone as Warren, Hammond's father, in Jack Kirkland's dramatization of the Kyle Onstott novel. Warren's antebellum Alabama plantation breeds slaves, many of them his bastards. Hammond and Blanche continue his tradition of interracial promiscuity. The play had flogging, incest, rape, murder. A generation before, Kirkland had made similar depravities oddly plausible and amusing in his 1933 adaptation of Erskine Caldwell's *Tobacco Road*, Broadway's all-time longest-running play (3,182 performances). *Mandingo* lasted eight performances.

THEATRE ARTS: The play is so offensively ill-written, wantonly violent, pointless and immoral that everyone connected with it should be ashamed.

Let It Ride! 10/12/61

George Gobel and Sam Levene in another musical based on *Three Men on a Horse*. Stanley Prager directed. 61 performances.

A Shot in the Dark 10/18/61

HAROLD CLURMAN: It was a very trivial play, let's say. But I was eager to do it because I'm attracted to a play if it's a vehicle for good actors. First the producer and author said they'd cast Judy Holliday; they couldn't get her. Then they mentioned someone else. And I said, "What about Julie Harris?" And they said, "Do you think she's sexy enough?" I said, "She's actress enough and she'll be good." I came to her and I said, "You're gonna do the part." And she said, "No, no. I'm not sexy enough." I said, "I'll tell you how to be sexy; gain five pounds. That's your characterization." I was hardly joking. And she accepted.

JULIE HARRIS: It was a funny play, but there was a tragedy in it. We lost Donald Cook, who had played M. Beaurevers. He was absolutely like a comet. I mean, when he was on stage, the audience just rocked the whole theater. I never saw an actor and a part come together so absolutely gloriously. He was *so* funny, but he was a very sick man, and he suffered a heart attack while we were playing in New Haven. Joel Thomas, the understudy, went on perfectly, but Donald died the next day.

And so the producer, Leland Hayward, was faced with having to replace him. And they found Walter Matthau. Now, Walter always says to me, "I know what you said. You said I couldn't play a 'gentleman.'" [*Laughs.*] Because when they asked me, "What do you think about Walter Matthau?" I said, "Oh, well, I was thinking of somebody like Brian Aherne, or Claude Rains, if he were alive–an elegant, suave European man." And I didn't [*laughs*] think Walter could do that. But actually he was superb.

CLURMAN: Donald Cook did the dirty trick of dying of a heart attack, and what are we going to do? We have to open in New York. The understudy is good but not brilliant. Somebody suggests Walter Matthau. "WHAT? An aristocrat! A French aristocrat! You're crazy!" But Harry Kurnitz, the adaptor of the play, said, "He really can do anything." I thought to myself, "How the hell do I make him seem aristocratic." You know he's such a New York boy; he likes to go to delicatessens. He had only one week to prepare, so after two days–he was learning his lines–I went to his dressing room and said, "We'll have to think of a gimmick, quickly. Basically, it's a very simple role in a very trivial play. All it needs is a certain style. Listen, Walter, do you like music?" He said, "Yes." I said, "Do you react to it?" He said, "Yes." I said, "I believe you. Can you think of a piece of music that you think is extraordinarily refined, unutterably light?" He said, "Yes." I said, "Play that. If it feels light and elegant, aristocratic, in other words highfalutin, stylish–all those things–that's enough. I want you to play that and walk in your room to it. Don't dance to it, just walk to it." He said, "Okay," and laughed.

And in rehearsal he walked as if he were gliding, as if he couldn't raise his foot above the carpet. The day before we opened in New York, Leland Hayward (he's dead, too, poor fellow) said, "Don't you think that's a bit exaggerated, that walk?" It's a lucky thing Kurnitz said, "Jesus, don't take that out! It's marvelous!" They didn't know I asked for that walk. If they'd thought I'd given it to him, maybe they wouldn't have been so enthusiastic.

Well, the audience opening night, I'll never forget: he stepped on the stage, took two paces and the audience was in an uproar of laughter. He won a Tony, then he got irredeemably into the movies, and now he gets $300,000 a picture. He drives a Mercedes and his wife drives a Rolls Royce.

Q: Did he ever tell you what music he'd been listening to?

CLURMAN: I think it was a Mozart piece. I wasn't interested in his musical taste; I was interested in the effect. The effect was perfect.

William Shatner (Paul Sevigne, a Paris magistrate), Donald Cook (Benjamin Beaurevers, a millionaire banker), and Julie Harris (Josefa Lantenay, Beaurevers' parlor maid). Sevigne, investigating what appears to be a routine crime of passion, upsets everyone when he finds that it was not Josefa who killed Beaurevers' chauffeur in her bed but Beaurevers' wife, who mistook the chauffeur for Beaurevers himself. This comedy about adultery in France was adapted by Harry Kurnitz from Marcel Achard's L'Idiote. It later became a Peter Sellers film. Harold Clurman directed. Leland Hayward produced. 389 performances.

Josefa pleads her case.

HARRIS: We gave an Actor's Fund benefit. And there was the wonderful photographer Carl Van Vechten—you remember?—an old gentleman who took surprising pictures. His wife had been an actress, Fania Marinoff, and they always came to the Actor's Fund benefits and sat in the front row. When I came on in the second act, I wore just a simple black dress, with a little coat over it. At the end of the first act I had been put in prison for the night; the next act starts when the guard brings me back for more interrogation the next day. And I remember when I came in the door, with the guard on the left side of me, I heard Carl say from the first row, "She's wearing the same dress!" He said it loudly, because by that time he was a very old gentleman and quite deaf. He thought an actress should be changing her costume, even in prison.

Kean 11/2/61

Alfred Drake as the Shakespearean actor Edmund Kean in this Peter Stone–Robert Wright–George Forrest musical based on a comedy by Jean-Paul Sartre which was in turn based on a play by Alexandre Dumas *père*. Jack Cole directed and choreographed. The critics loved Drake and little else. 92 performances.

BROADWAY OLD-TIMER: Steve Allen used to say that nobody looks at a woman like Alfred Drake. It turns out he looks at *everything* like that. It's a good look.

Gideon 11/9/61

Fredric March as the Old Testament God, who learns that man prefers to live without Him in Paddy Chayefsky's philosophical comedy. Tyrone Guthrie directed. 236 performances.

BETHEL LESLIE: Fredric March had the funniest voice exercise that I've ever heard in my life. Every night before he went on, you'd hear this very deep voice saying, "Hip ball. Hip ball. Lab-bo-tory, lab-bo-tory." He was just very businesslike.

The first day of rehearsal for *Years Ago*, he wondered whether he should light his pipe on the third word or the fourth word of his first speech. That's the kind of actor he is. It drove his wife, Florence Eldridge, crazy. She kept saying, "I . . . I just really am different from him. You see, I get *into* my character. He gets the outside of his character and then he finds the inside. I find the inside, *then* I find the outside. And I'm going crazy. I'm not going to work with him again." They'd only worked together, I think, for 25 years. Never work with him again!

A Man for All Seasons 11/22/61

Paul Scofield as Sir Thomas More, lawyer, humanist, scholar, Lord Chancellor to Henry VIII, and, afterward, saint. More chooses execution rather than bend his conscience to his king's command. Robert Bolt's play was even a bigger hit in New York than in London. Noel Willman directed. Scofield, though long a star in England, was making his first Broadway appearance.

368

Scofield and Olga Bellin as More's beloved daughter, Margaret. Here More comforts her just before he goes to his death.

George Rose as the Common Man, the cheeky cynic who narrates the play and takes the minor roles. As Headsman at the Tower of London, he dispatches More, then tells the audience: "It isn't difficult to keep alive, friends—just don't make any trouble. Or if you must make trouble, make the sort of trouble that's expected. Well, I don't need to tell you that."

CHARLES ADAMS BAKER: Paul's stardom comes at you very gradually. I've seen him not get entrance applause, and not just because he's disguised. Olivier comes on stage playing a butler, and you know its Olivier. His physicality is more overpowering than Paul's. Paul can play the same butler and you're not quite certain who it is, although ten minutes later you know it's the best actor you've ever seen in your life. Paul could play a two-year-old girl if he wanted to—he'd have some resources that could do it. But his talent doesn't explode on entrance.

Take Her, She's Mine 12/21/61

Elizabeth Ashley as Mollie Michaelson and Art Carney as her father, Frank, at a Dad's Weekend at Hawthorne College. Phoebe and Henry Ephron's comedy was directed by George Abbott. 404 performances.

BETHEL LESLIE: Mr. Abbott's been known to tell an actor, "Take three steps, turn, and say the line." And if he says this, and you do it, you get a laugh.

The Aspern Papers 2/7/62

Wendy Hiller (Miss Tina) and Maurice Evans ("H. J.") in Michael Redgrave's adaptation of the Henry James novella. Miss Tina, a middle-aged spinster, possesses the love letters that Jeffrey Aspern, a world-famous poet, wrote her aunt. H. J., a scheming publisher, intends to get the letters from her at any cost. To give the "publishing scoundrel" the initials H. J.—he has no name or initials in the novella—was Redgrave's pleasantry. Margaret Webster directed. 93 performances.

All American 3/19/62

Ray Bolger does his thing in a Mel Brooks–Charles Strouse–Lee Adams musical. Bolger was miscast as an Austrian professor of engineering in America's heartland. Joshua Logan directed. 86 performances.

CHARLES ADAMS BAKER: Ray was the original choice for Harold Hill in *The Music Man*. But he wouldn't do it because he said it didn't have an eleven-o'clock song. As an old revue-hand and vaudevillian he wanted an upbeat song he did by himself just before the finale. He'd had the all-time perfect one in *Where's Charley?*–"Once in Love with Amy." He'd get out there with the whole show as a warm-up, and he'd have the audience singing and he'd caper and improvise until some nights the song, instead of taking five minutes, took almost half an hour. He loved it and of course the audience went crazy. Well, we tried to tell him, "Ray, 'Trouble,' '76 Trombones,' 'Sadder but Wiser Girl,' 'Till There Was You'–they're *all* eleven-o'clock songs." He didn't think so.

A Funny Thing Happened on the Way to the Forum 5/8/62

Brian Davies (Hero, a young Roman) and Zero Mostel (Pseudolus, his slave). Hero pines for love of Philia, the newly arrived virgin in the flesh emporium next door. Pseudolus agrees to get her for him–but how?

Pseudolus. Wait! [*Thinks a moment*.]
Hero. Yes?
Pseudolus. A brilliant idea!
Hero. Yes?
Pseudolus. That's what we have to find. A brilliant idea.

This boisterous musical farce by Burt Shevelove, Larry Gelbart, and Stephen Sondheim drew from the comedies of Plautus. George Abbott directed. Harold Prince produced. 964 performances.

Gloria Kristy as Gymnasia, one of the girls next door, stupefies Pseudolus. Reviewer John Simon thought Mostel perfect: "Pungent, fatty, succulent, infinitely malleable, he is the memorial of (at least) twelve Caesars rolled into one, carved out of goat cheese, and lecherous like the goats it came from."

Ronald Holgate as Miles Gloriosus is about to kill Pseudolus. Jack Gilford as Hysterium, another slave, is prostrate with grief. The whores hide their faces, clinging to one another.

Pseudolus. Please, sir, please! May I be allowed a word.
Miles. A word?
Pseudolus. One word.
Miles. It had better be a good one.
Pseudolus. Oh, it is, sir!
Miles. What is it?
Pseudolus [*to audience*]. Intermission!

374

Pseudolus has Hysterium impersonate the virgin Philia.

Hysterium. They'll never believe I'm a
   girl. Look at me. Just look at me.
Pseudolus. I can't take my eyes off you.

They sing a love song.

The Desperate Hours 9/3/62
(Westport Country Playhouse)

Judith Robinson (Cindy Hilliard), James Waters (Dan, her father), Sammy Davis, Jr. (Glenn Griffin), and Remo Pisani (Sam Robish) in a revival of Joseph Hayes' suspense thriller. Griffin and Robish, escaped convicts, hide out in the Hilliards' suburban home and terrorize the family. The play was based on an actual incident made famous by its coverage in *Life* magazine. The 1955 Broadway production had Karl Malden as Dan, Patricia Peardon as Cindy, and Paul Newman as Glenn.

WILLIAM GIBSON: Sammy is a very gifted person. When I worked with him on the musical *Golden Boy*, I started out thinking, "Well, I'm going to see this typical nightclub performer." I didn't know what a typical nightclub performer was; that was a stereotype I went with. After I spent an hour with him, I thought: "This is a remarkable person." He never went to school; I don't think he lasted a year in public school. He can sound like Richard Burton if he wants to; he can be as English as anybody, speaking sentences of complicated and perfect syntax. At the same time he can be–just like that!–a guy from the corner of 125th Street and Lenox Avenue, and it's absolutely authentic. I like him best in that role, but I don't know who he is because he's 12 different guys.

He's driven, with a capacity for work that is phenomenal. His voice was ruined by the time I joined the show. They'd been out on the road six weeks already. They were fighting a mike problem: he was singing sometimes with a mike, sometimes without a mike. Still the sound wasn't right. He was beginning to croak. And even so, in Detroit, after the show, at one o'clock in the morning, he was out making a record with Count Basie and his orchestra because they happened to be there. He was doing what they call "marking" the songs, because his voice was so bad. His voice wasn't going on the tape, it would be added later. But he was needed, and he was there till 4 or 5 A.M. That's the kind of guy he is. Couldn't stop, couldn't stop.

Eddie Fisher at the
Winter Garden 10/2/62

Las Vegas comes to Broadway. Dancer Juliet Prowse (and comedian Dick Gregory) kept the audience amused until singer Eddie Fisher did his turn. 40 performances.

Come on Strong 10/4/62

Van Johnson (Herbert H. Lundquist, a struggling actor-photographer) and Carroll Baker (Virginia Karger, a less struggling actress) in Garson Kanin's failed satire on Hollywood. 36 performances.

378

Mr. President 10/20/62

Nanette Fabray (Nell Henderson, the First Lady) and Robert Ryan (President Stephen Decatur Henderson) in an Irving Berlin–Howard Lindsay–Russel Crouse musical, the biggest disappointment in a season of disappointing musicals. Joshua Logan directed. 255 performances.

NANETTE FABRAY: When I first read the script to *Mr. President*, I felt this terrible thing that happens inside: warning bells were going off, saying, "Danger, danger. Flop, flop. Wrong, wrong."

Never Too Late 11/27/62

Orson Bean (Charlie) and Paul Ford (Harry Lambert, his father-in-law). Charlie is trying to buck up Harry's spirits, without much success. Harry has learned that he, though pushing 60, is to be a father again. Sumner Arthur Long's comedy was directed by George Abbott. Elliott Martin and Daniel Hollywood produced.

WILLIAM GOLDMAN (1969): Freak things happen on Broadway. Paul Ford has been Paul Ford for a million years, always the same, always wonderful. But on the night that *Never Too Late* opened, the critics decided not to give the usual Paul Ford notice: "Mr. Ford struggles nobly with his material, but it is a losing battle." That night it's hats in the air and a 1,000-performance run and fortunes for everybody. There is simply no conceivable way of knowing when this contagion will strike the boys on the aisle. But one of the reasons that so many inconceivable plays get to Broadway is that when they're dying out of town they dream of the *Never Too Late*s and come on in.

The School for Scandal 1/24/63

Opposite, John Gielgud (Joseph Surface) and Ralph Richardson (Peter Teazle) in the imported British revival of Sheridan's comedy. Gielgud directed. Alexander Cohen produced. A limited engagement: 60 performances.

Richardson and Geraldine McEwan (Lady Teazle).

BRITISH VERSUS AMERICAN ACTING

Charles Adams Baker: The training in Britain is much more stringent than it is here. Most of our actors aren't trained at all. And I don't know where you'd send one to be trained. People find their own mentors: a lot of people swear by Lee Strasberg; a lot of people by Sandy Meisner; a lot of people think the American Academy is the only place in the world; a lot of people think Uta Hagen and Herbert Berghof are god and goddess. But that's personal. There's no way we can say, "You're going to start doing Shakespeare and Greek tragedy when you're in school," as the British do. I think the British *are* better trained. They are not always more interesting. There is something fierce about the personality quirks of American actors who become stars.

William Greaves: The British people, quite understandably, love the English language. When they say a word they seem to caress it. The word in itself is actually an *experience* for the British actor, one that he can very personally relate to. I think this is why their stage speech is so damn good. American actors are often more relaxed about language. They—particularly the so-called "Method actors"—try to get at the emotions, the psychic sensory experience, and they generally use words as channels or conveyors of the experience rather than as experiences in and of themselves. I guess this is at the heart of the difference between British and American actors. One is more interested in form—the speech and movement of the character; and the other is more concerned with content—the spirit, emotion, the inner life of the character.

Harold Clurman: The British have a different acting tradition. They set their parts in terms of speaking much more than Americans do. They're more professional in that sense, more exact. But I don't think on the whole—they have wonderful actors there—I don't think that they can be as moving, with a few exceptions, as the best of our American actors. I think, for example, that Laurence Olivier, who is considered a great tragedian, is really best in comedy and character roles. The same thing is true of Gielgud. The same thing is true of Richardson, who has, of course, pathos, but he's especially a character comedian.

The English look better, seem better in tragedy because they have the maturity, the bearing for it. American actors nowadays don't have much bearing—in the old days they did. That's because people in the street have no bearing. Our Presidents have no bearing. The only ones who have bearing are our army officers, and they're stuffed shirts.

We're a young country, and people are eager and dissatisfied, especially the actors. English actors, the better ones, are so secure they become like bureaucrats, very solidly professional—whereas, our kids are trying to put it over, if it's the last thing they do—even if a show runs only two days. They have a do-or-die attitude. And they're very dissatisfied with their lives as actors—even when they don't think about the social situation. Therefore, there's a flare that comes out of them, out of the best of them. The trouble is, they lack variety; they're not as skilled as the English actors.

The English skill can be quite dry. It's an odd thing: we overestimate the English and underestimate ourselves, because one envies what one lacks. We are impressed with their diction, bearing, and voice. I saw Scofield play in *Volpone* and everybody was falling off their chairs with worship, because it was like a vocal concert. It was beautiful and he looked handsome, but he had no characterization. When you go to London and see seven plays, one after another, as I did recently, you see they are all good concert players, but there's a certain complacency. The American actor is chewing up his gut. He's sometimes raw, but he's exciting.

But the American actor doesn't play frequently, and plays the same damn part over and over again. Al Pacino got the best actor award this year for doing the same thing he always does. And the American actor has another problem: the critics keep telling him he's "great." Everything is "great." You can't sell anything unless it is "great." But all this criticism of acting nowadays doesn't mean a bean because we have no standards of comparison. I saw Chaliapin and Stanislavski, when he was acting. Critics today compare what they're looking at with the show around the corner. What they should say is, "This is the best play on 45th Street." What they say instead is, "This is the greatest actor." Everybody is a "great" actor.

My first teacher, a Frenchman by the name of Copeau, said to me once, "You know, there have been fewer great actors in the theater than great playwrights, and the number of great plays is only about 100 since Aeschylus." I always say I'm not looking for something great; I'm looking for something that's good. I don't expect something "great" unless I live for 200 years.

Too True to Be Good 3/12/63

Lillian Gish (Mrs. Mopply) and Cedric Hardwicke (The Elder) in a revival of Bernard Shaw's allegory about the bankruptcy of capitalism. Shaw believed life no less miserable for the rich than for the poor; this play presents an array of wealthy, torpid people, Mrs. Mopply and The Elder among them. Albert Marre directed. 94 performances. The world premiere production by the Theatre Guild in 1932 had Minna Phillips as Mrs. Mopply, Claude Rains as The Elder, and Beatrice Lillie and Leo G. Carroll in other roles. It ran only 57 performances. Shaw noted that when this play was done the balcony always filled but not the expensive seats downstairs.

Marathon '33   12/22/63

Julie Harris (June, a vaudevillian down on her luck who takes up marathon dancing) and Lee Allen (the marathon's Top Banana) in June Havoc's play based on her autobiography, *Early Havoc*. The play re-created a 3,000-hour marathon. The music was by Conrad Janis and his Tail Gate Five. The Actors' Studio produced. 48 performances.

JULIE HARRIS: At the time we did *Warm Peninsula* together June was beginning to think of dramatizing *Marathon '33*, and I remember encouraging her because she felt it was too hard for her to do. I said, "No. You're a very gifted writer." And I think it was because of that association that she began to think of me as the one who should do June in the play.

I really felt kind of responsible because there was one point in the career of that play when Gower Champion wanted to do it, but he would have taken all control away from June. That was what she was unhappy about. I urged her to let him do it because I could see him making great success out of it. But she said no. She wanted to direct it herself; she wanted it done the way she saw it. And that's what she did. And actually I think it was a very exciting production. It was a great highlight in my career, being able to dance and sing. It had a kind of circus theme and I've always loved the circus. I loved it. It never quite came off, but we certainly tried.

Josephine Baker and Her Company 2/4/64

Josephine Baker thanks the audience for its ovation. This was the last New York appearance of the celebrated revue entertainer.

The Passion of Josef D. 2/11/64

Luther Adler (Lenin) and Peter Falk (Josef Djugashvili, alias Stalin) in Paddy Chayefsky's drama about the Russian Revolution. Lenin is protesting Stalin's excessive ruthlessness.

Lenin. We're as predatory as the capitalists, Stalin. Let's be as efficient.

Stalin. Is that our aspiration, to be efficient?

Lenin. Yes. Efficiency wouldn't have killed a hundred of the best Bolsheviks in Georgia. You, you bungler, did. You're not the politician you were, Stalin. You've become incorruptible, self-effacing, dedicated and inhumane. You're nothing but a priest.

Stalin. "You shall construct the Socialist Order, Stalin." Those were your words.

Lenin [*in a rage*]. They were not carved into a mountain with shafts of lightning!

Critic Henry Hewes said Falk conveyed Stalin's motivations "so well that we almost come to like the late dictator." Chayefsky directed. 15 performances.

The Deputy 2/26/64

Emlyn Williams (Pope Pius XII), Fred Stewart (the Cardinal), and Jeremy Brett (Father Riccardo Fontana, S.J.) in Rolf Hochhuth's controversial play attacking Pius XII for complicity in the Nazi extermination of Europe's Jews. Here, in the climactic scene, Fontana goes to his knees to beg the Pope to speak out forcefully against Hitler. The Pope refuses, wishing Hitler to consider him "impartial."

Fontana. God shall not destroy His Church only because a Pope shrinks from His summons.
[*Speechless, the Pope rises. He is unable to conceal the effect of these words which have struck him to the heart.*]

Many Catholic groups denounced the play, and American fascists in storm-trooper uniforms picketed the theater. Herman Shumlin produced and directed. 316 performances.

Anyone Can Whistle 4/4/64

HERBERT GREENE: I had trained Lee Remick and Angela Lansbury for the show and I didn't want to let them down. I went back and sacrificed a picture to do it. I thought the music was grubby and ugly, so I designed an orchestra that was so unusual that it would make the music sound as though there was something really going on. There were, I think, six cellos, four horns, five clarinets, three percussion and six brass—whatever the hell, I forget now, but it *forced* us to orchestrate in an innovative way. The music was less interesting than it sounded; now it's considered a kind of classic. I read about it a year ago; somebody was talking about *Anyone Can Whistle* as being way ahead of its time. And its musical level was such blah blah blah, I just *howled*!

Lee Remick as nurse Fay Apple succumbs to the wiles of Harry Guardino as J. Bowden Hapgood, a lunatic mistaken for a doctor, in this Arthur Laurents–Stephen Sondheim musical about politics, a phony miracle, and happy madness. Nine performances.

Angela Lansbury as Cora Hoover Hooper, a tough mayor in a dying town, sings "Me and My City" with her office pages.

CHARLES ADAMS BAKER: They were going to fire Angela in Philadelphia because the whole show didn't work. Very often in the theater, when the show doesn't work, the whipping boy becomes the person who's least experienced. And they said, "Oh, Angela's a movie star; she can't do this." And she was superb–but they were going to fire her! So I took Peter Glenville down because he was a client of mine and a friend of Angela's, and I said, "Somebody has got to pull some weight around here." We all went and had drinks after the matinee, and Peter, who is terribly authoritative and very Oxonian, told them, "You have discovered the newest musical comedy queen!" And they said, "You mean Lee Remick?" "No," he said, "Angela Lansbury!"

Folies Bergère, a French Revue 6/2/64

Patachou sings and Les Demoiselles des Folies hold themselves decorative in this importation of the opulent (15 tons of scenery, 1,200 costumes) Paris skin show. 191 performances.

Marcel Marceau 11/17/65

The French pantomimist.

MARGARET FEHL: Fred and I always enjoy hearing what the audiences say at intermission. We were in the balcony at City Center to photograph Marcel Marceau. Fred had gone to stretch his legs, and I was watching the cameras. One person behind us said to another: "You know, this is such an old theater, such a bad theater, it isn't worth coming to. The acoustics are so poor that you don't even hear what he's saying."

Man of La Mancha 11/22/65

Richard Kiley, as Miguel de Cervantes playing Don Quixote, and Irving Jacobson, as Cervantes' manservant playing Sancho. Cervantes and the manservant have been thrown in jail to face the Inquisition. Other inmates start to burn the manuscript to *Don Quixote*, and Cervantes and the manservant re-enact the story to prove its worth. Quixote's idealism gives Cervantes the strength he needs to face the Inquisitors. Dale Wasserman wrote the book based on the life and works of Cervantes. Mitch Leigh wrote the music and Joe Darion the lyrics. The tremendous hit: "The Impossible Dream." Albert Marre directed. Albert Selden and Hal James produced. The show ran 2,329 performances—so long that its ads began to say, "What! You've only seen *Man of La Mancha* once?"

The Playroom 12/5/65

Alan Howard (Charlot), Richard Thomas (Eric), Christopher Norris (Ellen), and Karen Black (Judy). Judy is so jealous of her father and step-mother–"smother and father," she calls them–that she and her spoiled teenage friends kidnap her stepsister, Ellen, and hide her in the tower play-room of an old New York apartment house. Ellen loves the attention suddenly paid her. To avoid capture the kidnappers decide to kill Ellen. Mary Drayton's competent perverse play didn't find an audience. 33 performances.

Illya Darling 4/11/67

Melina Mercouri re-creates in a musical the role she played in the popular 1960 Jules Dassin film *Never on Sunday*. She is Illya, the big-hearted Greek prostitute who doesn't want to change her ways. Orson Bean took the role Dassin played in the movie–the square American professor. Dassin wrote and directed. Manos Hadjidakis wrote the music, Joe Darion the lyrics. Kermit Bloomgarden produced in association with United Artists. 320 performances.

WALTER KERR (1967): I think they've made a slight mistake. They've left the show in Detroit, or wherever it was last warming up, and brought in the publicity stills.

Halfway up the Tree 11/7/67

Anthony Quayle as Gen. Sir Malla-lieu Fitzbuttress and Sam Waterston as his son, Robert. The General returns from four years of fighting guerrillas in Malaya to find Robert a flower child running to seed. The General dresses up like a hippie, hoping to shock the boy into proper behavior. What happens instead is that the General discovers he likes the hang-loose life style. Peter Ustinov's comedy was unusual in favoring the young side of the generation gap. Ustinov directed. Alexander Cohen produced. 64 performances.

SAM WATERSTON: It was a unique experience to have the director and the author be the same person. You'd sometimes find yourself asking the director for help in playing a scene, and the author would go to the back of the theater and return fifteen minutes later with a *new* scene. The ease with which Peter did it was wonderful to watch.

Q: How do you find the level of acting today?

PETER USTINOV (1977): Oh, I think it's perilously high. Only occasionally now when you're casting a play do you find a bad actor. When you do it's so refreshing, it's like a breath of spring air. And you say to him, "Oh, do come back tomorrow."

Golden Rainbow 2/4/68

Eydie Gorme and Steve Lawrence come forward singing the finale. This musical about Las Vegas and remarriage was based on Arnold Schulman's 1957 comedy *A Hole in the Head*. Ernest Kinoy did the book, Walter Marks the songs, one of which was "I've Got to Be Me." Arthur Storch directed. 135 performances.

JOHN LAHR (1968): At $11 a seat, better you should buy a bush for Israel.

Conclusions

WALTER KERR: The decline of Broadway was certainly steady from the time I came on the *Tribune* in 1951. In this sense: the first year I was on the paper I probably reviewed about 90 Broadway shows; the next year would be 84; the next year 79; the next year 68–there was a steady drop in the number of productions opening on Broadway. Now, that was compensated for to some degree by the fact that all of a sudden off Broadway began to grow. So by the time Broadway had dropped down to 70 or 60 shows per year, off Broadway shot up to the point where for a couple of years it was doing over 100 productions per year, a lot of them vanity, but nonetheless they were there. Then, of course, off Broadway finally ran into the same economic problems that Broadway had.

So the decline was absolutely steady until about three and one-half years ago–maybe a little longer than that now. You can date it from the summer that *Moon for the Misbegotten* was running. The year before it looked as if Broadway was totally dead. There was nobody on the streets. People weren't going into theaters. You saw no signs of health, no signs of energy, of life, vitality, coming from anywhere; no new playwrights; audiences obviously disaffected, most of them telling you they were afraid to come into midtown, they'd be mugged or something like that. And I can remember at the beginning of the season looking up and down 45th Street, which has more houses than any other, and nobody was on the street. There were several shows of the previous season running, but still–deserted, deserted, a ghost town. And everybody was in despair about it.

Then, all of a sudden, for no reason anybody knows or can yet explain, about three summers ago–as I say, you can date it by *Moon for the Misbegotten* which appeared earlier that year–that summer, for no reason at all, business on Broadway jumped by a million dollars from the previous year. And there were no new plays to account for it; no new stars to account for it–fewer even; no reviews because there were no new plays–actually there was no reason at all.

The only thing people kept saying was, "There's a recession, the economy is poor, people don't spend money on European vacations, they're stuck in New York so they go to the theater." Well, I don't think that many people take European vacations that regularly to account for all the difference, for all that new business. Furthermore, ever since then it's been going up and up and up and up, leaping by a million per year, and winters too, until the point where this last season has been the best in Broadway history–in terms of *grosses*, money.

And there must be some reason for it that the historians will tell us some day. We don't know what it is. All we know is, it doesn't seem to have anything to do with the price of tickets. The half-price ticket booth in Duffy Square has certainly helped, a lot. But at the same time regular prices are constantly going up–to $17.50 and even $25.00. It doesn't matter what you charge, the people come out.

CLIVE BARNES (1976): Broadway is now a commercial shop window. It is not a theater in which you can experiment.

PHILIP PROCTOR: I remember when I began to have second thoughts about Broadway. I'd always wanted a career in theater. I'd grown up in New York and been to shows–*Annie Get Your Gun, Oklahoma!*–as early as I can remember. I was a child actor for a short time, and I'd gone to a school known for its dramatics, where, a boy soprano, I played Gilbert and Sullivan's leading ladies. Then I went to Yale because of its Drama School and because New Haven is a try-out town. After graduation, I did small parts off Broadway; then understudied Rolf the singing Nazi in *The Sound of Music*; and finally got the lead in an original off-Broadway musical, *The Amorous Flea*, for which I was given a *Theatre World* Promising Performer Award–Paul Newman shook my hand. Then I got a role in a big Broadway musical *A Time for Singing*, which was based on the hilarious book *How Green Was My Valley*. You wouldn't think coal-mining disasters would be good musical material, and you'd be right.

It was during the run of this show that I began to change my mind about Broadway. We were a limited success, to be kind about it, and the kids in the chorus were constantly complaining. You see, we'd been in Boston at the same time as *Mame*, which everybody knew was going to be a smash. And the kids kept saying, "Oh, golly, if *only* we had lucked into *Mame*. We'd have five years' steady work. We'd make a record and get residuals. We'd be on the *Ed Sullivan Show*!"

I didn't feel this way at all. I didn't go into theater for a steady job. A steady job? I went into theater because I wanted to do many different parts, attempt different kinds of acting. I wanted to try things beyond my capacity and sometimes shine and sometimes fall on my face. I wanted a *career* with lots to do.

And I saw Broadway wasn't built that way any more. It *had* been. Back when it was economically feasible, everybody worked much more, took more risks. But now they couldn't afford it. The problem was the money: what shows cost, first of all, and what they could make. When you've got big money and the possibility of *tremendous* money, you've got commercialism and greed of course–and you've also got tremendous fear. Your highest aspiration is to have a nice safe Long Run that will take root and grow old. "By God, Stanley, we'll all be millionaires!"

That wasn't for me. I turned my back on Broadway, left New York and came to California–Los Angeles, which is the new media center. And I got into new kinds of media: records, concert tours, radio, books, TV, film. Peter Bergman and I began with the Firesign Theater, and we've been doing 20 different things ever since. Our answer is always Yes. We say we can do everything–direction, props, light design, costumes–and then we do it. What we've done really is create a theater on our own–defining *theater* very broadly, as I think it should be defined. It isn't easy, but if you produce wisely and promote properly, you'll find an audience. The costs don't have to rule you; we know we can control costs–we do the accounting.

And because experimenting and flexibility and breathing room are so important to me, I have to feel that a decentralized theater such as we're coming to have is much better than a New York–based theater–much more exciting artistically. And something else: the audiences are better. Out of New York they are less aggressive–they don't have a chip on their shoulder. They're more open and responsive. They can still be surprised.

Peter and I may "appear" in New York some day. Perhaps even on Broadway. But it must be as a *result* of our success, not as an attempt to attain it. And these days, with so much of the world to see and so much of the world we'd like to see us, it would have to be a limited engagement.

HAROLD CLURMAN: I'm one of the old propagandists for regional theater. In the days when I wrote for the *New Republic*, I kept on saying, "We must decentralize." I once said I didn't know what people were talking about when they said "regional theater," because New York, after all, is a region. I call Broadway "the ghetto of the theater."

We should have what Germany has. Every town with a population of 25,000 or more has its own theater–good theater, too; it doesn't just imitate the Berlin productions. Every town has its own subsidized theater and opera, and they do marvelous work. People do shows in Munich differently from the way they are done in Frankfurt or Hanover or other towns. It makes their theater very rich.

Decentralization has to happen because this country is full of talented people who want to be in the theater. New York theater is a bottleneck and there's no room for them. What have we got on Broadway? Musicals and comedies by Mr. Neil Simon or the like, and British imports. Fortunately, there is the Public Theater and there's Lincoln Center. Otherwise, we're in bad shape.

CHARLES ADAMS BAKER: Regional theater is almost all important now. In every respect it's important, but particularly where new plays are concerned. We have a musical that got a first-class production at the Spoleto Festival in Charleston, with Broadway actors and singers– all financed by the Fine Arts Council of the State of South Carolina. It will open in the fall at the Brooklyn Academy. We couldn't have gotten that show on in New York–too expensive.

I can't think of a musical on Broadway now, with the exception of *Chicago* and *I Love My Wife*, that *didn't* start somewhere else. Regional theater is where we're getting our actors; it's where we're getting the funds to put on shows. That was never more apparent than in *The Great White Hope* which came directly from the Arena to the Alvin without a single change. Of course, you get a sort of free ride now that New York critics go out of town. They go out to the Long Wharf, they go out to the Arena and they review. So before you put up all those thousands of dollars, you've got your review in hand. If Clive Barnes was mad for *The Great White Hope* at the Arena and you bring it in exactly as it was, he's not going to say, "Gee, I was wrong." So it makes your risk much less. You can get backers like crazy.

You see, money is very tough in the theater now. I don't think you could put on any kind of musical for less than $600,000 and that would be like a four-character play. I don't think you can put on a two-character straight play for less than $250,000. That's an awful lot of money. When I was a kid, you could put on a play for $25,000. In those days most producers put their own money in a show. George Abbott would put a play into rehearsal with his own money and then, if it looked good, he'd sell off shares. He'd ask some friends in and say, "Do you want to see a rehearsal?" And if they said, "We'd like to have a piece of this," that was fine.

There is so much waste in the theater; that's the heartbreaking thing. You have strong unions who won't give you an inch. I mean, actors will give you anything. They will go on for free if you're in trouble. But you can't get anything from musicians and stagehands. And there are the same problems on the road. If you open in the Shubert Theater in Chicago, there are the same unions and it becomes a strictly commercial endeavor. But to open something at the Long Wharf Theater in New Haven does *not* cost an awful lot of money.

Another way of getting around the terrific costs of putting on a play or musical–and I think it's the most thrilling story of the last two years –is to have the principals all go on minimum until payoff. They did that with Enid Bagnol's *A Matter of Gravity*, which opened in Philadelphia. Kate Hepburn, Enid Bagnol, and Noel Willman, the director, all went on minimum with expenses until payoff. That doesn't mean they starved; their expenses at the Barclay Hotel were not unlavish. But Kate's salary was something like $280. And the play paid off in three and one-half weeks. Of course, it takes a name like Kate's to do that. But that's a whole other way around financing plays: get it into payoff. It's sensible and no one gets hurt. I think that's going to be more and more what happens.

THE LUNTS (*their perennial advice*): If you really want to have longevity in the theater, stay off both coasts.

HUME CRONYN: We try to alternate between work in so-called regional theaters–Stratford, Ontario; Stratford, Connecticut; the Guthrie Theater in Minneapolis; the Mark Taper Forum; the Seattle Repertory; the Arena Stage–and things in the commercial theater. All last season we were at Stratford, Ontario, playing a classical repertory; now we're heading for Broadway with what we hope will be a commercial play. I don't mean to use "commercial" in the pejorative sense; it's just a different kind of production.

Q: You have been great exponents of this diversification of our theater.

JESSICA TANDY: On my part it's been luck. On Hume's part it's been good management. I think he really steers his life that way. But I think we both have been extremely fortunate in that opportunities to diversify have come along.

CRONYN: And to some extent, for a good many years, going right back to even before *The Fourposter*, we have been self-employed. Most of the plays we've discussed, we have launched. The time went by, long long ago, when actors could sit back and wait for managers to provide opportunities. I think you have to do it for yourself. You go where there's an existing theater, which means that you spend an enormous amount of your time traveling. We built a house in 1972, not very far from here actually. Well, we spent nine weeks in it in 1976, and five weeks in it in 1975, because we're always off somewhere else, either touring or playing.

HELEN HAYES: I don't think the theater's changed so much. I began on the road, touring all around the country, and when I do theater now it's all over the country again. Jimmy Stewart and I did *Harvey* two years ago at the University of Michigan, and we were nervous. We didn't know how this wonderfully *gentle* play would go. We saw the audience outside—young men and women with long hair and bands around their heads and tassels on their clothes—even bells, I shouldn't wonder. And bare feet! Well, Jimmy and I thought maybe the play was going to be out-of-date, or *we* were. Not for a minute. The curtain went up, the audience started laughing, they adored Jimmy, and they wanted the show to go on and on.

JULIE HARRIS: When I toured last year with *The Belle of Amherst*, we all wondered if—since it had been shown on television—if that would hurt the tour. But it only enhanced it, it seemed, because people were eager to see it live. I feel there's a great interest in live theater generally. And I think that it's a good thing that it's not just in New York City. In San Francisco this tour, we couldn't get a booking; there weren't enough theaters for all that was going on. So that's a good thing.

There are many theaters now that are renovated. The opera house in Lexington, Kentucky, has been all restored. It's absolutely beautiful for small operas or plays—wonderful acoustics. You find these surprising jewels all over.

BERT LAHR (1948): There's no reason why a city like San Diego shouldn't have a legitimate theater. I don't see how people can enjoy a play in a high school auditorium.

FREDERICK O'NEAL: I was responsible for Ford's Theater being re-opened as a legitimate house. I'll tell you how it happened. I was down in Washington with our representative Jack Golodner and he said, "They're talking about opening Ford's Theater as a museum." "As a museum!" I said. "Yeah, they'll have a recorded message. You'll pay fifty cents and all day long there'll be continuous talk about what happened here and what happened there." "My God," I said. "Why don't they have it as a theater, a live theater? That's what it was when Lincoln was alive." And he said, "Would you like to talk to Secretary Udall about it?" I said, "I certainly would."

We made an appointment and had a long talk with Udall. He was for the theater, but he said, "We just don't have the money to do it. The fire laws won't allow us to have a theater there because there aren't enough exits." So I said, "Why can't we work this out? Why can't we get an architect to look it over and make recommendations?" So we got an architect; Equity paid for him. He recommended exits on the side of the building next to a parking lot owned by somebody else.

Udall then made an arrangement with a foundation which bought and held the parking lot for the Interior Department until it got its next allocation of monies and could buy the land.

And it was going to be a museum, a mausoleum. Now it's a theater.

GEORGE BALANCHINE: In America, they always say *educational*, everything is educational. What happens after it doesn't matter, but everything has to be educational. Like at Hunter College, sometime, I remember some people came in and they said they would have lots of people coming one year for ballet and other people coming the next. And I said, "Why not continue these people? Make something out of them?" No, everybody must have a little bit of everything because we're all equal. Everybody equal, so everybody must have a little bit of art, a little bit of this, a little bit of that. And it's called educational.

So that's all. You see, you cannot find people that will sponsor performances. They build the theater because it's real estate, it's valuable land. But what's going to be inside, not planned and never will be. It's because it's real people and you have to pay people because they are going to have to eat, they have to live. It's very easy to find money for museum because it's educational, first, and it has pictures. They don't eat. They stay there and you don't have to do anything about them. But as soon as real people involved, nobody wants to give money because they think it lost—the money lost because they give to people and they play a game; they dance or play music. You play and it's gone; the sound is gone. You don't take home that sound in a package. Or, you don't have a chewing gum out of it, nothing—you don't have anything out of it. So, they say, "Why should I spend money on somebody who will whistle my money away?"

WILLIAM GIBSON: It's been many years, until just recently, since I've seen a Broadway show. When I came back from Israel, I went to see three or four plays, just to see what's going on. And I was very interested to see, by the way, that among the younger playwrights the avant-garde theater is as dead as a doornail. The Beckett influence has entirely gone out of the theater. Everybody is back to a kind of realism which stems from the thirties. David Mamet has a play, *American Buffalo*; Rabe's play *Streamers*; a play downtown called *Gemini* by a guy called Innaurato, another young American playwright. All these plays are one kind or another of social realism; this is the New Young Mood now. When you live long enough all these cycles of what's avant-garde become kind of comical, because they always come around and catch their own tail.

Back in the forties there was no regional theater; there were only civic theaters, community theaters. The Guthrie started in '59, but it wasn't an originative theater. I mean, they were essentially interested in doing Tyrone Guthrie's version of classics. It wasn't until the 1960s that plays started getting born out of places like the Arena. *The Great White Hope* was one of the first big successes to come out of a regional theater.

If you look at the Broadway listings now, nine out of ten shows are musicals, and the tenth is usually a comedy. So if you're looking for the new serious plays, you have to look to the regional theaters, because I don't know where else they're being done. There are advantages and disadvantages to this.

It seems to me you have to conceive the theater very differently when you're talking about regional theater, because up to this time the whole vitality has come out of what I was speaking of earlier: the cash basis of the theater—it pays its own way. The theater as a serious art form has always had its roots in that financial basis. And we haven't done too badly from Shakespeare on. We are now for the first time—in Anglo-Saxon theater history at any rate—seeing a theater which is publicly subsidized. I don't believe there was any publicly subsidized theater in the English-speaking world prior to the Second World War.

Now you're getting a theater which is not dependent upon people buying tickets at the box office to dictate its taste. You're getting theaters, scattered throughout the country—Long Wharf, Arena, Guthrie, Mark Taper, there are maybe 10 or 12 of them—which are funded essentially by large grants from the National Endowment for Arts and by some private grants from corporations. In these theaters the box office probably accounts always for less than 50 percent of the budget. When I was running the Berkshire Theater Festival, our budgets ran as high as $225–250,000 a summer, and we never took in more than $60–70,000 at the box office—25 percent of our costs.

There's a kind of separation happening. There's another layer coming in between the audience and the artist. Formerly the artist had to be very responsive to the audience, and one can think of all the bad things to say about that as well as all the good. But now a financial layer is coming in between, of national grants and institutional grants, and the artists are now not so responsible to the audience; they're more answerable in a way to the government and foundation bureaucrats who are able to produce that kind of money for the organization. So you're getting a different relationship between the artist and his product than obtained hitherto.

What the implications of this will be, I don't know. I don't know. It does seem to me that there is an obvious danger. In the past there *has* been such a thing as a non-public, non-box office theater. In Shakespeare's day, for example, there was the theater Shakespeare wrote for, which was a public theater, and there was also the court theater, for which various people, Ben Jonson among them, wrote masques. We don't read those masques anymore, even in college, because they are not living pieces of literature, as the plays from the Elizabethan stage are. There is no question but that the special-audience nature of those court operations vitiated the vitality of the works. The danger is that something like that could happen under this setup also. There is the danger that works will become very narrow in interest and specially directed to a certain audience—a paid-for audience, not a paying audience.

This movement toward special audiences began after the Second World War with a passionate interest in the theater that came out of Existentialism, a passionate interest in Beckett, Ionesco, Sartre—and from a different quarter, Brecht. This theater was very popular in this country in the colleges, but it never caught on in the commercial theater. I saw the first New York production of *Waiting for Godot*; it ran six weeks; even with Bert Lahr it couldn't last more than six weeks. That kind of play became the mainstay during the early years of regional theater.

Gradually, when the regional theater had created a viable operation, American writers began finding that there was a place for their work in these theaters. You began to see the emergence of an American avant-garde theater. These American writers kind of turned their back on the middle-class American audience who had been the support of the theater to that point—that is to say, the people who came in from Scarsdale to see *The Miracle Worker*. That's the audience I grew up with; I'm part of that audience. And when I was writing *The Miracle Worker* for them, I knew what everything in the play would mean to them.

But you've got a different situation when Ed Albee, for instance, begins writing one-act avant-garde plays like *The Sandbox*, *The Zoo Story*, things like that, for an off-Broadway audience. He knew that audience, too. It wasn't the audience that came in from Scarsdale; it was a *Village Voice* audience, and he was speaking very directly to it, so he had the same confidence as a playwright that Moss Hart and George S. Kaufman had in relation to their audience.

This is a very necessary connection. It goes back to what we were talking about with Clifford and Bill Inge, when I said they became obsolete. What happens is that the playwright changes, the audience changes, the class basis of the theater changes, and pretty soon the playwright doesn't know whom he's talking to. And he writes with uncertainty and groping, and "I don't even know if this joke is funny anymore"–that kind of feeling. You can see this in Albee's career. He moved into the Scarsdale audience, almost against his wishes, with *Virginia Woolf*, and became a Broadway playwright. And he's been in trouble ever since. He's never had another big success because he's addressing a middle-class audience for whom he has really great contempt. And justifiably so.

Q: Which audience no longer knows what it wants.

GIBSON: Right, yeah. But on the question of subsidized theater, I'll take a philistine attitude: great art has always been very popular art. I mean, Homer was not a coterie poet. Shakespeare was a hugely popular and financially profitable playwright. Tolstoy was read by millions and millions of people throughout the world every time he published a book, which wasn't often enough.

Q: Dickens, too.

GIBSON: Dickens! Dostoevski! There has to be some reason why the greatest of our art works, rooted in our most profound and universal experiences, were aimed at popular audiences. Generally when the art comes out of a society in some organic way there is a discernable connection between the art that's produced and the audience it's produced for; Whitman said, "To have great poets you must have great audiences." That connection has always been seen as organic. And now what has happened–by the way, this argument is full of holes and can be shot to pieces–but what has happened since the middle of the century, since the Second World War, is that a tremendous amount of money has gone into producing art for which there is no public outcry, art which exists because of the people who administer the money.

Q: And you prefer the groundlings with their pennies.

GIBSON: I think I prefer something that's gone through what Robert Frost called "trial by market." Trial by market is horrible; I mean, I *know* it's horrible. Anybody who works in the theater suffers from trial by market. All you get from everybody in the theater is what a terrible place Broadway is. Alan Schneider said to me once in a round table, "Broadway must be destroyed." I said, "Why?" although I could understand why. He said, "I go out working, directing a show, and in Boston I get sacked. There's no security; there's no continuity."

Well, that was 10 or 15 years ago. Broadway largely *has* been destroyed. And I don't know that people like Schneider or me are better off as a result. Or the theater in general.

Q: Harold Clurman said that in Scandinavia after three years an actor has tenure and you can't get rid of him.

GIBSON: Harold Clurman came to Israel to direct the Habimah, and I was in Israel a lot this year and heard this story. He said to the people of the Habimah, "You have a marvelous theater. Only one thing is lacking in your theater. You can't say those two magic words, 'You're fired.'"

Postscript: Mr. Stott's Acknowledgments

My first and deepest indebtedness is of course to Fred Fehl. Had it not been for his love of theater, his skill as a photographer, and his methodical conservation of negatives and prints, this book would not exist. Our collaboration began as an act of homage to the arts of theater and photography and to a time on Broadway that mattered to us both; because Fred and Margaret Fehl are the people they are, it immediately became an act of friendship as well.

After Fred, the person who did the most to make the book possible was W. H. Crain, Curator of the Hoblitzelle Theatre Arts Library in the Humanities Research Center of the University of Texas at Austin. Mr. Crain brought the Fred Fehl Collection of 50,000 negatives, 7,000 prints, and 900 theater programs to Texas. Much of this book was written in the Hoblitzelle, where Mr. Crain; Jane Combs, the Hoblitzelle's Administrative Assistant; and Ed Neal, Betsy Cornwell, and David Anthony of the Hoblitzelle staff were unfailing in their resourcefulness and cheer.

Fred printed most of the photographs in the book specifically for it. Over a period of eighteen months I shipped boxes of negatives to him; he shipped back negatives and prints. Gathering the negatives was complicated by the fact that they were being catalogued and readied for permanent storage in the Humanities Research Center's Photography Collections. These several tasks were done mainly by Roy Flukinger, a Research Associate–later Acting Curator–of the Collections. Roy answered my requests with steady good humor.

On photographic matters I was greatly helped by consultation with Joseph Abeles, James Colson, Harold Edgerton, Robert Elson, Roy Flukinger, Judith Mara Gutman, Jim Kaufmann, Dennis Longwell, Peg and Larry Madison, Barbara Morgan, Karin Ohrn, Lillian Owens, Tom Prideaux, Larry Schaaf, and Alan Trachtenberg.

On matters of identification I was helped by Fred Fehl, W. H. Crain, and materials in the Robert Downing Collection in the Hoblitzelle. The staff of the Hoblitzelle, Nanette Fabray, Alan Hewitt, Harold Prince, Frederick O'Neal, and Richard Rodgers offered counsel on specific pictures. All errors and omissions that remain are my responsibility. I trust readers will bring them to my attention so that they can be corrected in future printings.

Friends and colleagues at the University of Texas who gave advice, assistance, and encouragement include Roger Abrahams, Elizabeth Airth, Willa Beach, Klaus Bichteler, Martha Boethel, Richard Brettell, John Brokaw, Tom Cable, Joe Coltharp, Robert Crunden, David Farmer, William Goetzmann, Julie Hale, Goldia Hester, James Hitt, Dean Holland, David Hovland, Dan H. Laurence, Irwin C. Lieb and the University Research Institute, May MacNamara, Elizabeth Manning, Greta Morgan, David Nancarrow, Betty Nunley, Gaines Post, Karen Porter, Elspeth and Walt Rostow, Larry Schaaf, Carol Shinder, Victor Schill, James Treece, Barbara Turman, Enid Waugh, and Marie Williams.

The excellence of Fred Fehl's photographs, the respect he enjoys in the Broadway theater world, and the mild novelty of the book we were doing prompted many people to respond to my appeal and offer comments on the shows he photographed. My wife, Jane, and I conversed with Charles Adams Baker, George Balanchine, Harold Clurman, Marc Connelly, Hume Cronyn and Jessica Tandy, Mildred Dunnock, John Fischer, William Gibson, William Greaves, Helen Hayes, Seymour Herscher, Alan Hewitt, Walter Kerr, Frederick O'Neal, Alfred and Doris Palca, Philip Proctor, and Florence Williams. We were able to do this because our parents and, on a memorable occasion, Teddy and Arthur Woods took care of our children, Molly and Gordon. I conversed with Melvyn Douglas, Julie Harris, Russell Merritt, and Sam Waterston. Ann Reinke of the University of Texas Press conversed with Harold Prince. In addition, Margaret Barker, Virginia Spencer Carr, José Ferrer, Gusti Huber, Garson Kanin, Elia Kazan, Armina Marshall, Tony Randall, Gore Vidal, and Nancy Walker offered written comments for inclusion in the book.

Ronald Davis, Professor of History at Southern Methodist University, generously gave Jane and me access to transcripts in his University's Oral History Project on the Performing Arts, which he founded and now directs. Our work there was facilitated by the interest Ron and his associate Eleanor Solon took in it. On behalf of the Project and SMU, Ron has given me permission to quote excerpts of interviews with Yul Brynner, Red Buttons, Imogene Coca, Tom Ewell, Nanette Fabray, Herbert Greene, Gene Kelly, Bethel Leslie, Gregory Peck, John Raitt, and Bessie Mae Sue Ella Yaeger. Permission to quote excerpts of the Brynner, Fabray, and Kelly interviews was also given by the interviewees.

Several people were willing to lend their words to our book but not their names—whence the Broadway Old-Timer.

A good deal of the published material that is quoted in this book was gleaned from the clipping files of the New York Public Library of the Performing Arts at Lincoln Center. Paul Myers, Curator of the Theater Collection, and his associates were most tolerant of provincial researchers short of time.

The Carl Van Vechten photo of Paul Robeson is used with permission of Joseph Solomon of Lehman, Rohrlich & Solomon, executor of the Van Vechten estate, and Donald Gallup, Curator of the Collection of American Literature at the Beinecke Rare Book and Manuscript Library, Yale University. The excerpt from Maxwell Anderson's *Truckline Café* is used with the permission of Mrs. Maxwell Anderson and the Humanities Research Center of the University of Texas at Austin, where the manuscript is located.

From first to last this book profited from the knowledgeable interest taken in it by Archer Mayor of the University of Texas Press. Other Texas Press people who greatly contributed to it are Ann Reinke and Barbara Spielman.

Much of the book was done by Jane, who is as sad as I that now it is going out of our lives.

A portion of this book was written while I was on a John Simon Guggenheim Memorial Fellowship.

To all these people and organizations, and to our friends in American Studies and English at the University of Texas at Austin, Jane and I send our thanks and warm wishes.

Austin, February 1978

Index

NANETTE FABRAY: *Someday somebody will tell me where the theatrical tradition of hugging and kissing comes from. It's very nice, but I have a personal theory that it has to do with covering up the fact that you don't remember who the person is. "Darling!" you say, "darling!" And you fall on their neck. You give a lot of affection just in case somebody is somebody out of your past.*